Green
BABIES

Practical guidance for today's parents

Dr Penny Stanway

Illustrations by Nancy Anderson

CENTURY
LONDON SYDNEY AUCKLAND JOHANNESBURG

First published in 1990 by Random Century Group,
Random Century House,
20 Vauxhall Bridge Road, London SW1V 2SA

Random Century Australia (Pty) Ltd,
20 Alfred Street, Milsons Point, Sydney,
New South Wales 2061, Australia

Random Century New Zealand Ltd,
PO Box 40-086, Glenfield, Auckland 10, New Zealand

Random Century South Africa (Pty) Ltd,
PO Box 337, Bergvlei, 2012, South Africa

British Library Cataloguing in Publication data
Stanway, Penny
    Green Babies
    1. Babies, Home Care, Environmental aspects
    I. Title
    649.122

ISBN 0-7126-3918-7

AN EDDISON SADD EDITION
Edited, designed and produced by
Eddison Sadd Editions Limited
St Chad's Court,
146B King's Cross Road,
London WC1X 9DH

Typesetting by Tradespools Ltd, Frome,
England
Origination by Dot Gradations, Chelmsford,
Essex, England

Printed by Cambus Litho,
East Kilbride,
Scotland

For My Great, Great, Great, Great
Grandchildren

The book block (the printed pages inside the
covers) of *Green Babies* is printed on recycled
paper (115 gsm Welbeck Recycled Blade),
supplied by Gerald Judd Sales Ltd., London.
See page 183 **Consumer Guide** for suppliers of
recycled paper.

CONTENTS

INTRODUCTION

Of the 5.3 billion people on this planet, one in three is under the age of 16. Parents everywhere are understandably and justifiably concerned about the environment. They want children to grow, flourish and blossom, yet fear that this may not happen because of pollution, deforestation, global warming, over-consumption, famine and the depletion of fossil fuels and other non-sustainable resources (*see pages 185-7*).

According to many scientists, the environment is under serious threat. Science, technology and industrial growth have created some of these problems and they will undoubtedly contribute towards their solution. However, this is not the whole answer. Many of us, either unwittingly or knowingly, are helping to throw the ecological balance out of kilter and we must act promptly to remedy matters if we want our children to inherit an Earth fit to live on.

THINKING GREEN

I have been professionally and personally involved with parents, babies and young children for over 20 years. The subjects that continue to interest me – natural family planning, peri-conceptual care (care around the time of conception), pregnancy, labour and birth, breastfeeding, baby and child care, relationships, the needs of parents, food, health and education – are vitally important green issues and are the basis of this book. They bring the big green issues right into our homes and make them personally relevant. But whether we are parents or children, or whether we work or live alongside them, we are all intrinsically valuable natural resources. We have much to give and receive from each other, and much to lose if we do not. We also have much to lose unless we become aware of our deepest needs and our motivations for being green.

THE PRESENT

It is fascinating to consider why there is currently such interest in environmental issues. Apart from the obvious reasons, it may result from an effort to assert at least some control in the face of the power of governments, multinational corporations, the providers of health care and other services, and minor officialdom.

I suspect that the real reasons go deeper still. One is a fundamental desire to find meaning in life. Many people are searching for values which have nothing to do with worldly success and believe that the green movement, with its emphasis on the interconnections between everything on the planet, and the sanctity of nature, may help provide an answer. Jonathon Porritt, former director of the Friends of the Earth in the UK, asserts that 'What we're really up against is a crisis of the human spirit'.

There is more to our lives than the simple material reality – the obvious, visible, superficial or tangible dimensions of daily life. We have a spiritual dimension too and many people find themselves particularly aware of its importance and relevance when they become parents. To neglect this part of ourselves is to waste a natural resource. People discover their own ways of coming to know their spiritual dimension. Some are led and influenced by their children, many of whom accept their spirituality more readily than many adults. The possible existence of a higher being or divine energy, which is potentially part of each of us and can link us together, is too exciting and liberating to ignore.

Closely allied with spirituality are creativity, intuition and the ability sometimes to lose our breath through wonder and joy. Children are, I believe, born with each of these gifts as a sort of 'original blessing'. Parents are too. Yet how often do we stifle the very parts of our innermost beings which can make life worth living? Both we and our chidren can learn together to tune into a simple and vulnerable, yet awesomely powerful and often untapped well of personal resource deep inside ourselves.

Another possible reason behind the green movement is a reaction against the 'masculine', achievement- or product-centred paradigm that has dominated our existence for so long in industrialized cultures. People are searching for a more 'feminine' way of being – one which is concerned as much with the way in which things are done as with the end result, and one which values the reflective and nurturing side of people, both women and men, boys and girls.

Last but not least is the emotional factor. We are creatures of emotion and our lives are full of the many shades of colouration – from pale to intense, from monochrome to vivid hue – that emotions bring. Buried emotions such as fear or anger can prevent us from making the most of ourselves and our opportunities. Our fascination with pollution, waste and the end of the world may have deep psychological roots involving unacceptable and thus buried personal emotions, such as anger and a desire to despoil, and a fear that there is nothing beyond this world. The American writer Gore Vidal suggests that the current concern with green issues represents society's unconscious need for a common enemy in a time of relative peace.

Green parents try to recognize, accept and work on difficult aspects of themselves, as well as on those that really do exist in the outside world. They also try to stop their children's emotions from having to go underground in the first place.

WHAT CAN WE DO?

But whatever the reason for our 'greening', each one of us affects – and is affected by – our surroundings. And if we are not currently part of the solution, it is worth bearing in mind that we might be part of the problem. An intellectual understanding of environmental issues is not enough. Action and change occur only as a result of millions of families taking small personal decisions about how they care daily for their environment. Such change will not occur by leaving everything to the 'powers-that-be', whether at local, national or international level. Everyone, from the grass roots level in individual communities to those who are responsible for corporate, governmental and international policies, must work together. If we all do this, not only will our children benefit but so will their children. In this way our grandchildren will reap the harvest we have sown. Perhaps we could, with benefit, copy those North American Indians who think about the effect their actions will have on the seventh unborn generation – their great great great great grandchildren.

The global village is now such a reality that both developing and developed countries must take responsibility. Hopefully, as children in affluent countries grow up, they will learn that simply giving money to those in need may not always be enough. The wealthy third of the world needs to stop consuming so much. More important is to realize that we in the West do not have a monopoly of knowledge, experience and wisdom. We can learn a vast amount from the Third World. And few of us would be so arrogant as to claim that our First World exports have all been appropriate. As we teach our children about generosity and giving, we have an opportunity to teach them about humility and receiving as well.

Some people are put off any involvement with ecological matters because they fear that they might have to become unsophisticated and folksey. A back-to-nature image is not for everyone, but a concern for the environment may not necessarily rule out a hi-tech life-style. Indeed, with the increasing world population, state-of-the-art technology may even solve some of the problems it has created.

RIPPLES ON A POND

As parents, we can by our own example show our children most of what they need to know about safeguarding their environment. The very word 'ecology' (the study of the relationships between living organisms and their environment) stems from the Greek word for house, *oikos*. On a small scale at home we can demonstrate our concern and bring about change in many ways. For example, at the simplest level we can sort rubbish into different containers for recycling and we can buy unleaded petrol. Changing to become a more ecologically concerned family can feel strange at first. You find yourself making choices and changes not just once, but repeatedly. You also discover that as more people become involved, it becomes easier to incorporate green ideas into your way of life.

If millions of children grow up believing that their families can actively influence their environment, confidence will spread like ripples on a pond and the next generation of parents will be very different from us.

One of the most exciting recent changes in our society is the expansion of self-help, networking and pressure groups at local, national and international levels. The active involvement of 'ordinary' people makes such organizations a powerful force for good and for change.

THE FAMILY

As parents we are part of the biggest network there is and families can be vital units of change. In this book we will look step by step at how you can help achieve this. How about working out your family's individual plan of action as the book helps you reconsider your aims, take a look at various strategies and work towards new goals? New goals are essential if our children are to be able to say 'they not only took good care of me – but also of my world'.

We need to share a profound and honest regard and love for our world and each other. That is how our babies will be green.

Chapter One
PLANNING A GREEN FAMILY

The joys of parents are secret, and so are their griefs and fears.
Francis Bacon

What is a green baby? Not an alien, nor a baby who feels off-colour, but a baby whose parents are concerned about the future of the Earth. The parents of a green baby want to protect their child from the dangers in the immediate environment; and they are anxious to minimize any ill effects their lifestyle may have on the environment in which they live, and on the planet as a whole. Everyone is aware of the green movement; in fact, at the moment we can hardly escape it. Many of the most publicized environmental issues seem at first almost too distant, too large and important for ordinary families. Yet the big green issues (*see pages 185–187*) do turn out to involve people like you, me and our children. And myriad small green issues directly affect how we live our lives and plan our futures.

Having a baby is not something that should be taken lightly; similarly, being a green parent and bringing up a green baby should not be last-minute choices. It is best to start thinking about them in good time, way before pregnancy begins. When you become a parent you take on a serious responsibility; becoming a green parent means you take on not only the responsibility of your immediate family but a wider accountability to the environment. This chapter will address the vitally important choices you will have to consider before you start your family.

DECIDING TO HAVE A BABY

As well as having a natural urge to reproduce most people feel some pressure from society to have a baby. Couples who do not want a baby are often told they are selfish. I believe it is far more important that every child should be a wanted one and, ideally, wanted by two parents. There is no better recipe for the breakdown of a relationship than having a baby which only one parent welcomes. Imagine growing up sensing that one parent never really wanted you, or that you were responsible for your parents splitting up.

Before you get married or start a relationship you would like to be permanent, it is worth while making the time to explore how each of you feels about children. If having a baby is very important to one of you, but the other would prefer never to become a parent, perhaps you should reconsider the match. If the unwilling partner does not feel too strongly, you may be able to reach a compromise, but giving up the option to have a child altogether is too much for some people – both men and women – and they may wish to find another partner. If so, breaking up may be better done sooner rather than later.

Today, an increasing number of babies are born to mothers who are unmarried. That does not mean they lack a father who can be available to them as they grow up, because some unmarried mothers have a committed, live-in partner; many couples simply choose not to tie the knot legally yet or even at all. Being born into a single-parent family is far more significant from the baby's point of view (*see pages 101–102*). Whatever the reason why the parent – nearly always the mother – is alone, the baby misses out on the chance of having two adults intimately involved with his or her development and well-being.

If you are a woman and you would like to have a baby, but you do not have a permanent and willing partner, think twice before rushing into a decision and becoming pregnant. Life with a baby can be emotionally, physically, practically and financially hard on a woman living alone, especially if you have no close family nearby who would be supportive. If life is tough on you, you may not have sufficient reserves to give your baby – or yourself – what you otherwise might have wished to give in terms of time and attention.

CHILDREN VS. WORK

Women of today think of themselves not just as mothers but as people who will also spend much of their lives doing paid work, usually outside the home. Working women face a series of major decisions when they consider starting a family: when to break their career and have a baby; whether to leave work when they become pregnant, or to take maternity leave; whether to return to work and if so, when; whether to work part-time or full-time. Some women know from the outset that when they have a child they will not want to return to work. Others are sure they will, while some are – perhaps sensibly – undecided.

The fact is that most women do return to part-time or full-time work at some time after having children. It is sensible to spend time assessing your future role in the workplace before you start to plan your family. One option is to train for a career first. If you make this decision, you have a responsibility to yourself to consider contraception carefully. Some career women find it easier to return to work if, following their training, they gain a few years' experience and then have children. This can give them more credibility with employers. On the other hand, many women prefer to have their first baby when they are comparatively young. When their families are complete or when they are ready to return to work, some sign up for retraining or go on a refresher course; others embark on a completely new career; and some are content to pick up whatever work comes their way.

Staying at home to look after their children is not financially possible for many mothers. Working when the children are very young is frequently a financial necessity. This situation can create problems. Women who plan to return to work after their babies are born often find when the time comes that they really want to stay at home and look after their babies. It is sensible to bear this in mind as a very real possibility. Many couples decide to buy a house and take out a mortgage based on their joint earnings, but this means that unless the woman continues working after her baby is born, or the man's income rises substantially, the couple may be in financial trouble. In some countries and with some employers the period of paid maternity leave is much longer than others (*see page 21*). Even so, some women decide to spend a longer period at home looking after their babies. If paternity leave is available, or perhaps if the woman's income is high, some men may choose to take time off to care for their child. The point is to try to leave as much flexibility as you can.

Green parents plan their families to minimize conflict between paid work and child care. Before you start a family, consider how your role at work will change. A baby gets off to a better start in life if his or her parents are happy with their lifestyle.

The point of considering such long-term issues before you have children is that by doing some forward planning you may be able to avoid some of the practical problems over the child care/work conflict that so many women face.

Young adults are becoming increasingly mobile both in developed and developing countries. This may be necessary if they are to take full advantage of career opportunities and better standards of living. Inevitably, mobility leads to split families, with grandparents living perhaps hundreds of miles away from their children and grandchildren. Consider this if you are thinking of moving away from the area where your parents live. Grandparents can be a very real resource and support, both emotional and practical, when you have a baby. If you and your partner intend to go on working, bear in mind that, currently, grannies are statistically the most likely people to care for the children of working parents.

FAMILY SIZE

The number of children you decide to have is a green issue. It is important not only to you and your children but to other people as well. The World Fertility Survey found that in most societies there was a surprisingly strong wish to control the number of children in each family. In most families parents had more children than they would ideally have chosen. Various factors may influence your choice of family size. For example, some people are concerned about the rising world population (*see chart page 11* **Projected World Population Growth into the Twenty-First Century**). The nineteen-nineties are seeing the largest numbers of births ever, and more and more people will need more resources to live. We are already using non-renewable resources and eating into the Earth's capital assets. As the Duke of Edinburgh says, 'We have overstretched the carrying capacity of our habitat'. Each year 93 million people are born: $\frac{1}{4}$ million each day and 3 every second. Ironically, the non-renewable resources of the world are largely consumed by the small proportion of people living in developed countries. We must not allow the population problem to overshadow that of over-consumption.

It is very difficult for statisticians and demographers to predict population growth or shrinkage in a single country, let alone in the world, because so many factors have to be taken into account. Sudden alterations in conditions, such as famine caused by crop failure due to climatic swings, can lead to unforeseen movements of people and changes in population figures. Wars, such as the two world wars we have experienced this century, can lead to the death of a great many fertile people. Usually after a war there is an upsurge in the number of pregnancies, as if societies have a tendency to restore their numbers.

Some countries now have dwindling populations. This can happen because of an exodus of people moving toward what they think may be a better standard of living. The depopulation of the western islands of Scotland is one example; the recent exodus of refugees into the West from East Europe is another. A falling birth rate might also occur because bringing up children in the way sanctioned and determined by their culture is no longer attractive to parents. West Germany's population is diminishing by 0.3 per cent a year. Perhaps the sacrifices in having children outweigh the rewards for West Germans, one in three of whom thought them 'too much of an interference' in adult lives, according to a recent survey.

The present population in the UK, at 57 million people, is the highest it has ever been. As I write, at the beginning of the nineties, there is a boom in the birth rate; this is expected to decline in the mid-nineties. In other countries the birth rate is rising so fast that there is cause for concern that there will not be enough food and other resources to continue to feed and sustain the population. A country has a serious population problem if it fails to produce enough food to supply its population, and has insufficient industrial and commercial development to compensate economically. China, Bangladesh, Ethiopia and the Philippines are currently facing such a dilemma.

Even when a country exerts population control measures aiming to restrict the age at which a woman can have her first child, or the number of children she can have, many women want more children. In China, contraception is free and IUDs (intra-uterine devices) are the most popular form. Abortion and sterilization are readily available. A policy of one child per family has been accepted in principle, although it is not always practised. A couple who sign an official agreement to have only one child is immediately entitled to a higher income, more food, more land and better jobs. Couples who have more than two children are penalized by not being allowed to join the co-operative medical care systems. In spite of such rigorous attempts to control the birth rate, China's population continues to grow at a frightening rate.

In Bangladesh, which has an ongoing population problem, many factors account for large family size. Adherence to national customs and religion is one of the strongest, but fear of side-effects to health from contraceptive methods and inability to pay for treatments if complications were to occur are important factors. Added to these are: shyness; fear of ridicule; inability to pay for special food thought to be necessary for women using contraceptives; a lack of proper follow-up by the field workers of the family planning programme; sexual dissatisfaction; objection by the husband; fear of surgery; the complexity of the contraceptive methods offered; and an absence of easy and long-acting methods. In many other growing populations there is also a practical reason: the greater the number of children in a family, the more people there will be eventually to contribute to the family's income. Individual families may put themselves before the common good when comfort or even survival might otherwise not be guaranteed. In Bangladesh, however, a recent survey found that the poorer people had a clearer view of the population problem than did the middle class and the village leaders, and that they wanted fewer children than the middle-class people.

Stability in numbers in a population is perhaps more likely to result from pleasant living conditions, with enough food and other necessary resources for all the people, with low perinatal and child mortality rates, with enough work with enhanced status for women, and with the co-operation of religious leaders, than from governmental pressure. However, attempts to link fertility patterns to changing economic conditions have proved disappointing.

Recent statistics and predictions about world population suggest that the rate of increase is slowing down and that some of the more worrying forecasts may never come to fruition. That remains to be seen. The questions we must address are: should today's would-be parents incorporate any concern about world population into their decision-making about family size? And does the size of your own family matter?

If you are concerned about world population and you live in an already overpopulated country, you may wish to take some responsibility by limiting the size of your family and hoping that millions of other families do likewise. To stabilize the world population at about 9.1 billion people by the year 2050, the use of birth control must grow from one in two to three in four couples, and the average family size must decrease from four to two children.

Money is inevitably a crucial factor in decisions about family size. You may want to maintain your standard of living and feel that your finances will limit how many children you have. Work is another important consideration (*see page 8 under* **Children Vs. Work**). As a woman you may want to stay at home to look after your young children, but you may not want to lengthen this period by having another baby. It is also wise to consider how the size of your family will affect your ability to cope with the work

PROJECTED WORLD POPULATION GROWTH
INTO THE TWENTY-FIRST CENTURY

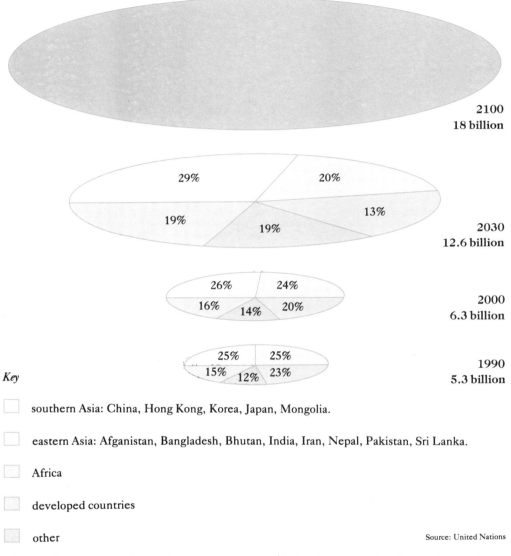

2100
18 billion

29%   20%
19%   13%
19%

2030
12.6 billion

26%   24%
16% 14% 20%

2000
6.3 billion

25%   25%
15% 12% 23%

1990
5.3 billion

Key

☐ southern Asia: China, Hong Kong, Korea, Japan, Mongolia.

☐ eastern Asia: Afganistan, Bangladesh, Bhutan, India, Iran, Nepal, Pakistan, Sri Lanka.

☐ Africa

☐ developed countries

☐ other

Source: United Nations

There will not be enough food for everyone at some point in the next century if world population continues rising at its present rate. The projected rate of increase throughout the world is shown in the chart (*above*). World population today is about 5.3 billion. The Population Crisis Committee in the USA has predicted that it will reach 6.3 billion by the year 2000, double by the year 2030 and nearly triple by the year 2100, unless birth control is used more widely. The rate of population growth has been rising since records began: by the year 1500, it had taken 1,500 years for world population to double; 350 years later it had doubled again; between 1850 and 1925 it did the same; and over the last 65 years it has more than doubled.

11

and emotional demands it entails. Many people say that the increase in workload from one child to two is greater than double the work created by one child, and that the change from two to three is even more surprising. You cannot know how you will manage until you try. However, if two children tire you out it is highly likely that three will be too many for you.

From a child's point of view it must be far better to be in a smaller family with parents who enjoy life than to be part of a larger family if those parents are going to be permanently exhausted. It may not be practical or feasible to have as many children as you would ideally like unless there were plenty of people around to help bring them up and take some of the responsibility off your shoulders. From another point of view, children in large families often look after each other. This is more likely if there are relatively big gaps between the eldest and the youngest. However, older children in such families sometimes find themselves bearing a heavy burden of child care.

FAMILY SHAPE

Your family shape is determined by when you have your first and last babies and by the gaps between them. You can shape your family much more reliably today than has ever been possible before. This is very important if you are to preserve your sanity and to make the most of your abilities and gifts both for yourself and for others. Men and women today often find themselves with a variety of roles and juggling them can be a full-time occupation. This is most true for the working mother, who may end up with very little time for herself to recharge her batteries.

There are pros and cons to any family shape and there is no one right way.

WHEN TO START A FAMILY

As far as the health of mother and baby is concerned, it is marginally better for a woman not to have a baby too early in her fertile life or too near her menopause. The problems of childbearing are greater at either end of a woman's reproductive life. A very young mother, especially if she is unsupported, is more likely to have social or emotional problems than physical ones; whereas some women leave it very late, only to be disappointed when they have difficulty in conceiving. The risk of miscarriage rises gradually from the age of 20 to 40, then rises much more steeply. In addition, the older you are when you have your first baby, the more likely you are to develop diabetes or high blood pressure during pregnancy; and the risk of conceiving a baby with Down's syndrome increases with the age of the mother.

Several researchers have pointed out that the older a woman is when she gives birth to a daughter, the greater is the risk of that daughter developing breast cancer in later life. A possible, though unproven, reason for this may be that younger pregnant women (aged under 20) have oestrogen levels in their blood one-third lower than those in older pregnant women (aged 20 to 29). It has been suggested that high levels of oestrogen in pregnancy increase the possibility of daughters getting breast cancer. American women have substantially higher levels of oestrogen during pregnancy than Japanese women; and the incidence of breast cancer in American and British women is five times higher than in Japanese women.

It is interesting to note that the incidence of breast cancer in Japanese immigrants in the USA approaches that of the average woman in the USA within one or two generations. This implies that genetic factors are not responsible. It may be that diet during pregnancy is a major determinant of a woman's oestrogen levels (*see page 30*), the supposition being that a diet high in animal fat could increase oestrogen levels.

Men can also run into trouble if they delay fathering a child. Geneticists have found that for paternally derived new mutations (such as achondroplasia or haemophilia A) there is often a positive association between the frequency of the mutation and the age of the father.

An important question for partners thinking of starting a baby is to ask themselves if they are ready for parenthood and the change in relationship a baby brings.

SPACING YOUR FAMILY

Before she even thinks about having another baby, a mother should give herself enough time for her body and mind to restore themselves and regain balance. Allow each baby enough one-to-one time before the next comes along. You cannot give two children the same amount of attention each that you can give to one. And even if you can give each one as much as he or she needs, you may feel overstretched by having two close together. While you are planning your family, learn about children's emotional development so that you will be able to recognize what your older child needs from you when the next one comes along.

Wait for a while after a miscarriage or a stillbirth, before starting another baby. Mothers who have experienced such a loss say that on balance it is better not to go ahead too soon. You need time to mourn the loss, as I found after our third baby was stillborn *(See also page 53.)*

The gaps you choose to have, or end up having, between your babies can have a profound effect on the family resources available to each child, not least in terms of parental availability and energy. Be creative in your family shaping. Your family need not have the same shape as all the other families around. Do what seems best for you and your family. Work out what help there will be for you if you are thinking of having several babies close together. Looking after them may be hard work, both physically and emotionally.

The spacing between children is particularly important in poorer countries, where parents are more likely to be uneducated and to lack adequate health care, sanitation and perhaps even food. In the Third World, a child is twice as likely as in developed countries to die before reaching five years of age, if the gap between that child and the older sibling is under two years. Experts have worked out how China could abandon its policy of one child per family without altering its targets for population growth. This could be done if each woman delayed having her first baby until she was 28 and if she had at least a four-year gap between her two babies.

Trying to make decisions about the size and shape of your family is pointless unless you know how to go about it. This means understanding fertility, allowing for infertility, and knowing about the different methods of contraception and which are more attractive from a green point of view.

INFERTILITY

If you and your partner do not conceive after a year of unprotected, unlimited sexual intercourse, you are said to be infertile. Infertility can strike before you have your first child, or afterwards; it can be temporary or permanent; and a person may be infertile with one partner but not with another. Infertility has been increasing in developed countries for some years and at present affects about one in six couples in developed countries. According to World Health Organization (WHO) figures published in 1985, one in ten people worldwide is involuntarily infertile. In some places, this figure fluctuates between 1.5 and 40 per cent. The higher figure represents levels of secondary infertility (people not becoming pregnant after having one child) in developing areas, such as the Congo, Gabon, Zaïre and Cameroon. In Mongo, Burkina Faso, 30 to 50 per cent of pregnancies end in miscarriage.

There are many causes of infertility, of which the environmental ones are particularly important. An infertile couple may not produce healthy eggs or sperm, or something may be preventing fertilization (the joining of egg and sperm). Infertility is just as likely to be a male problem as a female one. Male infertility is particularly susceptible to environmental influences, because sperms are vulnerable for a longer period than eggs *(see pages 27 and 30).*

Infertility is difficult to separate from recurrent early miscarriage. This has many possible causes – one of which can be defective sperm. Once a woman conceives, she may lose the newly conceived baby very early, without even realizing she is pregnant. The fertilized egg (the 'pre-embryo') may not implant in the lining of the womb; or the implanted embryo may be miscarried at a very early stage, leading to what seems like a normal or slightly heavy period.

Infertility can stem from a number of environmental and other green issues. These include diet (see opposite under **Fertility and Diet**), water (see page 127), toxins such as lead, aluminium and cadmium (see page 34), pesticides and herbicides (see pages 116–119), the Pill and the IUD (see page 23 under **Non-'Green' Methods**), lubricants, smoking (see page 33), radiation (see pages 134–135), VDUs (see page 148), infection (see page 23 under **Intra-Uterine Device (IUD)**), emotional stress and physical tiredness (see below), sex drive and when, how often and how you have sex (see pages 15–16 under **To Restore Sex Drive**).

The other side of the coin is that a 'green' lifestyle can prevent a great deal of infertility and the disappointment and frustration that often go with it. The key issues are to use 'green' methods of birth control until you decide to try to start a baby; to avoid polluting your body with toxins; and to make the most of your body's natural resources by following a healthy diet. Physical tiredness and exhaustion can reduce your fertility – and bear in mind that sometimes inactivity can make you tired – so you should not only get enough rest but also take enough exercise. Anxiety and stress can make you infertile, so seek skilled help if you have an emotional problem – and do not overlook the emotional stress of worrying about infertility.

LIGHT

If you are infertile and suffer from SAD (Seasonal Affective Disorder, see pages 97–98), you are most likely to conceive in the summer months with the longest hours of intense daylight. Children of SAD sufferers are most likely to be born from April to June in the northern hemisphere. Eskimo women are much more likely to conceive in the summer months; and in Finland the conception rate peaks in June and July when the average person is exposed to 20 hours of sunlight a day.

The reasons for these findings are not fully known, although it is well known to poultry farmers that hens can be encouraged to lay by giving them more hours of exposure to light in the form of artificial lighting. Perhaps infertile couples might experiment with spending more time outdoors in daylight, especially during the darker winter months. Many people in developed countries spend a disproportionate amount of time indoors under artificial lighting.

FERTILITY & DIET

The food you eat can affect your fertility. If you do not eat enough or if your diet is of very poor quality, lacking essential nutrients (see below **Guidelines for Diet**), you may not produce healthy eggs or sperms, or be able to conceive at all. Certain nutrients are specifically necessary for conception, while others interfere with it.

In general a man's diet is of greater importance for his sperm production than a woman's is for her egg production, so take particular care over your diet if you are a man. Men who are too fat (see chart page 31 **Recommended Ideal Weight**) have a greater risk of being infertile. At the other end of the scale, if a woman is too thin – especially if she is anorexic – her risk of infertility is high because egg production (ovulation) is more likely to fail. It is said that approximately one in every two women attending some infertility clinics are there because they have been slimming and have become malnourished as a result of following a nutritionally inadequate diet. A diet low enough in calories to allow weight loss should always contain enough essential nutrients.

GUIDELINES FOR DIET

Follow a healthy diet (*see pages 52–53* **Nutrients Checklist**).

● Keep refined carbohydrates (white flour, white rice and white sugar) to a minimum.

● Eat plenty of foods rich in vitamins A, B (especially B6) and C; arginine (an amino acid found in peanuts, chocolate, seeds and cereals); essential fatty acids; and zinc, chromium, manganese and selenium. These are vital for sperm formation and function. A lack of vitamin C can make sperms clump together. Vitamin A is said to be essential for female fertility.

● Eat plenty of foods rich in vitamin E. A lack of this vitamin may lead to a failure to produce sperm.

● Avoid too many processed foods containing additives: E154 (kipper brown, which can lead to genetic mutations); E220-227 (sulphur dioxide and the sulphites, which can reduce vitamin E); E239 (hexamine, which can lead to gene mutations in animals); E310 and E321 (propyl gallate and butylated hydroxytoluene or BHT, which can lead to reproductive failure); and 924, 925, 926 and 927 (potassium bromate, chlorine, chlorine dioxide and azo-dicarbonamide, which can reduce the amount of vitamin E available for the body to use). Some of the other additives can cause diarrhoea and other gut disturbances, which can interfere with the absorption of nutrients essential for fertility.

● Cut down on coffee, tea and caffeinated soft drinks, or cut them out completely. Studies of coffee intake and fertility give conflicting results, but one showed that women who drank seven cups or more every day had twice as much trouble getting pregnant as those who drank fewer. Two mugs of tea contain as much caffeine as a cup of brewed coffee; and one mug of tea contains nearly as much as a cup of instant coffee.

● Cut out alcohol. There is no known amount which is safe if you are trying to overcome infertility. Alcohol lowers the amount of zinc available from your food, and this can lead to low levels of the male hormone, testosterone, and so to lower sperm counts.

● Be particularly careful to choose a nutritious diet if you have any disorder of your gut function which might lead to poor absorption of nutrients.

● Lose excess weight. Obesity in a man can lead to impotence or a low sperm count.

FERTILITY & SEX

Many sex problems result from unresolved emotional or relationship problems, sometimes dating from way before you met your partner. A sex problem is likely to reduce the number of times you make love. This alone makes infertility more likely. Some couples have sex only rarely because one or both of them has a low sex drive.

Seek professional help through your doctor if you or your partner has a sexual problem. Impotent men should eat more foods rich in iodine, zinc and selenium, as well as the nutrients listed below.

TO RESTORE SEX DRIVE:

● Eat plenty of foods rich in vitamins A, B and E, magnesium, manganese, zinc and vegetable (as opposed to animal) protein. These are important for sex hormone production.

continued overleaf

- Avoid alcohol if you are a man. It may make you feel temporarily sexy but you may suffer from 'brewer's droop' afterwards.

- Optimize your chance of conceiving by clever timing so as to take advantage of the most fertile time of the month.

- Consider whether it might be worth getting psychosexual counselling. Sometimes a low sex drive results from buried emotional problems and can be improved.

- Learn how to cope better with the unavoidable stress in your life.

- Postpone trying for a baby if your lack of sex drive results from physical or emotional exhaustion or tiredness. Give yourself time to recover and take steps if necessary to change your lifestyle.

- Lose weight if you are an overweight man. Too much fat can raise the levels of female sex hormones in your body. This in turn can reduce your sex drive.

- Take more exercise to enhance your feeling of well-being; it may also make you feel sexier.

- Aim at having sex on alternate days during the most fertile time of the month.

- Have sex frequently. This means you are statistically likely to have sex at the most fertile time of the month. Many couples attending infertility clinics have sex only about once a month and then not during the most fertile time.

- A woman should lie down for half an hour after sex with her bottom raised on a pillow so that the semen does not trickle out too soon.

- A man should keep his scrotum relatively cool. Sperms can die if too warm. Try wearing loose boxer shorts instead of tight Y-fronts and do not wear tight jeans.

'GREEN' CONTRACEPTION

Contraception has been attempted for thousands of years, most often by women because, broadly speaking, if nature were allowed to take its course there would be far too many babies. This is, however, only really true of a society in which people are well fed and in which mothers tend not to breastfeed on an unrestricted basis, day and night, for a long time. In certain other societies things are different. When there is less food available, women tend to start their periods later in life and to finish them earlier. This means their potential reproductive life is shorter. If women breastfeed each baby for two, three or four years, the average gap between babies is about two to three years. If the society is poor and is without adequate health care resources, a proportion of babies (and mothers) dies.

Women in developed countries tend to have long reproductive lives; few choose to breastfeed in a way which could contribute towards the spacing of their babies; and they are unlikely to lose a baby or die in childbirth. This means that some other form of birth control is essential to control their fertility.

The past few decades have seen a great deal of experimentation with various new forms of contraception, such as the IUD, oral contraceptive pills, injectable hormones and hormone implants. All have proved highly reliable in preventing births, provided they are used properly; but they all have unwanted side-effects. Natural family planning is another new contraceptive method which promises to become popular rapidly. Sterilization and abortion (or 'termination', as it is euphemistically known) are increasingly being used as means of contraception, but they obviously have disadvantages too. The IUD and the 'morning after' Pill have similar disadvantages since they work by causing an abortion (*see page 25*).

Contraception considered from a green point of view should be reliable (*see chart page 24* **Which contraceptive?**), and should ideally have no side-effects on you or any baby you may have. I will now take a look at the various methods of contraception that are available today.

The simplest form of contraception is abstinence. That means saying 'no' to penetrative sexual intercourse in which the man climaxes inside the woman's vagina. It might be a blanket 'no' all the time, as for a young, unattached person who is sexually aware and attracted to the opposite sex but does not feel ready for an active sexual life; it might be following the birth of a baby; or it might be a cyclical 'no', as for people who choose only to have sexual intercourse during the woman's safe time and choose not to use any other form of contraception (*see below under* **The Safe Time Method**). It goes without saying that from the point of view of successfully avoiding pregnancy, saying 'no' is infallible.

However, some couples move from abstinence to sexual activity too quickly to organize the use of contraceptives such as the Pill, the IUD or even barrier methods. Obviously it pays to be prepared. The World Fertility Survey showed that one in seven of the Bangladeshi couples who delay conception, and 1 in 20 Filipino couples, practise abstinence.

Marital or couple therapists and other professionals whose wisdom is distilled from their experience of relationships suggest that it is better to have relatively few sexual relationships, especially early in adult life. Casual sex or sex outside a committed and loving relationship can lead to physical problems, such as an increased risk of cancer of the cervix and infection with sexually transmitted diseases (such as gonorrhoea, chlamydia, trichomoniasis, non-specific urethritis, herpes, gardnerella, candida infection and AIDS). It can also lead to psychosexual problems, such as a difficulty in ever being able to be emotionally intimate and to give, to trust and to be vulnerable.

From the green perspective, choosing to say 'no' to casual or uncommitted sex may protect your physical and emotional well-being, thereby conserving your personal resources in order to commit them more purposefully later on.

THE SAFE TIME METHOD

Also known as the safe period (a confusing name as it could be mistaken to mean the menstrual period); the calendar or rhythm method; and Vatican roulette, the safe time is the phase of the menstrual cycle when there is little chance of a fertile egg being fertilized by a sperm. This method is based on the supposition that women ovulate reliably and thus predictably on a particular day of their menstrual cycle, and that there is a risk of semen fertilizing the egg only during a certain time before and after ovulation. The safe time is calculated by counting 14 days back from your next predicted period to arrive at your estimated day of ovulation. You then add four or five days either side to arrive at your nine-day fertile time. The rest of the cycle is known as the 'safe' time. During your fertile time you need to refrain from penetrative sexual intercourse or else use a barrier method (*see page 18*).

This method of contraception has three major problems. First, ovulation is not necessarily predictable: some women ovulate irregularly; and some women ovulate regularly, but on cycles of, say, 10 or 16 days instead of 14. Some women ovulate 10 to 16 days before their next period. Second, it only works for women whose cycles are regular. But even a woman whose menstrual cycle – and, therefore, ovulation – are normally regular can ovulate early or late in her cycle. Some women ovulate after sexual intercourse, although ovulation may not be expected then. Third, sperms can live for up to six days inside a woman if the conditions are suitable.

If you do not mind too much when a baby comes along, the safe time method can be useful and it is certainly sound from a green point of view. But if you want your contraception to be as reliable as possible, this method is not at all ideal. Many couples who use the rhythm method have ended up with very large families. One source suggests that up to one in four women using this method get pregnant within a year.

THE TEMPERATURE METHOD

This is a refinement of the safe time method and accurately pin-points the end of a woman's fertile time. It is possible to detect when ovulation has already occurred by noting the rise in body temperature that accompanies it. The temperature rises between 0.2 and 0.4 degrees centigrade soon after ovulation as a result of the production of increased levels of the hormone progesterone. When three consecutive daily readings of temperature, taken first thing in the morning, have been high, they signal the end of your fertile time, and sex is safe for the rest of the cycle. Your temperature must be taken before you get up or have a drink. Several factors can disturb your temperature pattern, including fatigue, shift work and aspirin.

The problem with this method is that it cannot be used to determine the beginning of your fertile time because your temperature will not rise until after ovulation, by which time it may be too late. Furthermore, if you have a feverish illness, this method is obviously useless.

The temperature method relies either on abstinence or on the use of barrier methods as an adjunct during the fertile time. One problem is that during her fertile time a woman may be at her most likely to want sex. Some couples do not wish to use barrier methods, and abstinence may be too much for many couples to ask of each other.

SEXUAL FRUSTRATION

If a man or a woman find they cannot cope with sexual frustration easily, they may feel irritable or bad-tempered. Such feelings could spill over into their parenting. Of course, anyone who is motivated can either learn to live gracefully with their sexual inactivity, or can find alternative ways of relieving their sexual tension, such as masturbation (by self or partner), or withdrawal (coitus interruptus or the withdrawal of the man's penis from his partner's vagina before he climaxes). Withdrawal is probably the oldest method of contraception and is still the most common in some cultures, but it is not at all reliable: nearly one in four couples using this method will start a baby within a year.

These other ways of relieving sexual tension may be unacceptable, particularly at times of greatest stress in the family, such as when a couple are busy raising young children. In developed countries there is a statistically high rate of breakdown of relationships between parents of young children, especially in the first year after the birth of a baby. From the green point of view – that of conserving personal resources – it might not seem sensible to use a method of contraception which could make things more difficult.

CONDOMS, CAPS, DIAPHRAGMS

Barrier methods prevent semen from reaching the cervix (the neck of the womb). They include latex rubber condoms, caps and diaphragms and natural sea sponges. Correctly used with a spermicidal jelly, cream or gel, they have a high degree of efficiency and acceptability and are ideal for a couple who are sexually active and practised at using them. A couple who have sexual intercourse infrequently risk forgetting to use them or using them incorrectly, so that they fail to form an impenetrable barrier. There is also the possibility that the rubber of an old contraceptive may be weakened, or have perished, or that a new one may be punctured.

A problem is that some people are not very keen on barrier methods. A sheath or a condom is said by some to reduce the amount of sensation and, therefore, their pleasure in the sexual act; and it can be a nuisance to put on in the heat of the moment. A diaphragm or a cap can be fiddly to put in, especially at times of high sexual arousal, and some women do not like doing it. The result is often a relatively high rate of user-failure.

Perhaps the most effective use of barrier

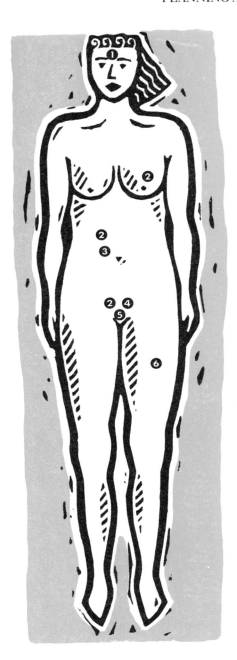

SIDE-EFFECTS OF THE PILL

Women who take the Pill have an increased risk of migraine *left*, (1); cancers of the cervix, liver and possibly breast (2); gall-bladder disease (3); erosion of the cervix (the neck of the womb) (4); thrush (*Candida albicans*) (5); blood clots in the legs (thrombosis) (6); strokes; high blood pressure; diabetes; food allergy; fluid retention; weight increase; skin disorders; depression; heart disease.

● Smoking while taking the Pill increases the risk of heart disease.

● Women on the Pill may have raised body levels of vitamin A (which may cause foetal abnormalities), increased levels of copper, a deficiency of vitamins and minerals, such as vitamin B2 (riboflavin), vitamin B6 (pyridoxine), vitamin B12 and magnesium. Some deficiencies, such as folic acid and zinc, have been linked to foetal abnormalities. The bodily requirement for vitamins C and B1 (thiamine) may be raised in Pill-takers.

● Other possible side-effects are alterations in the metabolism of tryptophan, one of the body's amino acids, and vitamin B12, as well as in the body's immune system.

● The effects of the Pill on vitamin and mineral levels can tip the balance for women whose nutrition is poor, into a state of deficiency. In women who stop the Pill to become pregnant, marginal nutritional deficiencies may reduce fertility or harm a newly conceived baby.

● Taking the combined Pill can reduce the amount of milk a breastfeeding mother makes. Synthetic steroids from the progestogen-only mini-Pill are present in her milk.

Although the Pill is a very effective method of contraception when properly used, the chart (*above* and *right*) details the many side-effects associated with its use in women in the West since its introduction in the nineteen-sixties.

methods is as an adjunct to a method which is fast gaining in popularity: natural family planning.

NATURAL FAMILY PLANNING

This form of contraception has nothing to do with the safe time method, described above. It combines a method called, variously, the mucus, the ovulation or the Billings method, with the temperature method described above and with a recognition of changes in other bodily symptoms to do with fertility. It is also called the sympto-thermal method. It is based on the changes fertility brings to the appearance and feel of the mucus produced by the cervix. This mucus varies in amount and texture according to whether or not you are fertile. It passes down the vagina and out of the body, so it can be examined regularly.

If you learn to recognize the sort of mucus you are producing, you can predict with a high degree of accuracy whether or not it is safe for you to have unprotected sexual intercourse. When your mucus is 'fertile' (meaning that it will keep sperms alive and allow them to swim through the cervix, and that ovulation is near), all you need do in order to have sex without risking conception is use a diaphragm or a cap, or ask your partner to use a condom. People with religious or other objections to using barrier methods will have to abstain from sexual intercourse during the fertile days of the month.

Fertile mucus is noticeably wetter than non-fertile mucus. Your vulva may feel wet, almost as if your period has begun, or as if you did not wipe your vulva well enough after passing water. Fertile mucus is also thin, slippery and stretchy. If you put some of it between your finger and thumb, then draw them apart, it will stretch out into a long 'string'; non-fertile mucus will not do this. The amount of this wet mucus increases each day until it reaches a peak. The next day it is less noticeable. Nine times out of ten, ovulation (the release of the egg from the ovary) occurs within 24 hours of this peak mucus production. Occasionally it occurs on the day of peak wetness; and sometimes within 48 hours. Even if you have multiple ovulations, they will occur during this time. When the egg is released it remains fertile only for 8 to 24 hours. Fertile mucus dries up after ovulation. In one study 97 per cent of women identified fertile mucus.

Since ovulation makes the body temperature rise, if you keep a daily early morning temperature chart thoughout your menstrual cycle, you will notice that your fertile mucus corresponds with the last six low readings. You are potentially fertile during that time, and during the first three high readings after ovulation, about nine days. Although an egg becomes infertile within 24 hours of ovulation, experts recommend waiting to have unprotected sexual intercourse until three consecutive daily temperature readings have been high to avoid mistakes occurring perhaps as a result of a temporarily raised body temperature caused by a minor infection. You are probably only potentially fertile for 7 days each month; menstruation normally begins 14 days after ovulating, but women vary from 10 to 16 days after ovulation (see page 17).

Fertile mucus is cloudy-white to begin with, then becomes as clear as raw egg white by the peak mucus day. It lasts for five to six days in all and can prolong the life of sperms in your reproductive tract for up to six days. Fertile mucus is alkaline, so it neutralizes the previously acidic conditions of your safe time to enable sperms to live in the vagina; it contains nutrients which feed the sperms; and it enables them to swim up to the cervix via mucus channels in the wall of the vagina.

To be safe from unwanted pregnancy, use a barrier method of contraception or avoid penetrative sexual intercourse from the day you suspect that your mucus is beginning to show signs of fertility until three days after your mucus peak. Unprotected sex before you have fertile mucus is safe because sperms need fertile mucus to survive. Without it they die within hours.

To assess your level of fertility even more accurately you can learn to examine your cervix. When you are fertile your cervix is softer and higher up in your vagina, and its opening is not as tightly closed as usual. Your awareness of certain other personal body symptoms can also add to your knowledge of your fertility. Some women bleed lightly at ovulation, for example. One in two experiences low, central abdominal pain a day or two before or after ovulation. Others have a one-sided pain – sometimes severe – related to the ovary which is ovulating. Tummy-bloating and breast-tenderness are two other symptoms.

Natural family planning is not so dependent on regular cycles as is the safe time method and – if you want to have sex in the first half of your cycle – the temperature method, because it depends on several symptoms of fertility. This means it can be used by women whose cycles are irregular. However, if you have recently come off the Pill you would be unwise to rely on the natural family planning method for several cycles after stopping the Pill. Oral contraception can suppress symptoms of fertility for some time after you have stopped using it. Similarly, such symptoms may be unreliable if you are breastfeeding or nearing the menopause.

The great green benefits of natural family planning are that it has no unwanted side-effects and that it allows unprotected but safe sexual intercourse for most of the cycle. It is a good idea to learn how to use natural family planning from a recognized teacher at your local clinic. When properly taught and used by a committed couple, the failure rate of this method, in terms of unwanted pregnancy, is equivalent to that of a barrier method, or to the IUD.

Also from the green viewpoint, natural family planning is an excellent form of spacing or preventing pregnancies. It is user-friendly, with no unpleasant side-effects. It makes no litter, it empowers the individual, and it encourages the use of your own resources and body-awareness. The couple who use this method benefit

UK MATERNITY RIGHTS

Most working women in the UK are entitled to 40 weeks' maternity leave. This period can begin 11 weeks before birth is due and must end 29 weeks after the birth. If a woman has worked for the same employer for at least two years by the 11th week before birth is due, she has the right to return to work at any time within 29 weeks of the birth. A woman cannot be made redundant because she is pregnant. If she is doing unsuitable or dangerous work, her employer is obliged to find her another job within the company.

Pregnant women in paid work can usually claim Standard Maternity Pay (SMP) from their employers, even if they do not intend to return to work after the birth. They must, however, have been in the same job for at least six months by the 26th week.

SMP can be paid for up to 18 weeks. A woman who has been working full-time in the same job for at least two years, or part-time for five years, will receive 90 per cent of her average weekly earnings for the first six weeks of payment. After this period, a basic rate applies (£39.25 per week in 1990). Women who have not been in the same job long receive the basic rate.

Women who do not qualify for SMP may be eligible for Maternity Allowance (£35.70 per week in 1990). Parents on low incomes may qualify for a payment from the Social Fund. All pregnant women may claim free dental treatment, prescriptions and milk.

Once your baby is born, you are entitled to Child Benefit (£7.25 per child per week in 1990). Single parents can claim One Parent Benefit (£5.60 per week in 1990) as well for the first child. If your baby is stillborn you remain eligible for most maternity benefits. You must obtain a certificate.

from the combined and ever-growing body of wisdom of the years of experience of millions of like-minded couples and the reports of doctors and researchers.

BREASTFEEDING

Breastfeeding is nature's contraceptive. If it is carried out on an unrestricted basis (with no limitation of the number or length of sessions the baby has at the breast, and no long gaps between feeds day or night) it can considerably delay the return of fertility after childbirth. Worldwide, it is a very important method of spacing babies and provides more than 98 per cent protection from pregnancy in the first six months after childbirth. To stabilize world population it is crucial to protect breastfeeding from the destabilizing effects of the marketing of infant formula (*see pages 86–87*). In Africa, it has been estimated that breastfeeding infertility prevents an average of four births per woman, and in Bangladesh six births per woman.

It is not safe to rely on breastfeeding infertility up until your first period after giving birth, because ovulation may not be preceded by a period. One woman in 20 ovulates before her first period. Ovulation returns on average eight to ten weeks after the baby's birth in the woman who does not breastfeed at all. She therefore needs to use contraception as soon as she resumes sexual intercourse.

In a fully breastfeeding woman the first ovulation after the birth is likely to be delayed very much longer. The earliest it will be is at ten weeks. By 18 weeks only 1 fully breastfeeding woman in 20 has started to ovulate. If unrestricted breastfeeding is continued for 6 to 8 months before the baby is given solids, and as a means of supplying drinks and comfort into the baby's second year, the average woman will not have a period until her baby is over 14 months old.

When your periods begin again, your menstrual cycle and mucus pattern may not be as obvious as when you are not breastfeeding. Your body may have several attempts at ovulation before it actually

occurs. However, a combination of unrestricted breastfeeding and natural family planning provides a natural and effective way of spacing babies.

The suppression of your ovulation by breastfeeding relies on fairly constant levels of the hormone prolactin, day and night. Prolactin prevents the release of the pituitary hormones responsible for your ovulation. A sudden dip can trigger the return of fertile mucus and ovulation. Dips in prolactin levels result from long gaps between feeds. These may happen for several reasons: you and your baby may sleep through the night; you may hire a babysitter for an evening; your baby may use a dummy (pacifier) or other soother and may not get enough non-nutritive sucking time (comfort time) at the breast; he or she may be ill or irritable and not want the breast; you may sometimes use a bottle for feeding, or foods other than your milk; or there may be a disturbance in your daily life such as a move, a holiday, or an unusual or busy situation, such as Christmas.

If one of these situations happens, avoid causing prolactin levels to dip: express milk from your breasts to stimulate prolactin production. Expression is not quite as effective a way of preventing prolactin dips as a baby's sucking, so take special care to monitor your mucus pattern afterwards. For example, a decrease in the number of feeds on one day may result in a feeling of wetness from increased (and possibly fertile) cervical mucus the next day.

If your periods have not yet restarted, or if your cycles are irregular, you will not know when to expect your wet, fertile mucus to appear. If you have intercourse one day, you must abstain the next day in order to be sure, because the presence of seminal fluid in your vagina makes the detection of fertile mucus difficult. Some breastfeeding women produce a little milky and infertile mucus most of the time. If so, intercourse should not be repeated within 24 hours. When mucus starts appearing, treat it as if it is fertile by avoiding sex or using a barrier method. Wait until the fourth day after the mucus dries up before having unprotected sex.

Bleeding or spotting may be associated with ovulation. Avoid sex or use a barrier method until the fourth day after the bleeding has stopped. When menstruation proper returns, your first few cycles may not be regular and your fertile mucus may not be as noticeable as when you are not breastfeeding.

If you are in any doubt about how to use natural family planning when breastfeeding, speak with a teacher trained in the method. Properly used, this combination works very well for many couples and is completely without any side-effects.

NON-'GREEN' METHODS

Any form of contraception that has the potential for causing damage to mother or baby is best looked at very carefully and ideally substituted with a more natural method. However, you may not be encouraged to do this. There are fortunes to be made for shareholders and top personnel in the pharmaceutical industry. This is especially true in the vast, largely untapped market of the developing countries, where companies often use expensive, top-level marketing techniques to encourage doctors to supply women with the Pill, IUDs, and injectable contraceptives. Women eager to control their fertility can readily become innocent prey at the mercy of the hunt for profit. By contrast, green methods of contraception, such as natural family planning, have no profit motive behind their promotion. Health personnel are only human, so some may be less enthusiastic. It is well worth bearing this in mind when you choose your method of contraception.

STERILIZATION

Both male and female sterilization (vasectomy or tubal ligation) are growing rapidly in popularity in developed countries. As a means of contraception sterilization is efficient, though not 100 per cent so. From a green point of view it helps with population control. From the personal point of view it enables many couples to be free from the worry of protecting themselves from unwanted pregnancy. Some people find that their circumstances change and they would like another baby. The operation is definitely not always reversible and side-effects, while rare, are not unknown.

THE PILL

The hormones in the oral contraceptive pill come in several combinations. They affect not only the reproductive system but also many other aspects of a woman's metabolism. The Pill has become one of the most studied drugs in history: women in developed countries have been the guinea pigs for its later use for women in the Third World.

Serious side-effects are rare. Indeed, the Pill gives protection against pelvic infection and certain cancers. However, the Pill alters body chemistry and many side-effects can occur (*see chart page 19* **Side-effects of the Pill**). They make some women feel less than well, with all that entails for them and their families. Some of these effects are relatively long-lasting and there is some evidence that they could affect a baby conceived too soon after stopping the Pill. Nowadays a gap of at least three and ideally six months is recommended before conceiving.

Most women stop taking the Pill after using it for between two and five years. In the USA the number of Pill users has been gradually falling since the heady days of the sexual revolution of the sixties, when it was the most popular method of contraception. Only nine per cent of fertile women now take it. Yet the number of Pill-users in developing countries is rising. All the different types of Pill are very reliable when taken properly, as the chart on page 19 shows.

INTRA-UTERINE DEVICE (IUD)

This type of contraceptive has a variety of other names, descriptive of its shape and content, the best known being the copper coil. Some IUDs contain slow-release con-

WHICH CONTRACEPTIVE?

Percentage of pregnancies per year when
method is used correctly

Method		
Combined Pill		Less than 1
Mini-Pill		1
Injectable contraceptives		Less than 1
Intrauterine Device (IUD)		1 - 3
Diaphragm or cap with spermicide		2
Sponge		9
Condom		2
Female sterilization		0.1 - 0.5
Male sterilization		0.1
Natural (sympto-thermal) method		2

Figures supplied by the Family Planning Service

The failure rates of the different methods of contraception shown in the chart (*above*), hold true only when couples use the contraceptives properly. The rates are significantly higher when the instructions on the pack or given by a health professional are not carefully followed. For example, the failure rate of the combined Pill rises to between 1 and 2 per cent with less careful use and it can be as high as 7 per cent if taken very erratically.

traceptive chemicals, such as progestogen. IUDs are made from plastic, plastic plus copper, or, in China, stainless steel. While they are generally very effective contraceptives, babies have been born holding one in their hands, so they are certainly not foolproof. Some women complain of heavy or prolonged periods when they have an IUD in place, while others complain of uterine aching. IUDs are sometimes difficult to remove. They make pelvic infection more likely and therefore increase the risk of infertility.

One invisible side-effect of the copper coil is the rise in copper levels in the body. High copper levels have been connected with premature labour, low birth weight, and neural tube defects such as spina bifida. This is a good reason for having your IUD removed six months before you plan to try for a baby. If you have an IUD put in soon after you have a baby – as mothers are sometimes encouraged to do – there is thought to be a higher risk of it perforating the womb than at other times.

The IUD is not a green method of contraception because of the way it interferes with body chemistry over a long period of time. It is becoming much less popular. This is partly because of the publicity given to a recent case brought before the US courts, dealing with the adverse side-effects of one make of IUD.

INJECTABLE CONTRACEPTIVES

These are contraceptive hormones (progestogens or progestogen plus oestrogen combinations), which may be injected into the body at intervals of three to six months to form a long-lasting depot. They can also be implanted in capsule form beneath the skin (of the forearm, usually). They have still not been given the seal of approval for marketing in the USA, the UK and several other countries, partly because of some doubts as to whether they might increase the risk of breast cancer in young women. They are officially approved in over 80 countries, including Sweden, Belgium and New Zealand.

TERMINATION

Termination – or abortion – has been used as a means of family planning for centuries, whether legally or illegally. Out of 1.2 million unintended pregnancies in the USA each year, half will end in abortion. In the UK, one in five known pregnancies are terminated. Some people find the idea of killing an unborn baby horrific and completely unacceptable from a moral point of view. From a green standpoint, if you accept that each person is a precious natural resource, killing an unborn person would seem unacceptable. A percentage of women find it very difficult to come to terms emotionally with abortion after the event.

An abortion can endanger a woman's fertility and in some cases her life or health. This is highly unlikely to happen if the operation is carried out by properly qualified health-care personnel, but that is not always the case. Any clamp down on legal abortions is inevitably bound to lead to a rise in back-street abortions. Medical methods of termination and surgical ones carried out early in pregnancy are both becoming more sophisticated.

You may be surprised to know that both the IUD and the 'morning after' or the 'visiting' pill act not as contraceptives (ie. preventing contraception), but cause what is technically an abortion. They prevent the newly conceived baby (the pre-embryo) from implanting in the lining of the womb, and this results in its death. The morning after pill is being marketed in China and Hungary. Its use is spreading in western Europe. Because it does not always work, it might damage the development of the pre-embryo.

THE PURPOSE OF PLANNING

Planning your life, postponing pregnancy as wisely and as naturally as you can and choosing the right time to conceive give you, your partner and your baby a good base for life, health and happiness. Thoughtful contraception is a way of loving and respecting others and yourselves.

Chapter Two
GREAT EXPECTATIONS

All the flowers of all the tomorrows are in the seeds of today.

A green pregnancy starts long before the genetic material in the sperm and the egg join at conception. Environmental influences can affect the very structure of these male and female cells, as well as their chances of joining up. They also affect the health of the mother-to-be and her unborn baby. It is during the earliest stages of life in the womb, before most women even know they are pregnant, that an unborn baby is at its most vulnerable to damage.

Cell division in a recently conceived baby is extremely rapid, yet this is the time when you may not even know you are pregnant and you are unlikely to be receiving any professional care. The newly fertilized egg (the pre-embryo) may only be a little round blob the diameter of the shaft of a pin, and the embryo at 28 days may only look like a big-headed worm the size of a pea (*see page 28*), but damage can be done in these early weeks of pregnancy, before you have missed your first or second period.

Looking after yourself before you conceive and caring for your baby in the very early stages of its life are therefore both vital, in my view. That is why I find the term 'peri-conceptual' (meaning 'around the time of conception') more apt and helpful than 'pre-conceptual' (meaning 'before conception').

You owe it to yourself and your unborn baby to be aware of environmental influences during the peri-conceptual period. You cannot make everything perfect, of course, but you can make the most of your health as a valuable natural asset. This chapter will discuss how both parents can prepare for conception and how a woman can care both for herself and her baby throughout pregnancy.

FITNESS TRAINING

Both women and men can do a lot for themselves and their baby-to-be in the months before pregnancy begins. You and your partner can reduce environmental hazards, optimize your health and cope with any problems that might affect your fertility (*see pages 13–15*) and the well-being of the baby you are trying to conceive.

Two of the cells inside your ovaries and testes are destined to develop into the egg and sperm that join to create your baby. Eggs and sperms are vulnerable to damage from a poor diet and from certain viruses, drugs, toxic chemicals and forms of radiation in the environment. The egg is vulnerable for about 100 days leading up to ovulation, but particularly during the three days immediately before ovulation and in the hours leading up to fertilization. This is because immature eggs may begin the chromosomal changes which will bring about their development into mature eggs several cycles before the cycle in which one will be released at ovulation. Eggs are at their most vulnerable when chromosomal changes are occurring. An egg does not finally mature (that is, lose half of its genetic material) until after it has been fertilized by a sperm in the fallopian tube. Only then can the genetic material of egg and sperm unite to conceive a baby with a full and unique complement of genes. Sperms are particularly vulnerable for up to 116 days before they reach maturity. This means that the four months or so before a baby is conceived are extremely important for both parents.

An unborn baby may be damaged as a result of a combination of adverse factors

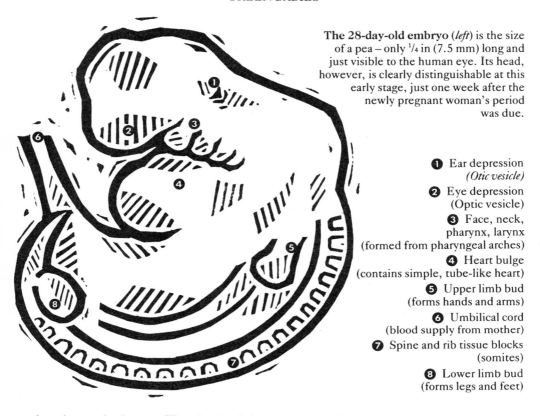

The 28-day-old embryo (*left*) is the size of a pea – only ¼ in (7.5 mm) long and just visible to the human eye. Its head, however, is clearly distinguishable at this early stage, just one week after the newly pregnant woman's period was due.

❶ Ear depression
(*Otic vesicle*)

❷ Eye depression
(Optic vesicle)

❸ Face, neck, pharynx, larynx
(formed from pharyngeal arches)

❹ Heart bulge
(contains simple, tube-like heart)

❺ Upper limb bud
(forms hands and arms)

❻ Umbilical cord
(blood supply from mother)

❼ Spine and rib tissue blocks
(somites)

❽ Lower limb bud
(forms legs and feet)

rather than a single one. That is why it is sensible to play safe and adopt a whole package of peri-conceptual care which begins before you start trying to conceive. Prospective parents are rather like athletes. They perform best when in peak condition; for that they need to train.

DIET

A good, healthy diet will maximize your chances of being able to supply enough of the nutrients needed by your baby without robbing yourself. Make sure your diet contains foods from the three major groups (*see pages 184–186 under* **Diet**), and that it is rich in nutrients essential to the baby's development, such as protein, calcium, iron, folic acid and iodine (*see pages 52–53* **Nutrients Checklist**).

Studies show that adequate levels of vitamins A, B, C and E, zinc, manganese, chromium, selenium and essential fatty acids are necessary for optimum fertility in animals. They also show that adequate levels of vitamins A, B, C, D, E, folic acid, the bioflavonoids, zinc, magnesium, iron, manganese, essential fatty acids and amino acids are necessary to maintain pregnancy and help prevent malformation and miscarriage. Foods containing all of these nutrients are listed on page 53 in the **Nutrients Checklist**. Numerous studies show that pre-eclampsia (a complex condition which can cause kidney damage in pregnancy), premature and stillbirth, and illness in a newborn baby, are all less likely if a mother's diet before and during pregnancy is sound (*see chart pages 52–3* **Preventing Complications In Pregnancy**). This is probably the case for humans too.

Early in pregnancy, when babies' organs and body systems are developing, they are most susceptible to damage from the environmental toxins which can cause congenital malformations (birth defects). Foods rich in vitamins A, C and E, selenium, zinc and manganese may protect you and your baby from toxic substances, possibly by enhancing their rate of breakdown and excretion.

Zinc levels in the human body can be lowered by eating a diet high in refined carbohydrates, food grown on soil deficient in zinc and food containing certain additives, and by consuming alcoholic drinks. Over-exposure to copper can also lower zinc levels in your body. Insufficient zinc in pregnancy can lead to babies being born prematurely and with a low birth weight. Traces of organophosphate pesticides (*see page 39 under* Biocides) can lower the amount of manganese the body can absorb from food. Manganese is necessary for optimum fertility and helps prevent birth defects.

Selenium deficiency may be connected with genetic damage. Chromium deficiency is associated with depressed sperm formation and can stem from eating a diet high in added sugar and alcohol. If you eat a lot of saturated fats, your body may be deficient in essential fatty acids. These are unsaturated fatty acids, such as cis-linoleic acid, which are essential to our health and present in foods of vegetable and animal origin. Animal fat, hydrogenated vegetable fat and some vegetable oils (such as palm and coconut) have high levels of saturated fats and little or no essential fatty acids. Eat foods which are as fresh as possible and always discard those which have any sign of mould. Some moulds produce toxins which can damage a recently conceived baby. According to some researchers fresh garlic is capable of counteracting fungal and bacterial toxins. No modern drug can do this, so it might be sensible to include garlic in your diet every day to protect your baby.

Any processing of food leads to some loss of nutrients. Even if this loss in any one food is small, many small losses soon add up if your diet contains a high proportion of processed foods. Try to choose foods which are free from unnecessary, purely cosmetic additives. Any additive capable of causing side-effects, however unlikely, is best avoided in case you become pregnant unknowingly.

Avoid too many canned foods. Some vitamins are usually lost in canning and also in freezing food. Choose really fresh fruits and vegetables, preferably organically grown, to avoid a build up of agrochemicals in your body (*see pages 116–119*); ideally they should be consumed as soon as possible after harvesting. Do not peel fruit and vegetables unless you have to, because many of the valuable nutrients are found just under the skin, but wash non-organic fruit and vegetables thoroughly. Cook them for a short time only in order to retain vitamins.

Buy 'organic' meat, fish and poultry, that is, meat from animals reared without the routine use of antibiotics, hormones or other drugs. If you can, take steps to avoid milk from cows which have been routinely injected with antibiotics to prevent mastitis. If you eat meat and drink milk, but are unable to buy organic supplies, include live, unpasteurized yoghurt in your diet as well as plenty of fresh, raw fruit and vegetables, to help maintain a healthy population of beneficial micro-organisms in the bowel. If you are a vegetarian, check that your diet contains plenty of foods rich in vitamin B12 (*see page 53*). Total vegetarians and vegans may be advised to take a vitamin B12 supplement.

THE JUNK FOOD DIET

Eggs and sperm need the right balance of nutrients from carbohydrates, proteins, fats (including essential fatty acids), vitamins and minerals in their blood supply. Nutritional deficiencies can result from a poor diet based on foods high in calories but low in essential nutrients. Such a diet is the typical diet of junk food containing: too much saturated fat (animal or hydrogenated vegetable fat); refined carbohydrate (added or recipe sugar; white flour and its products and white rice); drinks containing caffeine and food additives; and too little fresh fruit, vegetables, wholegrains, nuts and seeds. Choose instead foods which give your body the nutrients it needs to prepare a suitable environment for the baby you are waiting to conceive.

Unhealthy eating is all the more likely if you are living in difficult circumstances. If you have very little money and your choice of food is limited, bear in mind that junk food can cost more than simple wholefoods. It may seem easier to buy prepared food than to spend time choosing and preparing fresh produce, particularly if you have a family or a demanding job, or you live in a bedsit with limited storage facilities. But bear in mind that you can miss out in the long run on health and energy, so try to replace fast meals with healthier options whenever possible. If you are unhappy, bored or lonely and find yourself taking comfort in sweet, stodgy or fatty food, do not be afraid to seek help.

Remember that a little of what you fancy (in the way of junk food) does you good. A lot can harm you and your baby. If you are expecting twins, it is even more important to avoid junk food. Twins need twice as many nutrients and you need to avoid putting on too much weight.

WEIGHT

Women should not try to lose weight in the few months before conception (*see page 39 under* Biocides). Measure your height and weight and plot them on the chart (*opposite*) to estimate whether your weight is within the optimal range for your height, from the point of view of your health. If you want or need to lose weight, do it sensibly and gradually so as to finish at least four months before you start trying to conceive. Choose a slimming diet which gives you at least 1,000 calories a day and make sure that it has been worked out by a qualified dietician or other knowledgeable health professional, so you can be sure you will get the nutrients you need. It is more difficult for some women to maintain their optimal weight than it is to lose excess weight, so continue to follow a healthy diet once you have achieved your desired weight.

One American researcher has recently suggested that the daughters of women who were overweight in pregnancy may have a higher than average risk of breast cancer when they grow up. This may, it is suggested, result from the high levels of oestrogen associated with being overweight, or with the large amounts of animal fat commonly eaten by overweight people.

If you feel you are too thin, talk to a dietician about how you can gain weight easily and safely before you become pregnant.

WATER

Copper from copper water pipes is present in the water you use for drinking and cooking. It is an essential trace element, but too much can reduce the amount of zinc – one of the minerals necessary for optimum fertility – available from your food.

The water you drink may contain levels of aluminium (*see pages 36–37*) or fluoride high enough to interfere with the amount of magnesium you absorb (*see pages 52–53*).

Excessive lead in water can be a problem (*see page 35*) and pesticides can seep down from agricultural land into the water table or into rivers supplying reservoirs (*see page 127*) to contaminate the water supply.

Consider checking the levels of minerals and pesticides in your water supply with your local water board or with an independent water analyst (*see page 183* Consumer Guide). The Consumer Association of Canada will test tap water for 92 substances, including pesticides and PCBs (*see page 78*). If any levels are unacceptably high, filter your water using an appropriate filter before using it for drinking or cooking. Alternatively, use bottled water. The EC has adopted a number of measures prohibiting or limiting the dumping of toxins in rivers or seas.

ALCOHOL

Alcohol lowers the body's levels of zinc, a mineral necessary for sperm formation. Sperms take over three months to become *continued on page 32*

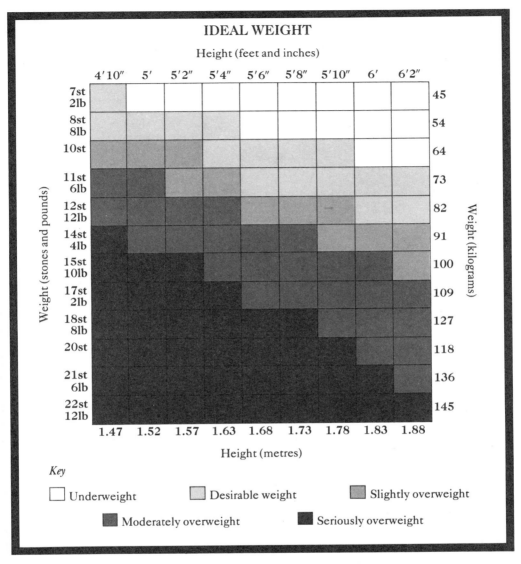

IDEAL WEIGHT

Height (feet and inches)

Key

☐ Underweight   ▨ Desirable weight   ▩ Slightly overweight

▨ Moderately overweight   ■ Seriously overweight

Weight problems can sometimes lead to complications before, during and after pregnancy. Use the chart (*above*) to find out whether you are of a desirable and healthy weight. Find your height on one of the horizontal axes, then your weight on one of the vertical axes. Draw a line from each point; the number of the square in which the lines meet indicates your weight category, and can be decoded by consulting the key. If you are underweight, you are more likely to be infertile. If you are of a desirable weight, you

have the best chance of enjoying good health and a healthy pregnancy. If you are slightly overweight, your health and pregnancy are not immediately affected. The trouble starts when you become moderately or severely overweight. You then have an increased risk of pregnancy complications, including pre-eclamptic toxaemia (a form of kidney damage), diabetes, prolonged labour, Caesarean section and complications after any operation you may need.

mature and can easily be damaged during this time. The sperms of men who are alcoholic are more likely to be damaged than those of men who drink little or not at all, but as little as one bout of heavy drinking may affect sperm.

An egg is especially vulnerable during its three days of active growth before ovulation, so the period when it is particularly vulnerable to damage by a potential poison such as alcohol is much shorter than that of the sperm. A fertilized egg can also be damaged by high levels of alcohol, which increases the risk of very early miscarriage. The safe amount of alcohol – if any – is not known. Women absorb more alcohol from their stomachs than men, probably because they have lower levels of the gastric enzymes that break down alcohol. Some experts therefore believe that women should drink no alcohol for at least four months before planning to have a baby and throughout pregnancy.

IMMUNITY

If you are less than healthy and your diet is poor, your immune system may be below par, making you vulnerable to infection (*see below*). The combination of a lowered immunity and a poor diet can lead to food sensitivity and damage to the bowel wall. This in turn can lead to a failure to absorb from your food all the nutrients necessary for a healthy conception and pregnancy. Food sensitivity, responsible for problems like diarrhoea, bloating, abdominal pain, headaches, joint pains, depression, insomnia, fatigue, eczema and asthma, can interfere with conception. Women with coeliac disease (gluten intolerance), for example, have an increased risk of infertility. It is worth tracking down a possible food sensitivity long before you start trying to conceive, so you can avoid both nutritional deficiencies and the need for medicines.

Traces of antibiotics from the meat or milk of intensively reared animals could lead to sensitivity to antibiotics, which might jeopardize any future treatment you might need for an infection during pregnancy. It is also possible that traces of antibiotics could alter the types of organism living in your gut and the balance of their populations. This could in turn reduce the amounts of nutrients you absorb.

INFECTIONS IN PREGNANCY

Rubella (German measles) is a viral infection that can damage your unborn baby if you catch it for the first time when you are pregnant. It can cause cataracts, deafness, heart disease, a small head, low birth weight and miscarriage. Rubella infection in the first three months nearly always damages the baby. Infection between 13 and 16 weeks of pregnancy damages a smaller proportion: one in six. Damage is rare if the infection begins after 17 weeks. Women who have rubella in early pregnancy may be offered a termination.

You can avoid rubella by making sure that your immunity to it is high. This is particularly important if you work with children, some of whom will not have been vaccinated against rubella. Immunity to rubella is raised if you have the infection or are vaccinated against it. You can have your immunity status checked by a blood test. If it is low, have a rubella vaccination, but make absolutely sure that you do not get pregnant for three months afterwards, or your baby could risk rubella damage.

Toxoplasmosis is an infection which, if caught by a woman just before or during pregnancy, can damage or kill her baby. She would hardly be aware she had the virus. It is caught by eating contaminated meat (lamb, beef or pork); from contact with the excreta of newly infected kittens or, rarely, older cats; or by eating vegetables grown in soil contaminated by the excreta of newly infected kittens. The virus is transmitted to kittens from their first prey, but they quickly become immune.

To avoid toxoplasmosis, make sure any meat you eat is really well cooked and wash your hands after stroking a kitten or handling its litter tray. You can have a toxoplasma antibody test to see if you already have protective antibodies in your blood.

In France and Austria pregnant women are tested routinely.

Pelvic infection, which is frequently sexually transmitted and symptomless, can lead to blockage of the fallopian tubes with subsequent infertility. Treatment is with antibiotics. If you have an unusual pain or discharge or if you believe your risk of pelvic infection is high, see your doctor or visit a special hospital clinic.

Other infections that can damage an unborn baby include cytomegalovirus infection (which attacks the liver, spleen and lungs); parvovirus infection (which can lead to miscarriage or stillbirth); and – rarely – chickenpox. There is little you can do at present to protect yourself and your baby from these infections.

SMOKING

Smoking affects the quality of sperm and makes infertility more likely. German researchers found that men who smoke between 10 and 20 cigarettes a day are more than twice as likely to have a malformed baby as men who do not smoke. You are more likely to miscarry or have a stillborn baby if you smoke, and your baby has a higher risk of dying from Sudden Infant Death Syndrome (SIDS or cot death), or from a breathing disorder. The babies of smokers tend to be lighter in weight at birth than the babies of women who do not smoke, and low-birth-weight babies (those weighing less than 5 pounds 8 ounces (2.5 kilograms) have a higher risk of the respiratory distress syndrome and may need intensive care to survive. Nicotine reduces the blood flow to the placenta and the baby's absorption of nutrients; and carbon monoxide in smoke lowers the oxygen-carrying capacity of placental blood. Cigarette smoke contains the heavy metal cadmium (*see pages 35–36*).

TOXINS

Toxins are best avoided for at least four months before you wish to conceive because they may take time to be cleared from the body and because you might get pregnant early. Toxins include alcohol and the chemicals inhaled from cigarettes (*see above*); the toxic metals lead, cadmium, aluminium and mercury; copper and selenium in excess; certain household and industrial chemicals; fungal toxins from mouldy food; excessively large supplements of calcium and vitamins A and D; and some medications (*see chart on page 41* **Medicines & Pregnancy**) and illegally used drugs. It can be difficult to establish a definite link between toxins and damage to an unborn baby, but there is good evidence that they can play a part.

Toxic damage to a newly conceived baby at the pre-embryonic stage (before it implants in the wall of the womb on about the seventh day after fertilization) has two likely outcomes. Either the damaged cells are replaced by new and as yet unspecialized cells and the damage is repaired; or the baby is rejected by the body and the woman has what seems like a normal or heavyish period, probably without even realizing that she has been pregnant. If the toxic exposure continues, she may have recurrent very early miscarriages and come to the conclusion that she is infertile and incapable of conceiving.

A toxin is most likely to cause serious damage to the developing baby from the time it implants (a week before your missed period was due) until the ninth week after fertilization (or from 3 to 11 weeks after the first day of your last period). The damage done depends on which organs or parts of the baby's body are at a critical stage of development at the time. Environmental toxins which can cause foetal malformation are also known as teratogens. High levels of industrial pollution of air and water make the south of Poland one of the most toxic regions in the world, with high levels of miscarriages, stillbirths, malformations and prematurity.

THE TOXIC METALS

The toxic metals lead, cadmium, aluminium and mercury are environmental pollutants which can damage an unborn

Toxins, such as lead, cadmium, aluminium and mercury, are invisible pollutants which can enter the body through the air we breathe and the food we eat. Those illustrated (*above*) can harm an unborn baby if they enter the mother's bloodstream.

baby if a mother's exposure to them is excessive. These invisible pollutants can build up slowly in your body over the years. The amounts in your body depend on your age and your levels of exposure. However high the levels are, heavy metals take time to clear from the system, so it is better to think about reducing exposure months before you wish to conceive.

Lead, when absorbed from polluted water, air or food, or through the skin, can lead to deformed or dead sperm, infertility, repeated miscarriage or stillbirth, or a low birth weight. Too much lead lowers the amount of zinc and manganese available from food. Zinc is essential for healthy sperms and successful pregnancy; manganese for the production of sex hormones.

The lead in the exhaust fumes from vehicles running on leaded petrol can enter your body through breathing air polluted by traffic fumes (*see page 37*); via fruit and vegetables if they have been grown on soil contaminated with lead from air polluted by fumes from traffic; or from dust and dirt containing lead in your home or place of work. City dwellers in Tokyo, where petrol has been lead-free since 1976, have low concentrations of lead in their blood compared with those of Mexico City. Mexican petrol has nearly the highest lead content of any in the world. The Swedish National Environmental Protection Board states that the exhaust fumes from diesel engines are about ten times as likely to cause genetic damage as the exhaust fumes from leaded petrol. Other airborne sources of lead are the smoke from coal-burning fires, industrial lead smelters, and lead scrap refineries. Traffic fumes also contain high levels of carbon monoxide (*see page 37*).

Plumbers, painters and motor mechanics are likely to face regular exposure to lead; men thus employed risk high levels of lead contamination of their seminal fluid. They should therefore consider using condoms as contraceptives until they wish to try for a baby and again once their partner has conceived; these will protect their partners from absorbing lead from semen into their bodies.

Have lead levels in your drinking water checked, or use a suitable water filter, to be on the safe side. Lead in water can come from old lead piping, from an old earthenware mains glazed with lead, in which the glaze is breaking down, from soft drinking water stored in tanks lined with lead, or from copper piping that has been joined with solder containing lead. Replacing the plumbing may be the best, if an expensive, solution. In the UK it is the responsibility of the householder to pay for the replacement of lead pipes in the internal plumbing system (everything from the principal stopcock inwards). The water authorities will pay for the replacement of lead piping in the communication pipe (from the water main to the principal stop-cock).

If you cannot afford major plumbing jobs or an efficient water filter, run the water from the cold tap for several minutes before using it for cooking, drinking, or boiling for hot drinks. This is especially important if the water has been sitting in the pipes for several hours and if the water is soft. Do not drink rainwater or melted snow if you live in an area with air polluted by traffic.

A healthy diet (*see pages 28–29*) can help the body fight the harmful effects of lead. It should contain enough foods rich in vitamins A, C, D and E, the bioflavonoids, iron, calcium, magnesium, manganese, selenium, chromium, zinc, protein and fibre. According to Japanese and Bulgarian research, fresh garlic in the daily diet can be particularly helpful in countering the effects of excessive lead in the body. However, in pregnancy your need for these nutrients is automatically increased. Unless your diet is nutritionally sound you may not have enough of them to carry out their protective role.

Cadmium can displace zinc from vital enzymes in the body and high levels of cadmium have been linked with stillbirth and low birth weight. Cigarette smoke is the most dangerous source of cadmium. It is

TO AVOID ABSORBING LEAD:

- Do not store acidic food in glazed earthenware, since the glaze contains lead.

- Do not eat blackberries picked from a hedge by a busy road.

- Do not use the lead-containing Indian eye cosmetics, surma and kohl, or hair blackeners.

- Keeping the windows closed and lining them with fine net curtains will keep out some of the lead from a house or office near a busy road. A high wall or hedge between the road and the house will act as a screen.

- Dusting with a damp cloth will stop dust containing lead from being dispersed into the air.

- Wear a silk scarf tied across the mouth and nose when walking along the street if you live or work in a heavily polluted city. Your best health option in this case would be to choose somewhere less polluted to live or work, and move away or change jobs, if this is practicable.

- Take care when stripping paintwork. In the UK all paints manufactured for indoor use are lead-free by law, but old paints and wood primers may contain lead. The use of lead additives in paints sold for domestic use was banned by the United States Consumer Product Safety Commission in 1977. If you are not sure whether the paint you want to remove is lead-free, wear a mask, gloves and protective clothing when working on it. Pregnant women should stay out of the home day and night until the burning or sanding to remove old lead paint is finished. The premises should then be thoroughly scrubbed with detergent several times to remove the fine lead particles generated by the burning and sanding.

also present in some domestic water supplies (from certain plumbing alloys), some plastics (especially those coloured red and orange) and some insecticides. It is found in refined cereal products, such as white flour and bread, alcohol, oysters, gelatine, some canned foods, kidneys of pigs which have been treated with a worm-killer containing cadmium, some cola drinks, and some instant coffees and teas. Artists should be wary of red and yellow pigments containing cadmium.

It is possible to avoid a build-up of cadmium in the body and to reduce existing high levels. First and foremost, do not smoke and avoid passive smoking (breathing in other people's smoke), especially in confined areas. Give up cigarettes and tobacco at least four months before you want to conceive. If you live or work with a smoker, you can help protect yourself by means of diet (*see page 38 under* **To Prevent Contamination**). Cadmium levels in drinking water can be measured by your water authority or an independent analyst; if they are high, use an appropriate water filter. If your water is soft, run the water from the tap for a while before using it for drinking in the morning, or else flush the lavatory to get rid of water which has been sitting in the pipes and absorbing cadmium all night. The same goes if you have been out of the house during the day for any length of time. Do not drink rain water collected in anything galvanized (roof, gutter, tank or pail). The zinc used in galvanization contains cadmium.

Adjust your diet to avoid an excessive cadmium intake by cutting down on refined foods and eating plenty of foods containing vitamin C, chromium, iron and zinc. Avoid alcoholic drinks as these may contain cadmium. Protect yourself adequately if you work with solder or insecticides containing cadmium.

Aluminium can be toxic if it is present in the body in high quantities. It has been linked with unhealthy placentas. You expose yourself to aluminium every time

Chemicals in exhaust fumes (*right*) make up 70% of air pollution. A catalytic converter can be used with unleaded petrol to convert 75–90% of harmful emissions to water, nitrogen and carbon dioxide.

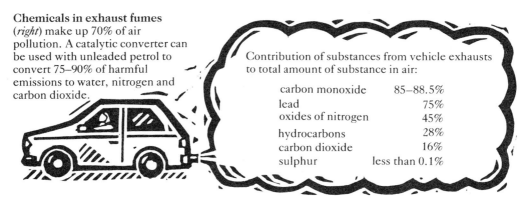

Contribution of substances from vehicle exhausts to total amount of substance in air:

carbon monoxide	85–88.5%
lead	75%
oxides of nitrogen	45%
hydrocarbons	28%
carbon dioxide	16%
sulphur	less than 0.1%

you cook in an aluminium saucepan, especially if the food is acidic (such as apples, spinach or rhubarb) and takes a layer of metal off the pan. Pressure cookers are particularly hazardous. Foods heated in cooking foil or foil trays or dishes will be contaminated with aluminium if any fat is in contact with the foil. And tea made in an aluminium teapot contains aluminium dissolved from the pot into the water, as well as aluminium from alum, a substance with which tea plants are dosed. Aluminium is used as an anti-caking or bleaching agent in foods in everyday use, such as salt, milk substitutes and flour.

Your water supply may contain unacceptably high levels of aluminium from the aluminium gel used as a flocculant to cleanse the water. Thames Water serving London in the UK stopped using aluminium in 1989.

Many anti-perspirants contain aluminium, but in these products it is said to be non-bio-available aluminium, which means that although it is absorbed through the skin it does not endanger health.

To minimize absorption of aluminium, steer clear of aluminium teapots and pans, especially when cooking acidic fruits and vegetables. Choose enamel, glass or stainless steel pans instead. Make sure cooking foil coverings are not in contact with fatty foods. Avoid eating bleached white flour and foods containing the additives 556 (aluminium calcium silicate), E173 (aluminium – C.I.77000), and 554 (aluminium sodium silicate). Eat plenty of foods rich in

magnesium (*see page 52*), which counteracts the harmful effects of aluminium. Consider having your water levels checked or using a suitable water filter. If you suffer from indigestion, ask your doctor to prescribe antacids that contain no aluminium.

Mercury in high levels has been associated with poor placental function. Mercury levels tend to be higher in foetal blood than in maternal blood. Industrial accidents leading to mercury poisoning have demonstrated that exposure to this heavy metal can lead to serious abnormalities in developing babies.

You expose yourself to mercury poisoning by eating tinned fish contaminated with mercury from water polluted by effluent from factories. Tuna fish is particularly likely to be contaminated. Three million tonnes of mercury are dumped by factories into rivers each year. This is enough to poison everyone in the world and it is steadily accumulating in the water cycle. Certain weedkillers and fungicides contain potentially dangerous levels of mercury. Farm workers need to take special care when handling seed wheat which has been dusted with mercury to prevent mould.

Dental fillings are often made from a mercury amalgam. If they are disturbed or removed just before or during pregnancy, the mercury can be absorbed through the lining of the mouth. Dentists and dental nurses are at particular risk of mercury overload.

Avoid mercury contamination by taking

adequate protective measures when handling fungicides containing mercury or seed wheat treated with mercury. As far as your diet is concerned, avoid tinned tuna fish and include plenty of garlic in your daily diet. Researchers believe this can prevent mercury from being absorbed by the body. Eat plenty of foods rich in vitamins C and E and selenium. Before dental treatment warn your dentist that you are or might be pregnant and prefer not to have mercury amalgam fillings drilled out. Some people believe it is preferable to refuse to have mercury amalgam fillings at any time. In Sweden, dentists are not allowed to use mercury in work on pregnant women and soon they will not be allowed to use it at all.

TO PREVENT CONTAMINATION:

● Your diet should be nutritious, with plenty of food rich in fibre (wholegrain cereal, peas, beans and lentils, fruit and vegetables); vitamins B1, B12, C and D; calcium, iron, manganese, magnesium, selenium and zinc.

● Pectin, found in apple pips, can protect your body from damage by toxic metal deposits, so stew apples with their pips.

● Eat plenty of garlic, onions, peas, beans and lentils, which may have a specific detoxifying effect.

TRACE ELEMENTS

Some essential trace elements may have adverse effects on a developing baby if they are absorbed in excess into the mother's body:

Copper is an essential trace element but its levels in the body can become dangerously high, thus lowering levels of zinc. It may also lead to low-birth-weight babies.

You may be putting yourself or your baby at risk of a copper overload: if you have a copper IUD (although this sheds a negligible amount of copper); if you take the contraceptive Pill (which alters the ratio of zinc to copper in the body and could increase the risk of post-natal depression); if your water supply comes through copper pipes and the water is soft and acidic (especially if you drink water from the hot tank, as copper is more soluble in hot water); if your copper pipes are less than two years old; if you use a water heater which may shed copper from a coil of small-gauge piping; if you use copper pans or a kettle; if you swim in water treated with an algicide containing copper; or if you wear copper jewellery.

Keep copper levels low by switching to a means of contraception other than the copper IUD or the Pill during the six months before you intend to conceive. Have the copper levels in your drinking water checked and consider using a suitable water filter. Do not drink water or fill the kettle from the hot-water tap. Do not swim in water treated with an algicide containing copper: alternative algicides are available. Steer clear of copper pans, kettles and jewellery. And eat plenty of foods rich in vitamin C, calcium and zinc, which reduce the body's absorption of copper.

Selenium, an essential trace element in the diet, which is toxic in excess, is present in some anti-dandruff shampoos. There is a suggestion that selenium can be absorbed into the body from photocopying machines. It can also be absorbed by inhaling North Sea gas from a leak (this applies to the UK only); from smoking; and from breathing air polluted with smoke or traffic fumes.

Avoid using selenium shampoos if you hope to start a baby in the next few months and do not use a photocopying machine unless it is situated in a separate and ventilated room. As far as possible, keep away from heavily polluted areas and busy roads so you do not have to breathe in the fumes.

COMMONLY USED CHEMICALS

Some of the domestic cleaning and personal cosmetic products you take for granted may contain chemicals capable of harming an unborn baby. Play it safe and avoid using the following products unless you are sure they are harmless:

Hair dyes contain chemicals that can enter your body through the skin of your scalp or through the air you breathe; some have been proved in tests on laboratory animals to be capable of causing genetic damage. The American publication, *Consumer Reports*, has advised against their use in pregnancy.

Hair perms are considered dangerous to pregnant women by some obstetricians in the USA. It is better not to colour or perm your hair while you are pregnant or trying for a baby, even henna is best avoided.

Disinfectants containing a substance called cresol are potentially dangerous. Cresol can lead to foetal malformation.

Many **cleaning products, paints, paint thinners, contact adhesives, marking pens, correction fluid, aerosols and solvents** such as benzene and toluene have a question mark against the advisability of men and women using them just before and after conception. Keep tops on all containers of such products when not using them, and use them only in a well ventilated room. Vinyl chloride (PVC) has been linked with lowered sex drive and impotence in men and with miscarriage, poor foetal growth and malformation of the foetus in women; chloroprene with a reduction in sex drive and infertility in men; and formaldehyde (*see page 141*) with infertility, miscarriage and poor foetal growth.

Biocides – the collective term for pesticides (insecticides and fungicides) and herbicides (weedkillers) – together with **nitrates** used in agricultural areas, can seep into rivers and underground water tables and contaminate your water supply (*see page 127*). Another source of exposure is air polluted with biocide spray, particularly in areas where the farmers practise aerial spraying (*see page 77*).

Pesticides are used in domestic fly sprays, fly repellents and anti-woodworm preparations; in lotions and shampoos for head lice; in powders, shampoos, collars and sprays for pets affected by insects; in greenhouse smokes and bombs (devices which give off pesticide fumes when lit), rose and fruit tree sprays and other horticultural products; and in moth-proofed clothing, curtaining and upholstery fabric, and carpets.

More than 1 pound (450 grams) of biocides are manufactured each year for every person in the world. Most of us are exposed to biocides via traces in our food and drink. Fruit and vegetable crops are often sprayed with harmful pesticides; and those chemicals that miss the target crop remain in the soil and are washed by the rain into our water supplies. A proportion (however tiny) ends up in our bodies. Today, virtually everyone has some organochlorine pesticide such as DDT in his or her body. Many biocides are stored in a person's body fat and can be released into the bloodstream if the fat is broken down: one reason why it is unwise to slim before conception, during pregnancy, or while breastfeeding. Pesticides in your body can damage the genetic material of the egg or sperm and increase the risk of infertility, foetal malformation, miscarriage and stillbirth. One study of women in India demonstrated higher levels of pesticide residues in the placentas of those who miscarried than of those who had full-term deliveries. In the USA a reduction in sperm numbers was found in one study to be linked with raised pesticide levels in semen.

Avoid touching pesticides or breathing in their vapour. If you can smell a biocide, you are at risk from any possible effects it might have. Do not be lulled into complacency by an absence of warnings on the container. Even in the USA, which has the most stringent testing standards in the world, few of the chemicals used in biocides have undergone all the legally required tests on their ability to cause birth defects; and even fewer have been tested for their potential to cause genetic damage. Never mix cocktails of different biocides.

Although you can do little about the levels of common agrochemicals in your water, you can contact your local water authority to find out known chemical levels in your supply (although tests are carried out only for a very few chemicals). If levels are high, or if your area is heavily farmed, use an appropriate water filter.

If you live or work in an agricultural area, ask the local farmers to let you know when they are spraying and leave the area, if possible. In still, dry air pesticides will linger. Avoid inhalation of dangerous chemicals in the home by having moth-proofed carpets treated with a silicone finish, avoiding anti-woodworm or anti-dry or wet rot chemicals, and by handling any biocides for domestic use carefully and according to the manufacturer's instructions. Do not use fly sprays in the home or unnecessary biocides in the garden. Always wash fruit and vegetables thoroughly before eating or cooking. Peeling fruit and vegetables reduces their biocide content but also lowers their nutritional value. You can avoid these problems by buying or growing organic food.

Polychlorinated biphenyls (PCBs; *see pages 78–79*) are widespread environmental pollutants and can cross the placenta. They have been linked with low sperm counts and poor foetal growth. One American study has linked PCB exposure during pregnancy with developmental delay.

Dioxins (*see pages 79–80*) are highly toxic chemicals which have been linked with genetic damage and birth defects.

ILLEGAL DRUG USE

It is difficult to be sure about the safety of drugs used for non-medical reasons before and during pregnancy, because many of the people who use or abuse them are susceptible to other high-risk factors. There is currently no definite evidence to incriminate amphetamines, for example; but dextroamphetamine and LSD (lysergic acid diethylamide) have been under study. Isolated cases of deformities have been reported in babies whose mothers took LSD.

The regular smoking of marijuana (pot, cannabis, hashish) can lead to high levels of carbon monoxide in the placental blood and, hence, to low-birth-weight babies. Men who are heavy smokers (15 to 18 joints a week) are more likely to be impotent and to have a reduced sex drive, fewer sperms and sperms which are less motile (less able to swim). One large study reported in 1987 concluded that cocaine abuse is associated with a higher rate of birth defects, stillbirth and low birth weight. The abuse of narcotics (heroin, opium, morphine and codeine) is linked with a lowered sex drive and infertility in men, and with an increased rate of birth defects, stillbirth, prematurity and low birth weight.

Medical researchers in Rhode Island, USA, tested 713 women in labour for cocaine, opiates, marijuana and amphetamines. Their report, published in 1990 by the Centers for Disease Control in Atlanta, Georgia, showed that 7.5 per cent of the women tested positively for at least one of the drugs. Among women with public health insurance (as opposed to private insurance) 16 per cent tested positive. Many more may have been habitual drugs-users because the tests only picked up drugs taken within the preceding 48 hours.

GENETIC DAMAGE

Only one in five fertilized eggs ever reaches its nest in the lining of the womb and half of these fail to implant successfully. This means that about nine out of ten fertilized eggs die very early in pregnancy, most of them before a woman is even aware that she is pregnant. One important reason for this apparent wastage is an abnormality in the genetic structure of sperms, eggs or fertilized eggs that prevents development.

There are two main reasons for genetic *continued on page 42*

continued on page 42

MEDICINES & PREGNANCY

Any medicine you take during early pregnancy will reach your baby, so try to avoid inessential medicines for four to six months before you conceive. During pregnancy the placenta acts as a barrier, but only to moderate doses of non-fat-soluble medicines. Only a few medicines have been proved to cause abnormalities, but thousands have never been tested for their safety in pregnancy. Medical and pharmaceutical knowledge about the safety of medicines is reliable only for long-established medicines.

Tell your doctor or pharmacist you are planning a baby if you need a medicine, or if you are already taking one. Non-toxic alternatives can be substituted. Do not buy an over-the-counter remedy without professional advice. A medicine labelled 'natural' is not necessarily safe.

A doctor may recommend a risky medicine knowing you may be pregnant because the risk to the baby would be greater from your untreated illness than from the medicine, or because the risk occurs in later pregnancy. If you are advised to continue taking phenytoin or trimethoprim with sulphamethoxazole, take a folic acid supplement and eat foods rich in folic acid (*see page 52*). Tricyclic antidepressants or MAOIs (monoamine oxidase inhibitors) tend to cause mothers and babies to cope badly with difficult labour and delivery, so discuss with your doctor psychotherapy or other ways of treating depression, preferably before pregnancy.

These medicines carry a high risk of abnormality in the baby: Anti-cancer drugs including actinomycin; folic acid antimetabolites, such as methotrexate; alkylating antimitotic drugs (all cause foetal death or abnormalities); tetracycline (cause discoloured teeth and damaged milk teeth enamel); radioactive iodine 131 (damages a baby's thyroid in later pregnancy).

These medicines may be risky for some babies: Antithyroid drugs and iodides (cause goitre); azathioprine and mercaptopurine (cause susceptibility to virus infection); large doses of barbiturates (newborn withdrawal syndrome); chloroquine (retinal damage; multiple abnormalities); coumarin anticoagulants (haemorrhage and, rarely, multiple abnormalities); large doses of diazepam and related benzodiazepines (newborn withdrawal syndrome; malformation); frusemide (reduced placental blood supply); ganglion blockers (paralytic ileus); glucocorticoids (virus infection and, rarely, cleft palate); narcotics (respiratory depression; newborn withdrawal syndrome); 19–norsteroids (male sexual characteristics in female); phenytoin and primidone (abnormalities, bleeding, newborn withdrawal syndrome); rauwolfia alkaloids (newborn depression syndrome); streptomycin, kanamycin, gentamycin and vancomycin (minor acoustic nerve damage and, rarely, deafness); large doses of vitamin D, dihydrotachysterol (skeletal abnormalities).

Medicines suspected of being risky: Oral contraceptives – the Pill (limb defects); oral pregnancy tests (multiple abnormalities); stilboestrol (adenocarcinoma of the vagina in teens); sulphafurazole, long-acting sulphonamides and trimethoprim with sulphamethoxazole; metronidazole (avoid until 17th week).

damage: inherited damage of a defective gene; and a new mutation (a change in the genetic material of a cell) caused by irradiation, ageing or toxins such as pesticides and vehicle exhaust fumes. Mutations are more common in cell division during the formation of the mature egg and sperm than in the fertilized egg.

You, your partner or your forbears may pass on a disorder to your baby; sometimes such genetic damage can be traced back through a family for many generations.

Genetic disorders such as achondroplasia (dwarfism), which are passed on to a baby by one parent, are known as dominant conditions. Others require both parents to carry the abnormal gene. These are called recessive disorders and include cystic fibrosis. Many sex-linked disorders are carried by females, who do not show any symptoms, and are passed only to males. Some genetic disorders, such as spina bifida, are thought to be caused by a combination of genetic defects and environmental factors, relatively few of which have been firmly identified in humans.

It is worth consulting a genetic counsellor before trying to conceive if you have a child with a genetic defect; if you or your partner has one; or if there is a family history of one. Genetic tests and assessments of the risk of bearing an affected child are improving all the time. If the risk of bearing a child with a serious genetic disorder were thought to be unacceptably high, you might decide that it would be better for all concerned if you decided against it.

In the UK, if you are a woman over 35, your obstetrician may suggest that you have a test called an amniocentesis, in which some of the fluid from around the baby in your womb is drawn off. This fluid contains discarded skin cells from the baby, which can be tested for chromosomal damage. Chorion biopsy, in which a sample of the membrane surrounding the embryo is taken via the cervix, is a way of looking for genetic damage very early in pregnancy. Both chorion biopsy and amniocentesis carry some risk of damage. Ultrasonic scanning helps reduce the risk of miscarriage after amniocentesis.

Having a test may put your mind at rest. It could also mean that you will be offered an abortion (a termination) if the baby is affected. Some centres offer counselling before tests are carried out.

IRRADIATION

The genetic material in an egg can be damaged by some types of irradiation when a future mother is still an unborn baby in her own mother's womb, or at any time from birth up to the point of fertilization by the sperm. All the eggs a woman will ever release for fertilization are present in her ovaries in the form of germ cells about ten weeks before she is born. They begin forming when the unborn baby girl is only three months old. The germ cells begin developing into egg cells before the baby girl is born, but further growth is suspended until puberty. After puberty, one or more of these eggs finishes maturing during the first half of each menstrual cycle.

Sperms begin to be produced in number from the matured germ cells in the testes from about the age of 15. Sperms have a short life of up to three months and some are newly formed every day. In other words, an egg is susceptible to damage from irradiation for a much longer time than a sperm, which can be damaged only in the short time between formation and fertilization. The genetic material in a fertilized egg is also at risk (*see page 27*).

One form of damage can come from ionizing radiation, including gamma rays (emitted by radioactive material) and X-rays. The amount of damage depends on the dose of radiation and the state of maturity of the egg or sperm or the age of the unborn baby. The younger an unborn baby, the more vulnerable it is to the effects of radiation, because the organs are still being formed. Pregnant air crew are at an increased risk of exposure to radiation, according to the US Federal Aviation Administration, and need to monitor their levels of exposure.

NUCLEAR POWER

It is possible that excessive ionizing radiation (which might occur after a major accident, a minor leakage or ineffective decontamination procedures at a nuclear power station) could lead to genetic mutation in the chromosomes in a man's or a woman's germ cells, sperm or eggs. It might also interfere with the development of the cells of a recently conceived baby. This might lead to miscarriage or, later, to leukaemia or other cancers. Children of men who work at the nuclear power plant at Sellafield in the UK and who have received cumulative radiation doses in excess of 100 millisieverts are six to eight times more likely than normal to develop leukaemia. There was no increased risk of leukaemia in the children of men who survived the atomic bomb explosions in Hiroshima and Nagasaki in Japan during World War II. However, people who were unborn babies at the time of these explosions have had an increased risk of cancer. Two British researchers have suggested that nutritional zinc deficiency may increase the risk of a man's sperms being damaged. Any man who works with ionizing radiation might be well advised to check with a dietician that he is eating enough foods rich in zinc.

X-RAYS

Research suggests if a mother has an X-ray in pregnancy, the danger of her unborn baby developing cancer or leukaemia later in life is minute, especially if modern X-ray equipment is used. There is, however, some risk of mental retardation in the baby, especially if the X-ray takes place between 8 and 15 weeks after conception; during the first 8 weeks after conception there is little risk of damage to the baby's brain.

To avoid X-raying a woman who might unknowingly be several weeks into the vulnerable part of pregnancy, any woman of childbearing age requiring an X-ray is asked whether she is, or might be, pregnant. This unofficial pregnancy rule is operated by radiographers and radiologists.

Many X-ray departments still use the ten-day rule, which suggests that no woman should be X-rayed, except in an emergency, unless she has had a period within the last ten days. Many radiologists believe that this rule is unnecessarily restrictive. A recent guideline states that the last period need only have been within the last 28 days.

However, some experts believe that there is a risk of X-ray damage to the egg during the seven weeks before its release (ovulation) prior to fertilization. If they are correct, women should defer trying for a baby until seven weeks after an X-ray of any part of the body between the waist and the knees (including a barium enema or meal, an IVP (intra-venous pyelogram, a type of kidney X-ray), or a cholecystogram (a type of gallbladder X-ray). It has been suggested that everyone should carry a personal X-ray record to avoid the potentially cumulative effect of X-rays over a few months. If there is a chance that you might be pregnant, especially if you have missed a period, reschedule any X-ray that is not essential and be sure to tell the radiologist and radiographer if you have to have an emergency X-ray.

One study showed that fathers of children with Down's syndrome were more likely to have been exposed to microwave radiation than other fathers. It is believed that any leakage from properly constructed microwave ovens in the period before conception is harmless, but research into its effect continues. Fluorescent lighting emits low levels of microwave radiation. Australian reports suggest that the number of miscarriages in women working in offices lit by fluorescent lighting is higher than average. Swedish research has found that men who work in high-voltage switch yards are more likely to be infertile and to have children with birth defects.

It has been suggested that pregnant women, including women who are trying to conceive, should avoid lying under an electric blanket. The electromagnetic field from the blanket may increase the risk of miscarriage and infertility.

VISUAL DISPLAY UNITS (VDUs)

The possible problems of working in close proximity to a VDU (visual display unit) during pregnancy are being researched, but as yet the results are inconclusive. VDUs release low levels of ionizing radiation (in the form of X-rays), ultraviolet (UV) light, visible light and radio waves. The levels of ionizing radiation and UV light emitted from VDUs are very low, much lower than those in normal background radiation. VDUs also create an electromagnetic field and the VDU screen has a strong electrostatic charge, causing a large static electric field between the operator and the screen.

One study, reported in the *American Journal of Industrial Medicine* in 1988, indicated that sitting in front of a VDU for more than 20 hours a week during the first three months of pregnancy could double the risk of miscarriage. There have been many reports indicating that the use of VDUs might be associated with miscarriage, infertility and foetal malformation. However, recent large studies in Sweden, Norway and Canada have failed to find any association between VDUs and adverse outcome of pregnancy. The effects of VDUs on the fertility and offspring of men have not been investigated. It would seem sensible to carry out some research into this, in case exposure to VDUs primarily affects sperms. Recent research indicates that the electromagnetic field of the VDU may be responsible for the possibility of an increased risk of miscarriages, perhaps because of the small electric currents it induces in the body. There is no way at present to protect yourself from this.

Researchers have pointed out that many VDUs are used in rooms with a positively charged atmosphere. A high concentration of positive ions has been linked with an increase in the level of serotonin in the body. In turn, high serotonin levels have been linked with recurrent miscarriage. This set of links is purely speculative, but if you wished you could decrease the concentration of positive ions in the room where you work by opening a window, turning the air-conditioning off, humidifying the air, decorating the room with pot plants (*see page 145*), damp-dusting (dry-dusting raises clouds of dust which contain positive ions), and having floor-coverings made of natural materials.

The UK National Radiological Protection Board states that a link between VDU ionizing radiation and pregnancy problems is unlikely because of the small amount of radiation involved. An idling car engine emits twice the quantity of radiation as a VDU; an electric whisk ten times as much. However, people tend not to sit in front of an idling car or an electric whisk for as long as they might sit in front of a VDU screen.

If you use a VDU a great deal in your job, consider changing the work you do well before you get pregnant, or take precautions such as having regular and frequent breaks away from the VDU (because with any radiation many short exposures are thought to be preferable to one long one). It might be sensible for men to avoid working with VDUs if they and their partner wish to start a baby within the next three months, although this suggestion is speculative. The fine mesh conductive (and earthed) metal or acrylic screen guards will not prevent any ionizing radiation reaching you, or reduce the electromagnetic field. Their job is to reduce glare and to minimize the electrostatic charge of the VDU. This charge attracts negatively charged dust to the screen and positively charged dust to your face and eyes, possibly causing skin rashes and eye irritation.

OVERHEAD POWER LINES

Several studies have linked exposure to the electromagnetic fields of high-voltage power lines with infertility and birth defects (*see pages 135–136*).

AGEING OF THE OVUM

This is the term given to possible damage to an egg which has been released from the ovary but has not yet been fertilized. If it is fertilized soon after its release, there is less risk of ageing and possible resultant genetic damage, so it is wise to avoid a gap of several days after ovulation before having sexual intercourse. If you are planning to conceive it makes sense to learn how to detect the time of ovulation (*see pages 17–21*), so that you can time sexual intercourse accordingly. Just as rabbits ovulate on copulation, some women ovulate as a result of sexual intercourse.

EXERCISE

Pregnancy involves carrying the increasingly heavy weight of the developing baby, the uterus and placenta, the amniotic fluid, the breasts and the extra blood and fat. You will be able to cope more easily with this extra luggage if you are fit. As part of your peri-conceptual routine, try to include regular exercise at least 3 times a week for at least 20 minutes each time.

If you go into pregnancy in the habit of taking regular exercise, you are much more likely to continue while you are expecting your baby. Exercise changes your baby's environment for the better, so making the most of the natural resources you have to offer. Even gentle exercise, such as walking and non-competitive swimming, increases the levels in the blood of endorphins (natural opiates or morphine-like chemicals produced by the brain) which, in turn, can make you feel happier or even elated. When you take exercise, your unborn baby will be exposed to endorphins via the placenta. We do not know what a baby experiences emotionally, but it is not fanciful to suggest that increased levels of endorphins could be pleasant.

The movements of your body during exercise are probably soothing to your baby. After all, many babies enjoy being rocked or jiggled up and down after they are born. Cushioned by the amniotic fluid and the walls of your womb, your baby is unlikely to come to any harm from any normal level of exercise – or even from potentially dangerous activities – if your skill (and that of any other people involved) will protect you.

FEELINGS

Your mood alters the chemical composition of your blood and this in turn affects your baby. No-one knows for sure whether it is better for a baby to develop inside a contented mother, rather than in one who is anxious or depressed, but some research suggests that this is so. What we do know is that a mother's feelings are inevitably picked up by her baby during the months after birth.

If you believe that your feelings are interfering with the way you would like to be, the time to do something about them is now, before conception. You may be able to work out how to cope better by yourself, or with the help of your partner or friends. You might decide to enlist a counsellor to help you with this. The point is not to push your feelings and moods away but to recognize their root cause and find a more efficient and perhaps less painful way of managing them. It can take time to do this, so the sooner you begin getting to grips with yourself and your situation before you get pregnant, the better. Research suggests that a poor relationship between the parents-to-be during pregnancy is linked with emotional problems in the baby later. Whether your baby is planned, unexpected, wanted or unwanted, now is the time to work towards a better relationship.

Are feelings a green issue? The way you feel and, therefore, the way you think and behave, shape your baby's environment in a more meaningful and immediate way than wider green issues. Of course life is about compromise and cannot be perfect, but what we can all try to do is optimize what we have to offer ourselves, our baby and the other people around us.

Feelings are not only important for women at this time. Men also have enormous influence over a baby's environment, both before and after birth. A potential father may be well advised to take time to face any painful or difficult issues that are shadowing his life so that he can help himself and his family.

Chapter Three
PREGNANCY AND BIRTH

*May Allah give me a true friend whether he's small or big
Even an infant sucking at the breast, or one lying in the womb.
When he comes forth we'll be friends.*
African pounding song

Many women say that from the time they first sense they are pregnant, they are constantly aware of the life within them. Their new mothering role in the first 25 weeks at least (counted from the first day of the last period) is vitally important because a baby born during this time is highly unlikely to survive outside the womb.

It is now possible for a woman's egg to be taken from her, fertilized with a sperm and returned, either back to her womb or to the womb of another woman, in the hope that the pre-embryo will implant into the womb lining. Scientists have not yet found a way of transplanting a human embryo from the lining of the womb to the womb of another woman or to an artificial incubator. This means that once an embryo has nestled into your womb lining, it is completely reliant on you for a safe environment.

You can do your best to choose, monitor and influence your external environment, both physical and emotional. Both will affect the micro-environment of your baby in the womb. But the baby is by no means passive in the relationship. Simply by being there, a baby alters your internal body chemistry, the way you feel and even the foods you wish to eat. Every woman's pregnancy is different. Some women are unwell as a result of being pregnant, others assert they have never felt better.

Looking at the different aspects of pregnancy from the green point of view, it is clear that many points about, for example, diet, exercise, feelings, toxins, infections and accidents in the peri-conceptual period (the period around the time of conception) continue to apply in pregnancy. Other issues, such as amniocentesis and ultrasound, are relevant only after conception.

You and your partner are responsible for the most important aspects of your baby's ante-natal care ('pre-natal' in the USA; meaning 'before birth'). This chapter concentrates on your contribution and takes it for granted that you will make the most of the professional resources available to you.

EATING WELL IN PREGNANCY

Carry on with the dietary recommendations suggested for before pregnancy (*see pages 28-30*). From a green point of view, eating well means making the most of what is available and learning which foods suit you and which do not. Women who eat too little during pregnancy are more likely to give birth to underweight babies. In Keneba in the Gambia, West Africa, researchers found that supplementary food (in the form of biscuits) eaten by women during pregnancy could boost the weight of their babies.

Nevertheless you should not waste your appetite, health or money by eating too many empty calories. During the World War II famines in Holland and in Leningrad the rate of birth defects increased by up to threefold and the birth weight of babies was much lower. One more recent study found that among women who could afford whatever they wanted to eat, those whose diet during pregnancy was nutritionally poor were twice as likely to have an unhealthy, deformed, premature or stillborn baby as those who had followed a good diet. It may be that even a mild deficiency of a particular nutrient could lead to inefficiency of the enzyme systems responsible for breaking down environmental toxins in your body. A healthy diet strengthens your body's resistance.

GOOD DIET GUIDELINES

• An excellent diet in very early pregnancy helps prevent low birth weight. Particularly important now are foods rich in animal and/or vegetable protein, vitamin A, vitamin B (niacin, riboflavin, thiamine, pantothenic acid, B6 and B12, and folic acid), vitamin C and the bioflavonoids, vitamins D and E, calcium, magnesium, manganese, zinc, iron, iodine, phosphorus and the essential fatty acids.

• If your unborn baby is a boy he will need five times as much zinc as a girl would have done (*see page 53* **Nutrients checklist**). Problems in young babies caused by a zinc deficiency in the mother's diet (such as skin problems, diarrhoea and poor sleep) are therefore more common in boys than in girls.

• You need at least twice and perhaps up to four times as much folic acid as before you were pregnant. Folic acid is found especially in leafy green vegetables, wholegrain cereals and in eggs.

• If you are vegetarian, eat enough foods rich in calcium, iron, zinc and vitamins B12 and D, as well as soya bean-based foods or combinations of grains and pulses (beans and peas), grains and legumes (lentils, chick peas and peanuts), pulses and nuts or seeds, or legumes and nuts or seeds. These combinations form complete proteins. Genetic engineering will probably soon produce beans containing all the amino acids humans need to form complete proteins. Vegetarian diet is covered on pages 130-131.

• Cut down on alcohol. Consider giving it up completely. Alcohol over-consumption has been linked with birth defects (the foetal alcohol syndrome). Researchers have not yet decided how much – if any – alcohol it is safe to drink during pregnancy.

• There is a great deal of speculation over the safety of large amounts of caffeine absorbed by the unborn baby. Finnish researchers have linked coffee-drinking in pregnancy to the later triggering of diabetes in the baby. If you must drink your coffee strong, limit the number of cups you drink each day to two.

• Steer clear of slimming diets during pregnancy. You may damage your baby if your diet is nutritionally inadequate, partly because your body stores will not be able to provide for all the needs of the growing baby, and partly because weight loss can lead to the presence of ketones (breakdown products of fats) and other toxins in your blood.

FOOD SENSITIVITY

If you know you are sensitive – allergic or intolerant, that is – to a particular food, it makes every sense to avoid that food during pregnancy, or at least to eat only small amounts of it at a time. This is especially important if you, your partner or any close relative suffer from asthma, eczema or hay fever. Undigested molecules of food can enter your baby's bloodstream by leaking through the placenta. If there is a family history of sensitivity, your baby has an increased risk of being food-sensitive. Try to avoid eating large quantities of foods that come high on the list of common food allergens. Wheat and milk – staples for many pregnant women – come right at the top

If you restrict the amount of milk in your diet, replace it with foods rich in protein and calcium (*see pages 52–53*). Researchers have recently suggested a link between an unhealthy diet during pregnancy and the later development in the offspring of breast cancer, heart disease and diabetes.

A HEALTHY APPETITE

Many women find they eat about the same amount of food during pregnancy as they did before. A lower energy output from less exercise as you become larger, combined with your body's more efficient metabolism during pregnancy, mean that your appetite will not necessarily increase. If you find you are more hungry, fill up with nutrient-dense foods rather than foods containing a lot of empty calories. Bear in mind that if there is a relative shortage of any particular nutrient in your diet, your body will go short whenever possible so that the baby's needs can be met.

Weight gain during pregnancy varies from woman to woman, but the average is about 12.5 kilograms (26 pounds 8 ounces). Women who are overweight before pregnancy tend to gain more weight during pregnancy than those who are not. The monitoring of weight gain throughout pregnancy is one of the reasons for routine antenatal care.

EXTRA VITAMINS & MINERALS

If you are well and are eating a nutritious diet there is no need to take vitamin or mineral supplements during pregnancy because your diet provides all you need (but see page 130). Iron is necessary only if a blood test reveals abnormally low haemoglobin levels. It is unwise to take iron during the first eight weeks of pregnancy because it could damage the baby by reducing the absorption of zinc. Multivitamin supplements containing folic acid are advisable for those women with an increased risk of having a baby with spina bifida or another neural tube defect. They should be taken for the first six weeks.

FOOD SAFETY

Listeriosis is a bacterial infection caused mainly by eating infected food. It is normally a minor problem for women, causing a 'flu-like illness, but it can lead to miscarriage, pre-term birth in pregnant women, and to septicaemia (the spread of infection through the body) – with or without meningitis – in a newborn baby. Listeria bacteria are widespread and about 1 person in 20 carries them in the gut with no ill effects.

You are most at risk of infection from 'cook-chill' or 'cook-freeze' foods (the commercial preparation of foods by cooking, then refrigerating or freezing). Many foods prepared by these methods are not cooked for long enough to destroy bacteria before being chilled or frozen. Manufacturers expect the purchaser to finish the cooking properly. Furthermore, these foods are often kept in the fridge or freezer for longer than is safe; and they are frequently stored at a temperature higher than that recommended by the manufacturers. Such conditions provide an ideal breeding-ground for bacteria.

Soft cheeses, raw egg, pre-packed salads and pâté have all been found to have high concentrations of listeria. Soft cheese, whether made with pasteurized or unpasteurized milk, has a lower acidity level than

FOOD SAFETY GUIDELINES

Following a few simple rules about food safety may protect you and your unborn child:

● Invest in a fridge or freezer thermometer to check the temperature at which food is stored. A fridge should be kept at a temperature of between 1 and 4°C.

● Always check the sell-by dates of cook-chilled or cook-frozen foods.

● Avoid unchilled pre-prepared food, such as sandwiches displayed in a shop window or an unchilled cabinet.

● When reheating refrigerated or frozen food make sure you heat it until it is piping hot right through (it needs to maintain a core tempterature of at least 70°C for 2 minutes), then serve it as soon as possible; at least within 15 minutes of reheating. Any food not hot in the middle should be put back into the oven.

● Be extra careful when using a microwave oven to reheat cook-chilled or cook-frozen foods. Some ovens have cool spots which do not heat food right through unless you follow the manufacturers' instructions properly. Always turn the container of food halfway through the cooking time and allow the recommended standing time.

● Cook foods made from processed meats, such as sausages and hamburgers, thoroughly.

● Do not eat pâté, raw egg (including mayonnaise and all other foods made with raw egg) and soft cheese, including Brie, Camembert, cottage, goat, curd and cream cheeses.

● Always wash salads thoroughly especially pre-packed salads, which might contain listeria.

hard varieties, so making it easier for listeria bacteria to thrive. Processed meat is more likely to contain listeria than whole meat. Food irradiation (*see pages 124-5*) is not the answer to listeria infection because listeria bacteria are not usually eradicated by the process. Further guidelines on food safety are given in Chapter 6.

PREGNANCY SICKNESS

Seven women in ten suffer from some degree of nausea or vomiting during pregnancy. In most the sickness can occur at any time of day. Two out of three women are still feeling sick at the end of the twelfth week. If you suffer from nausea you may find it helps to have frequent small meals high in unrefined carbohydrate and to eat and drink at separate times. Avoid fatty foods and added sugar. Chamomile or raspberry leaf tea and foods rich in vitamin B6 (*see page 53*) can all help. Ginger is an ancient remedy for nausea; try drinking grated ginger root infused as a tea, or use it in casseroles, stir-fries and salad dressings. Some people think that colours can influence nausea: hues and shades to avoid in your dress and environment include bright reds and pinks; go instead for blues.

SMOKING

If you smoke, the sooner you stop, the better (*see page 33*). If you carry on smoking during pregnancy you are more likely to miscarry. Your baby has a greater risk of being born prematurely and of having a low birth weight; and it has twice the risk of dying in the first week of life.

SOUNDS

Many mothers say that their babies seem to recognize and enjoy soothing sounds, such as pieces of music, which they first heard within the womb. It is certainly true that an unborn baby's environment is affected by the sounds and sonic vibrations reaching the womb. Your baby is able to hear from 24 weeks of gestation. Give your baby – and yourself – the benefit of pleasing sounds, as well as the reassuring ones that form part of your daily routine. Your voice and that of your partner and other children; music, laughter, singing and the sound of waves or birdsong can all be pleasing. If you enjoy a sound it will automatically do your baby good, because your positive emotions have a beneficial effect on the chemical constitution of your blood.

SEX DURING PREGNANCY

If you have had one or more miscarriages it is sensible to avoid penetrative sexual intercourse and orgasm during the new pregnancy, in the month corresponding to the stage of pregnancy when you previously miscarried. There is a small chance that an orgasm or the thrusting of the penis could dislodge a potentially unstable baby from the womb.

EMPLOYMENT

Whether or not you decide to continue with paid employment is up to you and may be dictated to some extent by your circumstances. If you like working, need the money and you do not get too tired from travelling to and from your place of work, as long as you are not exposed to overstrenuous, hazardous situations it is acceptable to carry on for as long as you feel you can. Both the employer and the pregnant woman must ensure that she and her unborn baby are not subjected to unnecessary risks as a result of her work.

Research into the effect of work on pregnancy has been inconclusive, but the most recent studies show that women in paid employment, whatever their social, educational and health backgrounds, have fewer premature and low-birth-weight babies, fewer stillbirths and fewer babies dying in the first week of life. Possible reasons include the beneficial social effects of work outside the home; the fact that the partners of working pregnant women are more likely to share domestic work; and the possibility that housework and the home environment may sometimes be hazardous to pregnant women.

If you intend to work during your pregnancy find out about your maternity rights in good time (see page 21). If you can, avoid work that obliges you to stand for long periods of time. This can lead to varicose veins and swollen ankles. Standing may also, according to a large study of women in four regions of the USA, be associated with growth retardation in your baby. If your job involves standing, ask for a chair to sit on when you are not busy. Rest with your feet up for a while every dayand take regular gentle exercise, such as swimming.

PROFESSIONAL CARE

Health-care professionals can monitor a pregnancy in a variety of ways, including using ultrasound scanning or amniocentesis when necessary as diagnostic tools.

ULTRASOUND

High-frequency sound waves, beamed off surfaces in the body to produce a variety of signals, can be employed to detect problems in the following ways:

1. Ultrasound is used in one heart monitor – a small hand-held device such as the Doptone – to produce audible foetal heart sounds. Continuous high-frequency sound waves are directed at the baby's beating heart, where they rebound from structures and surfaces, producing echoes which are recorded as audible signals.

2. Pulsed ultrasonic waves are used in the static ultrasonic scanner to produce a static ultrasonic scan: a visual picture of an unborn baby on screen or paper. The high-frequency sound waves are used to produce echoes which are measured and recorded on a visual display screen or paper as a static two-dimensional or cross-sectional view of the baby.

3. Rapid pulsed ultrasonic waves are used in the real-time imaging scanner to produce a moving or real-time ultrasonic scan: a movie of the baby's body.

The sound-wave pictures can detect abnormalities, such as an ectopic pregnancy
continued on page 54

PREVENTING COMPLICATIONS IN PREGNANCY

However well a pregnant woman looks after herself and the health professionals look after her and her baby, a pregnancy may not be straightforward. It is sensible to face this fact early in pregnancy, but to face it in a positive way by helping to prevent complications from arising (*see* **Prevention Checklist**).

Following a healthy diet is the most important step (*see opposite* **Nutrients Checklist**). Cutting down on alcohol consumption is the second. Research suggests that one in ten of all malformations in babies born in the UK and in the USA are the result of alcohol consumed by the mother when pregnant. Babies born with foetal alcohol syndrome have multiple minor malformations, such as an unusually small head, short eye slits, joint abnormalities and a hole in the heart. One US expert claims that 'the fetal alcohol syndrome is the third leading cause of mental retardation and neurological problems in infants after Down's syndrome and spina bifida'.

NUTRIENTS CHECKLIST

A healthy diet is one key to a healthy pregnancy. A study at the Harvard School of Public Health found that women who could afford a healthy diet did not suffer from pre-eclampsia (a complex condition which can cause kidney damage in pregnancy), whereas one in two women on a poor diet did. Follow a healthy diet during the peri-conceptual period (*see pages 28-30*), as well as during pregnancy: a shortage of any single essential nutrient, even if only for a few days, may lead to faulty development in an unborn baby.

To ensure a healthy pregnancy, check these lists for foods rich in:

The bioflavonoids (crystalline substances formerly known as vitamin P): broccoli, cabbage, peppers, tomatoes, citrus pith, apricots, blackcurrants, cherries, melons, grapes, plums.

Calcium: milk, cheese, tinned sardines, shellfish, beans, peas, green leafy vegetables, carrots, parsnips, seaweed, seeds, nuts.

Essential fatty acids: egg yolk, fatty fish, meat, wholegrain cereals, beans, peas, green leafy vegetables, root vegetables, mushrooms, avocados, garlic, pepper, seaweed, tomatoes, blackcurrants, seeds, nuts, some polyunsaturated margarines, cold-pressed vegetable oils.

Folic acid: green leafy vegetables, eggs, wholegrain cereals, beans, peas, lentils, fruits, nuts.

Magnesium: fish, meat, wholegrain cereals, beans, peas, nuts, green leafy vegetables, carrots, potatoes, seaweed.

Iron: meat, shellfish, whole cereals and rice, beans, seeds, nuts, green leafy vegetables, seaweed, dates, figs.

Manganese: wholegrain cereals, beans, peas, lentils, green leafy vegetables, carrots, potatoes, garlic, pineapple, seeds, root ginger.

Vitamin A: milk, cheese, eggs, meat, green leafy vegetables, carrots, avocados, peppers, seaweed, tomatoes, bananas, apricots, blackcurrants, cherries, melons, plums, butter, margarine.

Vitamin B: *thiamin:* meat, wholegrain cereals, brown rice, peanuts, seeds, nuts, peas, beans, lentils, potatoes, seaweed, mushrooms; *riboflavin:* milk, cheese, eggs, fish, meat, wholegrain cereals and rice, green leafy vegetables, mushrooms, seaweed, nuts; vitamin B6: egg yolk, fish, meat, wholegrain cereals and rice, beans, peas, green leafy vegetables, carrots, potatoes, mushrooms, avocados, bananas, seeds and nuts; *vitamin B12:* wholegrain cereals, beans, peas, sprouted seeds, peanuts, green leafy vegetables, seaweed, mushrooms, root vegetables, bananas, meat, fish, eggs, cheese, milk, meat, yeast extract.

Vitamin C: fresh fruit and vegetables.

Vitamin D: cheese, eggs, fish, seeds, nuts, milk.

Vitamin E: milk, cheese, eggs, wholegrain cereals, green leafy vegetables, soya beans, seaweed, seeds, nuts, vegetable oil.

Zinc: milk, cheese, egg yolk, fish, meat, wholegrain cereals, beans, peas, carrots, turnips, potatoes, garlic, seaweed, seeds, nuts, root ginger.

PREVENTION CHECKLIST
These lists give useful guidelines – in addition to a healthy diet – on ways of preventing or treating:

MISCARRIAGE:

● Eat foods rich in vitamin C, the bioflavonoids and iron to strengthen the blood vessels in the placenta.

● Eat foods rich in manganese, zinc and the essential fatty acids.

● Eat foods rich in vitamin E, thought to promote the healthy growth of the placenta.

● Lower your exposure to potentially harmful toxins, such as copper, lead and irradiation.

● Cut down on alcohol. The safe amount, if any, is not yet known.

● Do not smoke, actively or passively.

● Guard against listeria (*see pages 49-50*) and rubella infection (*see page 32*).

● Do not use a VDU for too long.

PRE-ECLAMPSIA (formerly called toxaemia of pregnancy)

● Watch your weight (*see page 31*). If necessary, cut back on empty calories.

● Eat plenty of foods rich in calcium, vitamin B6, magnesium and natural salicylates (most fruit and fruit juice, vegetables, other than green leafy ones; potatoes with skins, nuts, seeds, honey).

● Eat fatty fish (coldwater fish such as herring and mackerel).

HIGH BLOOD PRESSURE

● Eat a variety of calcium-rich foods.

● Drink lime-blossom tea several times a day to widen the blood vessels of the uterus and improve the blood supply to the placenta.

LOW BIRTH WEIGHT & PRE-TERM LABOUR

● Eat plenty of foods rich in zinc, calcium, magnesium, folic acid, the bioflavonoids and essential fatty acids.

● Avoid over-exposure to copper, lead or cadmium.

● Do not drink too much alcohol.

● Guard against toxoplasmosis (*see p32*).

MALFORMATIONS IN THE BABY:

● Eat plenty of foods rich in vitamin A, riboflavin, pantothenic acid, folic acid, vitamin C, zinc and manganese.

● Reduce your alcohol intake; give it up completely if possible.

● Keep away from dangerous pesticides.

● Do not use a VDU for too long. The electromagnetic field from these machines may increase the risk of malformation.

COPING WITH LOSS
It is a sad fact that some women lose their babies from miscarriage, still-birth or early death, despite all the care they and the professional advisers take before conception and during pregnancy. If this happens to you, you need time to mourn your loss and to readjust after the hormonal, physical and emotional changes of pregnancy. If you have had a termination, you must not miss out on this crucial period of mourning and readjustment. Bear in mind that fathers also need the opportunity, permission and support to mourn.

You and your partner may not have enough emotional and physical resources to support each other at this difficult time. Make the most of any support – both practical and emotional – offered by friends, family, and professional and lay helpers. If this is not forthcoming, try to summon up the courage to ask for it.

(a pregnancy in which a pre-embryo implants in the wall of a fallopian tube); a cleft palate; spina bifida; heart defects and other malformations. It can also detect twins; the position of the baby; the rate of growth (using a series of scans); the location of the placenta; and the baby's age and sex. But doubts still exist as to the safety of this method. Ultrasound alters the environment in the womb and can cause heating and vibration of the cells in the baby's body. Although there are no apparent short-term hazards to a mother or her baby from diagnostic ultrasound in pregnancy, there are few studies of possible delayed or cumulative effects in humans.

One study of nearly 35,000 babies in the USA suggests that routine foetal monitoring does not improve a baby's chances of being born healthy or alive. And similarly, studies of routine ultrasonic scanning have failed to show that its use consistently benefits the outcome of the pregnancy.

Two other researchers noticed that after cells in a test-tube were exposed to diagnostic levels of ultrasound there were lasting effects on the DNA (the genetic material) of cells and on cell growth. This means that further research is needed to establish whether diagnostic ultrasound might damage the eggs of an unborn baby girl. There has also been insufficient investigation into ultrasound's effects on behavioural and neurological development, on the immune system and on the blood. The work of one British researcher suggests that there could be a higher incidence of leukaemia in children who were exposed to diagnostic ultrasound in the womb.

Continuous ultrasonic monitoring of the foetal heart, in which the device is strapped to the mother's abdomen using a broad elastic belt, allows the ultrasonic beam to focus on one spot for many hours. This process can be uncomfortable for the mother, who has to lie in bed for hours on end, and is not very reliable. Equally worrying is the tendency of some midwives to take more notice of the monitor than of the person to whom it is strapped.

When any investigation or technique is used routinely by health professionals in pregnancy or labour it restricts a woman's choice of the type of care she receives because she is unlikely to be offered any alternative and may feel too intimidated to ask about the possibilities.

Much of the research suggesting possible dangers of ultrasound has been criticized, but it is important to realize that no-one can say that diagnostic ultrasound is entirely safe. Until the risks are more adequately defined it makes sense to accept routine diagnostic ultrasound only if there is a good medical indication for it. However, statistics indicate that ultrasonic scans and monitoring can improve the outcome of high-risk or complicated pregnancies.

New equipment and techniques recently introduced to ultrasonic scanning have led to better-quality pictures (sometimes only because more powerful ultrasound output has been used), improved reliability and quicker results. All these advantages serve to encourage the use of more scans. Yet most health professionals agree that the risks are difficult to assess.

Although the experts do not agree that the routine use of diagnostic ultrasound is a good idea, routine early scanning in pregnancy is increasing, both in the UK and in several other countries:
● The World Health Organization has stated that in view of the lack of information regarding the safety of ultrasound in pregnancy, routine ultrasound examinations should not be carried out.
● In the USA so many medical indications are accepted as reasons for ultrasound scanning that they could be taken as applying to virtually all pregnancies, perhaps partly from fear of litigation. The indications are based primarily on clinical judgement rather than on evidence from well conducted research.
● The West German Maternity Care Guidelines, the *Mutterschaftsrichtlinien*, state the right of each pregnant woman to be offered at least two ultrasound tests during pregnancy.

● The Danish Minister of the Interior has stated in guidelines for the maternity services that ultrasound must not be used routinely.

AMNIOCENTESIS

This procedure involves inserting a needle through the abdominal wall to draw some amniotic fluid from within the amniotic sac which surropunds the baby. The fluid and the cells suspended in it undergo several tests, including those for Down's syndrome and for alpha-feto-protein (a foetal protein normally present in the amniotic fluid) which is raised if the baby has an open neural tube deformity, such as spina bifida. An amniocentesis should be carried out in conjunction with an ultrasound scan, to avoid piercing the baby or the placenta. There is, however, still a risk of damaging the baby or causing a miscarriage. Every woman offered an amniocentesis must weigh up, with the aid of a professional, its pros and cons. If you are very anxious, an amniocentesis could put your mind at rest for the remainder of the pregnancy. If you would want a termination (abortion) if the baby were found to be affected, the test is worth having. However, if you do not want reassurance, or if you are against abortion, the only point in having the test is the early discovery of any serious defect that might require surgery immediately after delivery. It is important to consider these options calmly before the test, not afterwards, when emotions inevitably obscure decision-making.

LABOUR & BIRTH

Doctors have spent most of the second half of the twentieth century trying to make childbirth safer for mothers and babies. In many countries they have succeeded, but ironically the credit goes more to improved general health than to modern obstetric technology. Women in the developed countries are healthier than they used to be because they have higher living standards, a better diet and fewer children. The average woman enters pregnancy more able to withstand the demands the baby will put on her body than her counterpart even half a century ago.

The question now is how best to make pregnancy safer and better for mothers and babies. It seems to me that there are three ways. First, we need further improvements in living and working conditions, diet and general health. These will take time, effort and money. Second, we need obstetric technology to become ever more sensitive and able to prevent damage or death in babies. This will be expensive and time-consuming. The third way, which is the most immediately possible and, to my mind, the most exciting, is the green way.

IMPROVING CHILDBIRTH

Mothers, fathers, midwives and increasing numbers of obstetricians are beginning to agree that the most hopeful potential for safer birth lies in optimizing the environment in which women labour and have their babies.

Labour and birth are natural events which can (and surprisingly often do) go wrong. Modern obstetric technology is capable of improving the outcome of pregnancy for mothers and babies. It can save lives and it is one of the wonders of modern medicine. Obstricians can helpfully intervene in a vareity of situations, including oxygen lack in the baby due to placental insufficiency, a poorly positioned placenta, multiple birth, rhesus incompatibility, maternal diabetes, pre-eclampsia, pre-term birth, prolapse of the umbilical cord and an abnormally prolonged or difficult labour.

However, it is becoming ever more apparent that technological intervention in childbirth is used too often and taken too far. In hospitals around the world women with a low risk of anything going wrong are being encouraged and sometimes even pushed, to accept obstetric intervention (*see page 56*). This is well-intentioned but vague, based on the often scientifically unsupportable hope that it will make labour and birth safer. The benefits sometimes outweigh the risk of side-effects, but

CASCADE OF INTERVENTION

One snag with unnecessary medical intervention in labour is that any side-effects tend to make further interference essential. For instance, breaking the waters to speed up labour is sometimes done without good reason, yet obstetricians are loath to leave a woman with her waters broken for too long for fear of infection. So begins a cascade of intervention, as mapped out in the illustration (*below*).

3. Oxytocin causes extra-painful contractions, so pain relief is required.

4. An epidural prevents mother from moving around or being upright, so reducing efficiency of contracting uterus.

5. Intervention necessitates electronic monitoring of baby's heart rate, preventing mother from getting out of bed.

6. Mother's immobility makes second stage of labour more difficult.

2. Risk of infection increased when waters broken, so labour started or accelerated with oxytocic drip.

7. Difficult labour necessitates assisted delivery by forceps or vacuum extraction, and episiotomy.

1. Labour triggered by breaking the waters.

8. Pain-relieving drugs can pass into baby's bloodstream, inhibiting breathing, sucking and responsiveness.

not always, especially if intervention is a routine, as it is in many hospitals. Unnecessary interference in normal labour can upset its delicate balance and exhaust a woman's physical and emotional resources, so that she has to rely on obstetric help. This is a waste of highly trained professional experience, a waste of money and, most importantly, a waste of what should be a very different experience for all concerned.

Many women for whom intervention is non-essential say they would have preferred the option of a labour without technological intervention. It is easy, however, to be wise after the event and difficult to assert your need for an informed choice in the middle of labour. Some of the responsibility for stemming the vast amount of unnecessary intervention in labour must rest with the professional birth attendants.

In the UK, the rate of intervention varies widely from one hospital to another. The rates for Caesarean section in large units during 1982 and 1985 varied between 7 per cent and 17 per cent, depending on the hospital. The rates for private practice tend to be higher. The rate for forceps or vacuum extraction varied between 3 per cent and 19 per cent. Induction rates were between 5 per cent and 39 per cent. In the USA the average Caesarean rate is 24 per cent. The American Public Health Association, not surprisingly, notes that many of these operations are not medically necessary. In Texas, one in two white, middle-class, insured women delivering in a private hospital has a Caesarean. Even this figure is superseded in a few Brazilian hospitals in which more than four out of five women are delivered by a Caesarean section. Unnecessary operations may not benefit mother or baby but they certainly help the doctors' pockets and the malpractice insurance companies.

THE OVERDIAGNOSIS PROBLEM

There is not enough space to examine fully the implications of obstetric intervention during labour, but a brief look at electronic foetal heart-monitoring will suffice as an example. This monitoring, invaluable during high-risk labour or when problems occur in low-risk labour, is becoming routine procedure in many hospitals, increasing the likelihood of a Caesarean section by two or threefold, even though a proportion of monitored babies is subsequently found to have been in no danger.

One reason for this overdiagnosis may be that routine foetal monitoring methods still lack precision. Unnecessary Caesareans are bad because they cause post-operative discomfort to mothers and (although rarely) problems resulting from the anaesthetic. They also inhibit the mother/baby relationship, including breast-feeding. Unless continuing research proves that routine monitoring makes low-risk labour safer, it seems sensible only to do it for high-risk cases.

In a Danish study one in three mothers said they would prefer their babies to be monitored by the midwife using a foetal stethoscope – a simple trumpet-shaped instrument – to hear the heart, although they would very reasonably accept electronic monitoring if any problems were detected.

The best way forward for better birth care, both in developing and developed countries, is to integrate traditional and modern approaches so as to allow each to benefit from the other. We need technology only if it is appropriate. This way both lives and money can be saved. As Brigitte Jordan, Professor of Anthropology at Michigan State University says, 'By the time a particular technology reaches the Third World it has often been superseded in its country of origin, so that the transfer amounts to dumping. It is ironic that, at a time when 'natural' childbirth, upright delivery positions, the importance of midwives, having babies at home and the avoidance of high technology are all becoming popular and receiving increasing scientific support in the USA and in western Europe, the Third World is bent on adopting high-technology obstetrics'.

BIRTH ATTENDANTS

The best choice of professional birth attendant for a woman interested in a 'green' birth is one who will:
● Be with her in labour, or wait in the wings if a woman prefers to labour in the company of someone else.
● Support her in her choice of environment and in her preferred way of labouring.
● Encourage her to be aware of her body and discover her own best way of giving birth.
● Listen to her.
● Consult and inform her fully about any proposed intervention.
● Accept that giving birth and being born can be spiritual events as well as physical and emotional ones.

DEFENSIVE OBSTETRICS

In practice, only women who can afford to pay their birth attendant have any say in who that person is. Others are allocated the midwife and doctor on duty at the time unless they have a special arrangement with their own health professionals. This happens in some areas of the UK, where a woman's own doctor or midwife delivers her in hospital. For women who decide to have their babies in hospital, there may be some choice of obstetrician when they first attend for ante-natal care. In the USSR many women deliver alone because there are not enough nurses.

Even if you do have some choice, it is becoming more limited in some countries. In the USA, where defensive obstetric practice is on the increase, obstetricians are fearful of allowing normal labour, hence the extraordinarily high Caesarean rate in the USA. Their reason is based on experience. They have been sued too often in the past when they have avoided intervening in a low-risk labour but something – through no fault of their own – has gone wrong. One in eight obstetricians has now stopped delivering babies because of their ever-increasing malpractice insurance premiums.

Similarly, in the UK, fewer doctors are choosing to go into obstetrics. Many say that they are profoundly dissatisfied with the interventionist method of obstetrics and with increasing malpractice claims, which foster an atmosphere of suspicion and fear. Ironically, but not surprisingly, this interventionist obstetrics has not led to better infant health. In fact, the level of infant mortality has been rising in the USA compared with that of other countries.

I am sure this situation is not simply based on the fact that women are jumping at the chance to make money out of their obstetricians' insurance companies. I believe the reasons go deeper. Many obstetricians stopped listening to women a long time ago. They wanted increasingly more control over labour and did not want to wait around while nature took its course. It is my belief that women are now metaphorically and unconsciously hitting obstetricians where it hurts most – in the wallet – as a way of telling them to behave in a different way. Women used never to punish obstetricians when something went wrong with pregnancy or labour. Something profound is now being communicated; whether obstetricians listen to the message is up to them. The politics of the labour ward reflect those of world-wide environmental issues. It is crucial that scientists, manufacturers and obstetricians learn to heed the voices of ordinary people and to work with them as fellow human beings in harmony.

I believe that defensive obstetrics is based on a scientific misunderstanding, as well as on a misunderstanding of what women want. Much obstetric intervention aims to prevent brain damage (cerebral palsy, mental retardation, learning disorders and epilepsy), thought to be caused by a lack of oxygen supplying the baby's brain during a difficult birth. The basic assumptions behind this aim are increasingly being seen as faulty. The neurologist and psychoanalyst, Sigmund Freud, said as early as 1897 that problems in the baby attributed to a difficult birth may in fact be present way before birth and be the cause of the difficult birth, not the result.

The real cause of most brain damage, such as cerebral palsy (one of the major handicaps of childhood, affecting one in 500 children) is not known. Children with cerebral palsy have ten times the risk of being born early. Premature babies with cerebral palsy are more likely to be born with a congenital malformation and to be underweight for their degree of maturity. These three factors suggest that such babies may have been damaged by environmental factors, such as toxins during very early pregnancy (see pages 33 to 44), rather than simply by the process of labour and birth.

Whatever happens in the USA usually filters through to other developed countries before long, and the developing world does not lag all that far behind. In the Third World, 60 to 80 per cent of babies are currently being delivered by traditional birth attendants. The commonly held yet often unquestioned goal of universal hospital delivery by personnel trained in modern obstetric methods may be far from ideal. In many American States home births with a midwife in attendance are illegal, though many midwives and other women are working hard to change this ridiculous state of affairs. So what alternative do women have if they want to influence the kind of birth they want?

TALK TO THE PROFESSIONALS

One option is to make a contract with the obstetrician. This is frequently done in the UK as an unofficially agreed birth plan. Some obstetricians feel uncomfortable with birth plans, knowing how often they end up being scrapped because labour does not turn out as expected. This can be overcome by accepting that, should things not go according to plan, you will consider other options that are in general accord with the way you would like to be treated. Perhaps the most important factor lies in the attitude of the birth attendant, who is ideally affirming, encouraging, loving and respectful, whether or not intervention becomes advisable and is agreed upon.

Talk to acquaintances who have had babies and try to find out which obstetrician is most likely to be sympathetic toward your ideas about the birth.

Try to arrange for a midwife, rather than an obstetrician, to be with you while you are in labour. Midwives are trained to help with normal labour. Obstetricians are trained to manage risky or complicated labours and may find it difficult to stand back and let normal labour take its course. Of course it is sensible and comforting to have access to obstetric help if necessary.

You will be more relaxed if you feel at ease with your midwife and this is most likely if you have had a chance to get to know each other during your pregnancy. If this seems impossible, try to get the message across to the people responsible for personnel in the hospital that improvements are badly needed to make maternity care better for other women.

If at any time you feel you are being patronized by a doctor or a nurse, say so, politely but assertively, and say how you would like to be treated. Make sure that you are not engendering that attitude by acting in an unnecessarily dependent or even aggressive fashion.

PERSONAL ATTENDANTS

Some women choose to have close family members or friends with them as they give birth, alongside a professional birth attendant. Maya Indian women in Yucatan in Mexico sometimes go to the hospital with labour problems too late because they know that the modern health-care system will not allow their family and midwife to stay with them. Over the past 20 years or so there has been a fashion in developed countries for encouraging the partner to be present in labour, although this is not always to the liking of the woman or the man. If you would like someone – perhaps your partner, mother, sister, friend or older child or children – to be present while you labour, just say so. Some women like to be alone, while others prefer company to help while away the long hours of labour. There is no reason why your request should be refused unless the person or persons would somehow interfere with your labour or with any necessary professional assistance. In such a case the person could anyway just be asked to leave for a while.

HOME OR HOSPITAL?

There is a great deal of controversy over whether hospital or home provides the safest environment in which to give birth. The statistics indicate that if your pregnancy is low or moderate risk, home is safer for you and your baby, perhaps because it is a much less disturbing environment than hospital in which to go through the process of labour and birth. Many women who go into hospital while they are in labour find that their contractions stop, albeit temporarily. One problem is that once in hospital the great medical temptation to restart your labour artificially can lead to a cascade of intervention. Marjorie Tew, a UK statistician, says that even the babies of women with high-risk pregnancies may not necessarily be safer if born in hospital. A UK government-funded study published in 1988 concluded that a hospital is not necessarily the best place in which to have your baby.

There is a much-reduced chance of infection with bacteria resistant to antibiotics in you or your baby if you give birth at home. Breastfeeding is likely to get off to a better start and you will probably have more sleep. One snag is that you may not give yourself enough time to recover, especially if you have other children who need to be looked after. If you have your baby at home, make sure that you have someone to look after you, the house and your other children.

● In the Netherlands nearly two out of five women have their babies at home. No more babies are damaged at birth there than in European countries in which most babies are born in hospital.

● In Sweden the number of babies born in hospital has been rising for 20 years, but there is no evidence that levels of cerebral palsy (a possible result of birth damage) have fallen in this time.

● Birth is intrinsically a sexual and a sensual event, yet this is frequently denied by all concerned. Sexuality and sensuality by their very nature fit better into a home environment than a hospital one. Some women who are in tune with their bodies help start or restart labour by having an orgasm – a hospital environment is not exactly a conducive place for this.

COPING WITH LABOUR

A relaxed woman labours more easily and efficiently than one who is tense. Antenatal classes (such as those given by National Childbirth Trust teachers in the UK) help women to maximize the natural resources which enable them to cope during labour. You will have a better chance of relaxing and working with your body if your environment is pleasant. When you are relaxed, emotionally and physically, your body produces higher levels of naturally occurring chemicals called endorphins. These help you cope with the pain of labour and, unlike artificial painkilling drugs, have no side-effects. Many women find the following helpful while they are in labour:

● A low level of lighting.

● A peaceful atmosphere with no loud or jarring sounds; perhaps with some music of their choice.

● The opportunity to get on with everyday life (if they want to) during the early hours of labour.

● Familiar smells rather than the odour of antiseptic.

● A comfortable temperature with enough fresh air.

● Pleasant surroundings with suitable furnishings and colourings, conducive to relaxation.

● The presence of someone who is trusted (and preferably known and loved), who will be there to listen and will give focussed attention, encouragement and support when they are needed.

● Light massage of the lower back. Quick

'butterfly' strokes can be very helpful as a means of pain relief and compares with TNS (trans-cutaneous nerve stimulation, *see page 187*) in its effectiveness. Both raise the level of endorphins circulating in the blood.

● The freedom to move around – to stand up, walk about, bend over a chair, kneel on all fours – to help cope with the contractions and make both the first and the second stages of labour more efficient.

● Solitude when requested, to sleep or just relax.

● Privacy to be with someone or to have a cuddle with their partner.

● A bath – provided that their waters have not broken and there is someone with them in case they need help.

● Food and drink according to their appetite and liking. If labour is complicated, so that a general anaesthetic may be necessary for a Caesarean section, food is better avoided and drinks only sipped.

ACTIVITY & POSITION

The freedom to move around and change position is essential to reduce the pain of contractions as the cervix dilates. During the second stage of labour, as your baby is being expelled from your womb down the birth canal, it helps if you experiment to find the least uncomfortable position. The baby's head twists round and passes down the birth canal asymmetrically; as it moves down, the source of your discomfort alters. By repeatedly changing position to avoid the pain, you give more room to the part of the baby that is causing the discomfort. Good and bad positions are illustrated on page 62.

Some hospitals are experimenting with expensive beds that convert into birth chairs. The position a woman adopts when she is in such a chair is, however, only semi-upright and is not the same as her position if semi-squatting or kneeling. Surveys comparing the labours of women in birth chairs with those on their backs do not cast any light on the advantages of labouring in a naturally upright position. Old-fashioned birth stools allow a better position than modern birth chairs.

TO PUSH OR NOT TO PUSH

Contrary to popular belief little pushing is normally needed in the second stage of labour. The force of the contracting womb, gravity and, hopefully, sensitive changes of position (to avoid hampering the progress of the baby by an unhelpful configuration of the pelvis) combine to expel the baby. If you strain to push you can reduce the amount of oxygen reaching the baby via your bloodstream. Try to go with your bodily sensations and do what seems natural at the time, rather than push because you think you have to. When you are in tune with your labouring womb you find your body automatically bears down without you thinking about it.

THE UNKIND CUT

An episiotomy is a cut made in the perineum – the skin and muscle between the vaginal opening and the anus – to widen the vaginal opening and so prevent it tearing when the baby's head emerges. An episiotomy is best avoided unless it is absolutely necessary. There is little evidence to suggest that it is useful to mother or baby unless it is done to prevent severe tearing of the perineum, severe stretching of the muscles supporting the bladder and back passage, or a dangerously long second stage of labour. Forceps deliveries require episiotomies, however, and breech or pre-term babies are often helped by a cut. The episiotomy rate varies greatly – from about 30 per cent to 70 per cent in developed countries – and from one birth attendant to another.

The pain from a healing episiotomy can be severe. I remember having to use a rubber cushion to make sitting down bearable for ten days or so after my first baby was born. I also remember waddling like a duck. Such pain is difficult to ignore. It can spoil the early days with your new baby and even hinder breastfeeding. What is more, the pain seems to drag on for weeks or

BIRTHING POSITIONS

Lying on the back in order to give birth (*top left*), a position still encouraged by birth professionals in many hospitals, gives the baby little space to get out: not a very welcoming start. This position puts pressure on the sacrum (the back of the pelvis) and coccyx (the base of the spine) and decreases the size of the pelvic outlet. The baby is, in effect, being pushed upwards against gravity. Bringing the knees up toward the chest while in this position further reduces the size of the pelvic outlet.

A kneeling position, leaning forward slightly from my hips and taking some weight on my hands, which were resting on a low object in front of me (*centre*), was the position I adopted when I had my last baby. This is a similar position to the supported crouch. Full squatting is not as good because it puts more tension on the perineum (the part of the body between the vulva and the anus), increasing the risk of it tearing. Maya Indian women give birth while pulling on a rope suspended from rafters.

The supported crouch, semi-squat position (*bottom*), creates more room for the baby. This entails remaining upright with knees half bent and the weight on the feet, your birth attendant(s) sharing some of your weight by supporting you under the armpits. The space in the pelvic outlet can increase by as much as 30 per cent in this position.

months and can frustrate attempts to return to sex. The old idea was that an episiotomy would heal better than a torn perineum, although studies show that this is not true. Not only can healing take longer than for a natural tear but breakdown of the healing wound is more common.

You can help yourself deliver without an episiotomy by relaxing and going with the waves of your contractions. If you are upright or on your side in the second stage of labour you give your vaginal outlet a better chance of dilating smoothly and evenly than if you are on your back.

YOUR BABY IS BORN

At the moment of birth a child can see, hear, feel, smell and taste. Like many of us, newborn babies can sense the emotional atmosphere, so the environment your baby is born into matters a great deal. The renowned French obstetrician, Frédéric Leboyer, reminded us to be sensitively aware of the baby's feelings. Such feelings are important whatever the birth was like.

The most important thing to help ease the baby's shock of being born is to have you there. Your baby has been used to the sounds and movements of your body for many months. The sounds of your heart, your voice, your tummy rumbling, your laughter and your breathing are reassuringly familiar. There is no reason for you to be separated from your baby after the birth unless the baby needs essential medical care which cannot be given while you are there. Many mothers find that however tired they are immediately after the birth, they feel wide awake and want to talk, think, eat and be with their babies. These early hours give you the chance to hold your baby and for you both to get to know each other face to face.

Left lying on your tummy, your newly delivered baby will slowly find the way up to your breast and then to the nipple. The smell of the breast is attractive and the darker colouration of the nipple acts as a target. The Norwegian midwife researcher, Ann-Marie Widström, suggests that calmly and patiently letting newborn babies do what they want may be better than encouraging them to go to the breast before they are ready. Lighting levels are best kept low. Newborns like to open their eyes without lights glaring into them.

It seems sensible to allow only essential people into the room. The sounds and smells of strangers may interfere with the baby's transition from being dependent on you inside your body to being dependent on you outside it.

SPECIAL CARE

You can help the doctors and nurses make the environment pleasant for your baby, if he or she needs special medical care. Visit the baby frequently in the special care unit. You may be able to have the incubator by your bed, or you may be encouraged to nurse the baby between your breasts inside your clothing in the 'kangaroo' position – in the way pioneered in hospital in Bogotá, Colombia, and in the UK. Research suggests that being with the mother reduces the risk for many low-birthweight babies and helps them to develop. If your baby has to be in an incubator, try to visit and do as much of the essential nursing as possible. Every time you touch or stroke your baby you communicate something important.

SERENDIPITY & INDEPENDENCE

Being born does not, of course, make a baby independent. Babies need to be fed, kept warm and protected for years to come. Birth marks the point at which the baby begins to breathe air and take food directly, not via the placenta. After birth, a baby shares the mother's environment rather than having a personal micro-environment within her. Breastfeeding provides a gradual and smooth transition from one state to another. This is why the breastfed baby has been called the 'exterogestate foetus', or the 'unborn baby outside the womb'.

Chapter Four
FEEDING YOUR BABY

My breasts will grow full
For the sake of one more of us
Tanikawa Shuntaro

Mother's milk is a vital natural health resource and a valuable economic resource; and breastfeeding is an important part of mothering. Yet around the world increasing numbers of women are turning – some unwillingly – to bottle-feeding with infant formula. In this chapter we will look at the importance of breast milk and at some of the reasons behind the move to bottle-feeding.

Breast milk helps protect a baby against certain infections, diseases and developmental problems. Both experience and research conclude that mother's milk is preferable to infant formula. The milk of every mammal is formulated for its own young. Thus, when we breastfeed, we are supplying our babies with milk that is specifically made to suit human young.

Infant formula, on the other hand, is an adaptation of cow's milk, which is formulated by nature specifically for calves. The hi-tech manipulation of cow's milk makes the levels of the major constituents of infant formula similar to those of mother's milk, but the constituents are not all identical to those of mother's milk in kind, let alone in quantity. The type or amount (and sometimes both) of proteins, free amino acids, nucleotides, fatty acids, carbohydrates, major minerals, trace elements and vitamins in cow's milk formula are not the same as in mother's milk. However hard the manufacturers of infant formula try, they can never replicate mother's milk.

A NATURAL PROTECTION

Breastfeeding protects against diarrhoea (gastro-enteritis) and chest infection. It also protects against infections of the urinary tract, according to a recent US study. This means that breastfeeding could save the lives of hundreds of thousands of children who die around the world every year because they are bottle-fed. Infective diarrhoea, chest infection, meningitis (an infection of the meninges, the coverings of the brain and spinal cord) and septicaemia (blood-poisoning) are statistically more common in babies bottle-fed on infant formula than in breastfed babies, wherever in the world they live.

Factors such as these account for the results of a British study, which showed that a formula-fed baby is more likely to be admitted to hospital, regardless of social factors. Another study looked at infant feeding by mothers of different educational levels in a developed country. Bottle-fed babies of less well educated mothers were four times as likely to catch an infection as their breastfed peers. And the bottle-fed babies of the well educated mothers still had twice the risk of serious infection as the breastfed babies of mothers from the same group. Many surveys have shown higher rates of serious illness among bottle-fed babies than among breastfed babies. In the Philippines, for example, bottle-fed babies are 40 times more likely to die than breastfed babies. These are some of the reasons why:

Diarrhoea triggered by infection is less likely to occur in the breastfed baby whose 'green' gut contains millions of useful organisms which help prevent infective varieties from taking a hold. These friendly, protective organisms cannot readily make their home in the gut of a bottle-fed baby, which is washed regularly and repeatedly by infant formula. This is because the composition of mother's milk creates ideal conditions for them to live, whereas infant formula creates an environment inside the gut which favours the growth of less friendly organisms. A bottle-fed baby, lacking the protection of breast milk and with its gut full of organisms which are less protective than those in a breastfed baby's gut, has a high risk of diarrhoea in adverse situations. These include physical weakness from insufficient infant formula in conditions of poverty (*see pages 86-87*) and exposure to infection from dirty water and unhygienic food preparation.

If diarrhoea lasts for a long time, it will weaken a baby and further lower his or her resistance. Infection causes inflammation and irritation of the gut lining, which increases the normal peristaltic movements of the muscles in the gut wall. The inflamed and over-active gut cannot absorb nutrients properly because the gut lining cells which normally take up nutrients from milk are damaged and because the milk travels too quickly through the gut for optimal absorption to occur. A single attack of diarrhoea can damage a baby's gut lining in such a way that its failure to absorb certain nutrients continues even when the adverse conditions causing the initial precipitating infection are over.

The temporary inability to absorb sugars (sugar malabsorption or sugar intolerance) is a common result of infective diarrhoea. When sugars are not properly absorbed into the baby's blood by the damaged cells of the inflamed gut lining, they remain in the gut and act as irritants. Sugar attracts water, making the gut contents more copious. The combination of high-volume contents and the irritant factor of sugar results in continuing diarrhoea and further weakness of the baby. There is one confounding point: bacteria like a sugary environment. Re-infection is therefore highly likely and a vicious circle sets in:

Infant formula in gut plus another adverse precipitating situation leads to infective diarrhoea, which leads to low resistance plus malabsorption (inability of the gut lining to absorb), which in turn lead to reinfection and diarrhoea.

Dehydration (a dangerous shortage of water in the body) caused by diarrhoea, coupled with malnutrition, leads to vast numbers of babies throughout the developing world suffering from what has come to be known as 'bottle-baby disease', a pitiful sight. Breastfeeding for more than 13 weeks helps to protect a baby from gastro-enteritis throughout the first two years of life.

Chest infections such as pneumonia and bronchiolitis (an infection of the bronchioles, the smallest air passages in the lungs) caused by the *Haemophilus influenzae* bacterium, or by the respiratory syncitial virus (RSV), are more common in formula-fed babies than in breastfed ones. Organisms such as *Haemophilus* stick to certain receptors on cells lining the breathing passages. Breast milk contains sugars called oligosaccharides. These are absorbed into the body from the gut and are taken to the lining cells in the lungs, where they bind on to these receptors and prevent harmful organisms from doing their damage. A baby fed on infant formula is denied this protection.

Allergy may be less likely in a breastfed baby. Arguments over the anti-allergic effect of breast milk continue to rage. One problem with the research has been that many studies deem babies to be breastfed even if they have only had a few feeds at the breast. Modern trials distinguish between babies reared exclusively on their mother's milk, those who have only had a few breastfeeds, and those who have both breast- and formula-feeds. The best trials support the view that breastfeeding can provide some protective effect against allergy, especially if there is a family history of allergy (*see page 67*). Even one bottle of formula may in some cases alter the nature of a baby's immune defences.

A baby's immune system is immature for the first four to six months of life. Breast milk not only boosts this immunity but also seems to pattern its future development in some way. Only a proportion of allergic disorders in older children and adults are caused by food allergy, but the type of food (milk) given in early infancy seems to affect the development of both food-related and non-food-related allergy.

It is difficult to predict whether a baby will develop allergic problems such as eczema, respiratory allergy (wheezing caused by croup or asthma), and hay fever (allergic rhinitis). If one parent or one parent's family has a history of allergy, the baby runs twice the risk of developing an allergy as a baby with no such family history. If both parents have a family history, the baby has four times the risk. Some babies, however, develop allergies with no such family record.

If there is no family history of allergy it is advisable to breastfeed exclusively for three to six months, then carefully to introduce other foods and drinks while continuing to breastfeed. It is wise to avoid foods containing wheat for the first eight months, citrus fruit and juice for nine months, fish for ten months, cow's milk for eleven months, eggs for a year, and nuts, fruit and vegetables with pips or seeds for an even longer period. Ideally no one protein food should form too important a part of a young child's diet. In many developed countries, children tend to be given a disproportionate amount of cow's milk or wheat.

If there is a family history of allergy, particularly of serious allergic problems, it is best to breastfeed exclusively for a year. Research shows that this gives a fairly consistent protective effect. During this time mothers should try not to eat too much of any one protein food, because traces of undigested protein molecules could enter the milk from the bloodstream. It is important that the mother's diet continues to be highly nutritious if she is breastfeeding an older baby. Nutritional supplements for mother and/or baby may be advisable.

Food allergy is only one type of food sensitivity. Some other manifestations of food sensitivity include colic, dermatitis, diarrhoea, catarrh, convulsions, tummy-ache, urticaria (nettle rash or hives) and roughness of the skin. One study showed that bottle-fed babies are twice as likely to wheeze as breastfed ones.

Disorders such as coeliac disease (an intolerance of the small intestine to gluten) are less likely in a baby who is breastfed. Research continues into the effectiveness of breastfeeding as a protection against: ulcerative colitis and Crohn's disease (inflammation and ulceration of the lining of the gut); heart disease; dental decay; faulty jaw development; multiple sclerosis; pyloric stenosis (the narrowing of the outlet from the stomach to the first part of the gut); and plugs of meconium – waste matter – in the bowel of a newborn baby.

Cot death or Sudden Infant Death Syndrome (*SIDS, see page 92*) and its possible link with feeding method has been the focus of much research. The cause of SIDS is unknown and a number of factors are known to be involved, but many older surveys have suggested that it is less common in breastfed babies. However, it is well known that breastfed babies can die in this way and some surveys have shown no link with bottle-feeding.

I think one hopeful line of research lies in looking at the intervals between feeds. Researchers have noted that in many cases of cot death, the last feed was given many hours before the death. Bottle-feeding mothers and those breastfeeding mothers who feed on a controlled, scheduled basis often leave long periods between feeds, especially at night. This is in comparison with mothers who feed their babies on an unrestricted basis, often many times during the day and night. Further research is required to see if this time factor is linked with cot death; to investigate the place of death; and to see whether young babies are safer when with their mothers than when left alone for long periods in their cots.

Childhood cancers are five times more likely to occur in bottle-fed babies than in babies who are breastfed for more than six months. Among the most common is lymphoma (cancer of the infection-fighting lymph nodes or 'glands' situated along the course of the lymphatic vessels that carry tissue fluid as lymph to the veins).

BREAST IS BEST FOR BABIES

After birth, a baby's natural environment is by the mother's body, next to her skin and at the breast. Bottle-feeding inevitably interferes with this environment. Women who breastfeed unrestrictedly give more than just food and drink. They meet their babies' needs and their own needs in a way that is sensitively responsive and ever-changing. In the USA and many other parts of the world, breastfeeding is known as 'nursing'. This is an excellent term because it conveys some sense of the mothering aspect of having a baby at the breast. In German, *stillen* means 'to breastfeed', as well as 'to soothe' or 'to calm'. Bottle-fed babies inevitably have very different early experiences from those who are breastfed. A Canadian study showed that the longer a woman breastfed, the less likely she was to be hostile towards her young child, to want to control, or to reject the child.

The differences may not be great, but several studies have indicated that children who are breastfed walk sooner, are more intelligent and more successful at school, and are less likely to be fearful, jealous or spiteful, than children who are bottle-fed. Such differences are hard to quantify and explain, but it is significant that mother's milk contains amino acids of a particular type and in a particular balance, which are crucial to the optimal development of the fast-growing brain in the first year or so of a child's life.

An American study showed a statistically significant difference in the development of breastfed and bottle-fed babies as measured by Bayley's Mental Development Index (a method used by psychologists to ascertain a child's developmental level). A British study indicated that the length of breastfeeding affected a child's performance in tests of both vocabulary and hand-eye co-ordination.

Babies need company and sensitive interaction on a one-to-one basis. Breastfed babies spend less time asleep and less time lying by themselves, according to researchers. The amount of time available for learning and interaction is therefore greater.

The psychological benefits of breastfeeding must be greater if a child is nursed on an unrestricted basis and for a long time, perhaps until he or she is ready to stop. Babies who can have the breast when they need it benefit from skin-to-skin closeness and intimacy, and a sense of contentment and empowerment at being able to control the flow of milk from the breast. Their sensual experience is very different from that of bottle-fed babies.

Researchers have noted that if babies are breastfed unrestrictedly, that is, without sticking to a schedule, and are put to the breast to be emotionally comforted as well as physically nourished, they cry less. This makes sense. Crying is a signal that something is wrong: a baby brought up without crying for long periods each day is more likely to grow up feeling basically secure.

Breastfed babies do not waste resources. A bottle-fed baby relies on cows for milk. Cows need pasture. As the population of the world increases and more women bottle-feed, more cows are needed to produce milk to make infant formula, so wooded lands are cleared to provide grazing. This deforestation leads to erosion of the soil and the depletion of its nutrients, as well as to an increase in greenhouse gases (*see* **Glossary** *pages 185-187*). Bottle-feeding causes a serious wastage of the world's resources; breast milk is readily and freely available for every baby.

Breastfeeding creates no unnecessary waste. Bottle-fed babies create a large amount of waste in the form of (usually unrecyclable) formula tins (*see page 82*).

THE VALUE OF BREAST MILK

The milk of every mammal is formulated for its own young. Thus, when we breastfeed, we supply our babies with milk specifically made to suit human young. Infant formula is an adaptation of cow's milk, which is formulated by nature specifically for calves. Hi-tech manipulation of cow's milk makes the levels of the major constituents of infant formula similar to those of mother's milk. But the constituents are not all identical to mother's milk in kind or quantity. The type and/or amount of proteins, free amino acids, nucleotides, fatty acids, major minerals, carbohydrates, trace elements and vitamins in formula milk are not the same as in mother's milk. If you want the highest-quality product for your baby, breast milk is the one to choose, for many reasons:

Breast milk is the perfect food, providing exactly the right nutrients in biologically correct amounts. If a mother's diet lacks nutrients vital to her baby's development, her body makes up the loss from its own stores.

Breast milk contains hormones and active enzymes which are beneficial to human infants. Enzymes in cow's milk are inactivated by the process of making infant formula. Hormones and enzymes tend to be species-specific: effective only in the species which produces them.

The contents of breast milk change to suit the needs of the baby: daily between morning and night; from birth to when you stop breastfeeding; from the beginning of a session at the breast to the end; and according to the physical or emotional hunger of the baby. Infant formula remains constant because although the milk produced by a cow varies to meet the needs of its calf, infant formula is made from the pooled milk of many herds of lactating cows.

Infectious illnesses are less likely in a breastfed baby because the active cells in mother's milk are accompanied by a cocktail of antibodies against infection. Most infant formula is made from heat-treated cow's milk, so its cells are not only bovine but they are also dead. Both mothers and babies are exposed to certain disease-provoking bacteria and viruses in their home environment. A mother is likely to have resistance to infection in the form of protective antibodies, but her baby's immune system cannot produce antibodies in the first few months. A breastfed baby is protected by the mother's immunity passed on in her milk.

BREASTFEEDING IS BEST

Many women, especially those who feed in a natural, unrestricted way, find that breastfeeding is enjoyable and sensually gratifying, giving rise to positive feelings about their breasts and body. It has been said that a mother-infant relationship without enjoyable breastfeeding is in some ways similar to marriage without enjoyable sex. Not to breastfeed your baby is to deprive yourself of a beneficial experience. Breastfeeding brings a sense of peace and contentment to many women. They like meeting their baby's physical and emotional needs with their own bodies. They are proud of usually being able to comfort their babies by day and night. Many women comment on the boost to self-esteem and faith in their feminine competence that breastfeeding gives them. Perhaps if more women took up and continued with the intrinsically feminine process of breastfeeding, with its emphasis on the process, rather than the product and the present, rather than the future, it would help counterbalance the excessively masculine attitude prevailing in the developed societies of the modern world.

Women who breastfeed into their child's second or third year or longer say that the emotional benefits to the child of breastfeeding include security, happiness, an earlier transition to relative independence and enhanced mutual love. Women comment that natural and unrestricted breastfeeding leads to a type of mothering which involves the whole self – mind and body – and increases their confidence during the next stage of child-rearing.

In some ways breastfeeding is much easier for the modern woman than bottle-feeding. A breastfed baby is eminently portable and needs no bulky bottles or sterilizing equipment. Moreover, women are becoming increasingly aware of their power as consumers and are encouraging shops, restaurants, leisure centres, libraries and other places to be more welcoming and to provide more facilities for the mother and her breastfed baby. In many countries babies and children, breastfed or otherwise, have always been accepted in public places. Today's breastfeeding woman expects to take her baby wherever she goes and if she needs to breastfeed she certainly does not expect to be consigned to the toilet.

Research is beginning to suggest that years of having menstrual periods may not be healthy. The continual surges of hormonal activity created by menstrual cycles may predispose women to certain gynaecological disorders by disrupting the cells of the breasts and uterus each month.

Breast and womb cancer have puzzled the medical profession for a long time. Breast cancer is extremely common and many women suffer greatly from the effects of mastectomy. One in five women in the UK has a hysterectomy at some time in her life. It looks now as if research is close to discovering more clues as to the causes of these distressing problems.

Nature intended women of reproductive age to be either pregnant or breastfeeding for most of the time. We have foiled that intention in several ways. First, most women in developed countries are well- (often over-) nourished. This means that they start their periods younger and they continue to have periods for longer, until they are 50 years old, on average. Most women have only one or two children. The majority either avoid breastfeeding altogether or do so for a short time only, perhaps up to 16 weeks.

As a result, the average woman in the developed countries may have as many as 450 periods in her lifetime, compared with her ancestor several centuries ago, who might have had only 20 or 30. Combined research at centres around the world now suggests that the type of breast cancer that strikes women before the menopause is related to the number of years spent breastfeeding: the more time spent breastfeeding, the less likely is it that pre-menopausal cancer will develop.

Many women today think of breastfeeding as something they will do for one or

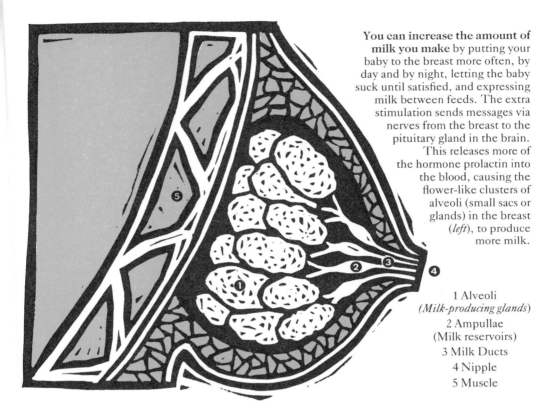

You can increase the amount of milk you make by putting your baby to the breast more often, by day and by night, letting the baby suck until satisfied, and expressing milk between feeds. The extra stimulation sends messages via nerves from the breast to the pituitary gland in the brain. This releases more of the hormone prolactin into the blood, causing the flower-like clusters of alveoli (small sacs or glands) in the breast (*left*), to produce more milk.

1 Alveoli
(*Milk-producing glands*)
2 Ampullae
(Milk reservoirs)
3 Milk Ducts
4 Nipple
5 Muscle

two babies for a few weeks or months; it is certainly not seen as a long-term practice. This is a big change in attitude compared with that of years ago and compared with the prevailing expectation in many other countries today.

Chinese women who have breastfed for a total of nine years or more have only one-third of the risk of getting breast cancer of women who have breastfed for a total of three years or fewer. By contrast, in the USA, only between 17 per cent and 35 per cent of women breastfeed their babies for as long as six months. Perhaps this helps explain why the incidence of breast cancer is so high there.

Although it is not a foolproof contraceptive device, breastfeeding is a useful and a very green one. When combined with other methods, it is an excellent choice (*see pages 22–23*). An international group of scientists meeting under the auspices of the World

Health Organization in 1988 concluded that breastfeeding provides more than 98 per cent protection from pregnancy in the first six months after childbirth if a woman is exclusively breastfeeding and her periods have not yet returned. Thereafter the protection lessens somewhat. In Africa breastfeeding prevents an average of four births per woman; in Bangladesh, more than six.

THE ART OF BREASTFEEDING

Breastfeeding is certainly the greenest way to feed a baby. The big snag in developed countries is that the art of successful and natural breastfeeding was all but lost in the swing to bottle-feeding that occurred early in the twentieth century. Those women who did breastfeed began to use their breasts as if they were bottles: they gave feeds every four hours and limited their babies to ten minutes on each side. This sort of breastfeeding is unsuccessful for more than a few days or weeks in the majority of women because their milk dries up with relatively infrequent stimulation of the breast. Babies were increasingly separated from their mothers at night and strongly encouraged to sleep through the night, which made breastfeeding likely to fail. As breastfeeding, particularly successful breastfeeding, declined, knowledgeable helpers and wise women became rare. Many midwives were seduced by child care 'experts' and by the manufacturers of infant formula into believing that breasts should be used like bottles and that infant formula was the equivalent of breast milk. The net result was that many women completely lost confidence in their ability to mother their babies at the breast.

Another setback to the promotion of successful breastfeeding was the realization that bottle-fed babies sleep longer than most breastfed babies. This not only suited many bottle-feeding women very well but it also made breastfeeding women believe that there was something wrong with their milk when their babies spent more time awake and woke more often at night.

All this time, society made demands on women: during World Wars I and II they were encouraged to go out to work and in the late forties and fifties they were encouraged to stay at home again. From the sixties women have increasingly seen themselves as career women, but many have found themselves having to compete for careers with men in ways which have denied their childbearing and breastfeeding roles. Ultimately women, men and children will benefit if we find together creative ways of healing the split between work on the one hand and childbearing, breastfeeding and child-rearing on the other.

In the UK today an average of 64 per cent of babies start off being breastfed, but only three in five babies are being breastfed by six weeks of age. The main reason given for stopping is insufficient milk. Virtually all the women questioned would prefer not to have stopped so soon (*see pages 82–83*).

This is a preventable problem. Only 50 years ago more than nine out of ten babies were breastfed from birth, many until well into the second half of the first year.

In Western Australia, as a result of a drive by health professionals to improve long-term breastfeeding statistics, 85 per cent of women are nursing their six-month-old babies. This is the highest figure in the Pacific, as well as in the western world.

I look here at some very basic breastfeeding know-how, together with some essential information about current green issues and breastfeeding. For detailed information on how to breastfeed, and how to cope with breastfeeding problems, consult a practical manual (*see page 182–183* **Further Reading**). In many developed countries most babies are born in hospital. More mothers stop breastfeeding in the first week of their baby's life than at any other time, so the period in hospital is particularly important.

HOW SOON TO BREASTFEED

The earlier after birth that breastfeeding can begin, the better its chances of success in the long term, although this is just a statistical observation and does not mean that a baby cannot be successfully breastfed if the first feed is delayed. If you had a strong pain-killer such as pethidine (meperidine) toward the end of your labour, your baby may be too sleepy to suck well at first, so be patient, keep the baby near you and keep offering the breast gently. Mothers who have their babies with them after birth, instead of in the hospital nursery, have been found by researchers to have lower levels of gastrin (a stomach hormone which is increased during stressful situations). If, as the research implies, they are less stressed, this must inevitably benefit the beginning of the breastfeeding relationship. A government-funded survey of over 7,000 mothers in the UK in 1985 found that only one in two had their babies with them all the time. However, this is an improvement on 1980, when only one in six mothers could keep their babies by them.

Hold a baby's body so that it faces yours and the baby does not have to turn his or her head (*top*). Change positions to avoid the build-up of milk in an un-emptied part of the breast. Nursing as you lie down (*centre*) can be restful and useful at night. Try the 'football hold' (*above*): tuck your baby's legs to the side of the breast at which you are nursing.

HOW OFTEN? HOW LONG?

American research shows that the average healthy full-term baby, encouraged to feed as often and as long as he or she desires, takes between eight and thirteen feeds a day during the first two weeks of life, and between six and nine feeds a day during the second month. The same research found that babies spend an average of 112 to 212 minutes at the breast each 24 hours during the first 2 weeks of life. In the second month feeds were slightly longer. In the UK one in five breastfeeding mothers is told to feed her baby only at set feeding times. This is poor advice and makes breastfeeding twice as likely to fail than if feeds are unrestricted.

If you limit the time your baby spends at the breast in the first few days (or, indeed, at any time), you are likely to become engorged and your milk supply will begin to fall. Engorgement means the breasts swell up like balloons, go red and become very painful. During the bad old times of the fifties and early sixties engorgement was a common sight on post-natal wards, but it is almost entirely preventable. If your baby is unable to go to the breast, all you have to do is express your milk little and often so that it cannot build up in the breasts. Expressing by hand is a knack which it is important to learn. You may find it easier to learn with the help of a midwife, or on your own. It is more effective for most women than pumping with a hand or an electric pump.

If you give your baby a dummy (pacifier), you may find that your milk supply diminishes because your breasts lack stimulation. Experience shows that large numbers of women cannot breastfeed for as long as they wish because they are not producing enough milk. This does not mean that they cannot produce enough. The distinction is important. Milk production is dependent on many factors, not least of which is the amount of stimulation received by the breasts. A woman whose milk is drying up can increase the amount she makes by putting her baby to the breast more often and for longer periods and by expressing milk from the breasts. Within two or three days the milk supply increases.

MIXING FEEDING METHODS

Infant formula should not be given to newborn breastfed babies (unless for specific medical reasons in a tiny minority of babies) because it interferes with the initiation of breastfeeding. However, in the UK nearly one in two breastfed babies is given some infant formula in the first week after birth. Statistics show that a mother is three times as likely to stop breastfeeding in the first two weeks if her baby has had any infant formula.

FEEDING SPECIAL CARE BABIES

Pre-term (premature) or small-for-dates babies need breast milk as much as, if not more than, other babies. Yet they are less likely to receive it. This is because breastfeeding is a much more skilful business for these babies, who may be too immature, frail, or unwell to suck efficiently or at all. Yet breastfeeding is possible, even if the milk has to be expressed and given by tube. Your success depends largely on your enthusiasm and tenacity, on how well you look after yourself (or allow yourself to be looked after) during this difficult time, and on the knowledge, enthusiasm and skill of your midwife or doctor.

Young babies are attracted to the scent of the lactating breast. Your baby has the best chance of starting to suck (when he or she is mature enough to do so) if you have been in the habit of holding him or her at your naked breast several times a day. First attempts at sucking will be in very short and inefficient episodes of 'fluttering' sucks. This is an excellent beginning and the sucking will strengthen over the next few weeks. A group of researchers has pointed out that anxiety, tiredness and emotional stress are common among mothers whose babies are in special (intensive) care units. They used audio cassettes of relaxation training and visual imagery to help mothers relax. The mothers in their experiment produced one and a half times as much milk as other mothers.

DIET WHILE BREASTFEEDING

Your body has the ability to store certain nutrients but not all of them. This means that if your diet is inadequate in some way, your body will be able to give up some of its stored nutrients to meet the baby's needs. However, this might be at the expense of your health. If your diet contains insufficient quantities of nutrients that are not stored, both you and your baby will suffer.

You need to follow a healthy diet and consume 300 to 600 extra calories a day to meet the energy needs of the growing baby, depending on his or her age and activity levels. Make sure that the food you eat is high in quality and rich in nutrients, including zinc and vitamin B, and not laden with saturated fat, refined carbohydrates and added sugar. If you consume too many empty calories neither you nor your baby will get what you deserve.

If you are a total vegetarian or a vegan, and your diet contains plenty of foods rich in calcium, iron, zinc and vitamins B12 and D (see page 53), there is no need for you to take these nutrients in the form of nutritional supplements.

DIETARY GUIDELINES

The zinc requirement for unborn baby boys is five times as high as for baby girls. Some boys are born relatively short of zinc and this may lead to poor sucking, poor growth and colic. Given that some nutritionists consider many people eating refined diets to be short of zinc, it makes good sense to check that your diet contains foods rich in this element (see page 53).

Cost does not have to be a prohibitive factor when taking in extra calories. In fact, highly refined junk food is often more expensive than basic nutritious foods. Even though you need to eat more than the bottle-feeding mother, it is still vastly cheaper to breastfeed than to give infant formula.

DRUGS & BREASTFEEDING

Mothers should be wary of taking any drugs while breastfeeding, because most of them pass into the milk. Some are known to be harmful to the baby; not enough is known about the effects of many others. When breastfeeding women need drug treatment it is usually possible to choose a relatively safe form, but in a very few instances there is no choice but to stop breastfeeding. Find out from this alphabetical list which drugs are unsafe, best avoided or should be used only under careful medical observation.

Aloe, calomel, cascara, danthron, phenolphthalein and senna: likely to cause diarrhoea.

Amantadine: can cause vomiting, urine retention and a rash.

Anticoagulants: heparin and warfarin are safe.

Anti-thyroid drugs: can be used if the baby's hormone levels are monitored.

Aspirin: high doses can cause a rash or intestinal problems.

Atropine: may decrease milk flow and cause constipation and urine retention.

Barbiturates: can cause drowsiness and can alter the metabolism of other drugs.

Bromide: can cause drowsiness and a rash.

Carbamazepine: should not be taken in high doses or with other anti-epileptic drugs.

Chloral hydrate: can cause drowsiness.

Chloramphenicol: avoid if your baby is under four weeks old.

Chloroform: can cause deep sleep.

Corticosteroids: (steroids): could theoretically cause retarded growth.

Corticotrophin: alters sodium and potassium levels in breast milk.

Cytoxic (anti-cancer) **drugs:** busulphan and methotrexate seem safe.

Diazepam: has led to lethargy and weight loss.

Dichloralphenazone: can cause drowsiness.

Dihydrotachysterol: might theoretically lead to decreased milk production through its prolactin-lowering effect.

Diuretics: can decrease milk supply.

Ergot alkaloids: leads to diarrhoea, vomiting, weak pulse and unstable blood pressure.

Gold: can cause a rash.

Indomethacin: one report of convulsions.

Lithium: can lead to lithium toxicity, including lethargy and floppiness.

Metronidazole: high doses cause risk of blood problems, vomiting and diarrhoea.

Nalidixic acid: reports of anaemia and raised intracranial pressure.

Nitrofurantoin: not to be used for babies with glucose 6 phosphate dehydrogenase (G6PD) deficiency.

Novobiocin: can lead to jaundice.

Oral contraceptives: the combined Pill can decrease the milk supply and its levels of protein, fat and minerals; in one unconfirmed study the use of the Pill before pregnancy was associated with breast milk jaundice; the old high-dosage Pill was associated with breast enlargement in male babies, overgrowth of the vaginal skin in females and bone changes in isolated reports. No Pill has been cleared of dangerous long-term effects on the breastfed baby.

Penicillins: may cause allergy.

Phenylbutazone: possibility of a blood disorder.

Pyridoxine – vitamin B6: one report of a decreased milk supply.

Propranolol: may only be used if the blood sugar and heart rate are monitored.

Radioactive drugs: *6^7 gallium citrate[1]:* discard milk for 72 hours to 2 weeks; *^{125}I-labelled albumin:* discard milk for at least 10 days; *^{131}I[2]:* discard milk for at least 24 hours after a small diagnostic dose; 1 to 3 weeks after a large therapeutic dose. *^{131}I hippurate[25]:* discard milk for 24 hours; *($^{99m}TCO^2$ technetium 99^2):* discard milk for 32 to 72 hours; *$^{99m}TCO^4$-labelled macro-aggregated albumin 1:* discard milk for 24 hours.

Reserpine: one report of a stuffy nose; slowing of the heart and an increase in lower respiratory mucus.

Sulphonamides: may increase jaundice; can cause anaemia or a rash.

Tetracyclines: may cause mottling of unerupted and erupted teeth.

Tricyclic antidepressants: high doses may theoretically accumulate in the body.

Dieting to lose weight can be harmful to the breastfeeding mother because fat-soluble toxins stored in her body fat may be released as the fat stores are broken down.

Food allergy or sensitivity in the breastfed baby may be triggered by certain foods eaten by breastfeeding mothers. Neither of these are strictly toxic reactions, but some foods eaten by some breastfeeding women are toxic to their babies. For example, some breastfed babies in eastern Mediterranean countries can be affected by their mothers eating large amounts of broad beans. Eating any one protein in large amounts can lead to an allergic reaction in a susceptible baby.

Wheat and cow's milk are common allergens. With this in mind, ignore any advice about drinking more cow's milk in order to produce more breast milk. You can get all the nutrients you need from a diet containing little, if any, cow's milk. Indeed, many women breastfeed successfully without ever seeing a glass of milk because they get adequate amounts of protein and calcium from other foods.

Some specialists in allergies say that traces of undigested foods present in a mother's milk help her baby to learn to cope with foreign foods gradually.

Drinking-water can contain toxins (*see page 77 and 127*). Breastfed babies are relatively protected in areas where the water contains high levels of nitrates from fertilizers used in farming, because the mother's body can break them down, but bottle-fed babies can be exposed to high levels when water contaminated with nitrates is used to make up their feeds. If the water in the area where you live contains very high levels of nitrates, you might consider using brands of boiled bottled water containing safe levels of salts to make up feeds, although this proves an expensive alternative.

In Central Asia salty water irrigating land reclaimed by draining the Aral Sea has contaminated the underlying water table and affects breastfeeding women in the area.

Their milk contains three or four times the expected amount of salt and many babies suffer, sometimes fatally, as a result. The bottle-fed babies are no better off.

Coffee, drunk in large amounts by a breastfeeding mother, may make her baby restless and abnormally wakeful. Caffeine from coffee, particularly if it is boiled or filtered, seems to be more of a problem than caffeine in tea, instant coffee or caffeinated soft drinks.

Alcohol can alter the let-down reflex (a neuro-muscular reflex mediated by the pituitary hormone, oxytocin, which allows stored breast milk to be released from the milk glands to feed the baby) if the breastfeeding mother drinks enough of it to make her feel tipsy. If she drinks a great deal, the reflex could be completely blocked. Alcohol inhibits the production of the hormone oxytocin. Some babies react badly to some drinks, becoming uncomfortable, colicky or irritable. Nevertheless, plenty of breastfeeding women who enjoy a daily alcoholic drink do their babies no harm at all. Although alcohol can get into breast milk, aldehydes (the toxic metabolic break-down products of alcohol in the blood) do not appear in breast milk, because they are screened out by the breast.

CIGARETTES

Smoking releases nicotine into a woman's bloodstream and may interfere with her letdown of milk. Nicotine reaches higher levels in breast milk than in blood, and heavy smoking (more than 20 cigarettes a day) can make a breastfed baby feel sick or vomit. It has been suggested in the medical literature that nicotine might lead to restlessness and circulatory disturbance in a baby. Smoking can increase the effect of caffeine, so if you feel like unwinding with a coffee and a cigarette, think of your baby's health first and choose something more nourishing. In the USA it is estimated that between one in five and one in three nursing mothers smoke. The amount of nicotine in breast milk depends both on the number of cigarettes smoked each day and the time between the last cigarette smoked and the next breastfeed. If you wish to smoke and you also wish to breastfeed, it is sensible to smoke mainly after feeds rather than before (*see page 96*), but you will be making your baby smoke passively.

COLIC

One in every three babies – breastfed or bottle-fed – suffers from colic at some time (*see page 166*). It rarely helps to change the bottle-fed baby's formula brand. If you are breastfeeding and your baby is colicky, check your diet and be careful to avoid any foods that you think are likely to upset your system. Traces of cabbage (and the other vegetables in the brassica family) chocolate, citrus fruit and juice, tomatoes, caffeine, alcohol and dairy products made from cow's milk can affect breast milk and upset some babies. Experiment by eliminating just one of these groups of foods for five days, but be careful to replace necessary nutrients with other foods; ask for skilled help if necessary. It is sensible to try to spread your food intake throughout the day rather than have one or two larger meals. Make sure you always have something to eat between your baby's feeds. One study found that one in three breastfed babies with colic is sensitive to cow's milk protein in mother's milk.

It is best to be with your baby if he or she is suffering from colic, but if you come to the end of your tether, ask someone else to come and help out, if you can. Being with a grizzly baby can be exhausting, particularly since colic often strikes in the evening.

Dicyclomine is a treatment commonly recommended for colicky babies, although it is thought to be unsafe for babies under six months old. In very rare cases babies dosed with this drug have breathing difficulties or convulsions.

DANGERS FROM TOXINS

The exposure of a baby to toxins is a hazard of both breast- and bottle-feeding. Toxins are most likely to enter the body of a woman – or a cow – via food, but they can also enter from the air, from water, or through the skin, especially from sources such as incinerators and wood-pulping sites. Many drugs are given to dairy cows and some pass into their milk. Antibiotics are under particular suspicion; they may cause problems in formula-fed babies.

The levels of toxins in breast milk and infant formula depend on the contamination of the environment of women and cows. Human milk tends to contain higher levels than cow's milk of pesticides, heavy metals, pollutants such as PCBs (polychlorinated biphenyls and dioxins (*see pages 78–79*). This may be partly due to our diet and partly due to the limitations many women place on breastfeeding.

INSECTICIDES & HERBICIDES

Organochlorine insecticides tend to accumulate in breast milk to a greater degree than in cow's milk. This may be because a breastfeeding woman loses insecticides stored in her body fat via her milk for a relatively short time, compared with a cow, which produces milk for most of its life.

Pesticides can enter breast milk via the air a woman breathes (for instance, during the spraying, particularly aerial spraying, of insecticides); through her skin, should she handle the chemicals with her bare hands; via the water she drinks; and – by far the most likely method – via her food from chemicals which have entered the food chain. Vegetarians have very low levels of insecticides in their milk. The foods in which these toxins collect include freshwater and inshore fish, fats and oils, eggs and meat. Some of the most dangerous chemicals, such as DDT, are no longer used in developed countries; however, in countries such as Kenya, DDT in breast milk is over the upper limit in most women.

In Central Asia, around the partially drained Aral Sea, cotton is grown as a cash crop on reclaimed land that lacks humus and requires vast amounts of pesticides and herbicides to boost its fertility. Defoliants

Breastfeeding women who live in agricultural areas should steer clear of crops that have been sprayed recently, since pesticides can enter the bloodstream and contaminate breast milk. It is best to go away while spraying is taking place (*above*), particularly if it is aerial spraying. The vapour trail from an overflying aircraft is a form of aerial pollution.

are sprayed from light aircraft and come into contact with women working in the fields. Infant mortality is high, at 54 deaths in the first year per 1,000 births. This is the highest rate in the USSR and ten times that of most developed countries. A contributory factor might be the babies' exposure to poisonous chemicals in their mothers' breast milk or infant formula made up with poisoned water.

FUNGICIDES

In Turkey many breastfed babies were taken seriously ill and some died after their mothers ate wheat that had been treated with hexachlorobenzene. In Iraq a similar outbreak of poisoning followed the use of a methyl mercuric fungicide on wheat.

PCBs

Polychlorinated biphenyls and organochlorine compounds were once widely used as an insulating or protective fluid in electrical and hydraulic equipment (including batteries and fluorescent tube fittings); in paints, plastics, plasticizers, adhesives and printing inks; in protective coatings for wood, metal and concrete; in flame retardants; and even in kiss-proof lipstick. The main environmental sources today are the burning of waste PVC (polyvinyl chloride) plastic, dry-cleaning solvent and treated wood.

Although production was almost stopped in the UK in 1976 and their use banned in 1986, PCBs remain a hazard because they are still seeping into the environment via the air and water, and they are almost indestructible. Of the PCBs that have been produced, 35 per cent are already within the environment, working their way up the food chain; some have been destroyed and about 60 per cent are waiting to escape. Old electrical equipment, such as fluorescent tubes, can leak PCBs in appreciable amounts. The American Center for Science in the Public Interest recommends not eating fish caught in water near industrial areas. In Holland people are advised only to eat fish once a week and to avoid eels, bream and carp completely.

Breast milk contains higher levels of these toxins than cow's milk, although research seems to point to the fact that the hazard to babies is from transfer across the placenta before birth rather than from breastfeeding after birth. So far, there has been only one recorded case of a woman having to stop breastfeeding because the PCB levels in her milk were very high.

DIOXINS & FURANS

Dioxins and furans are toxic and widespread organochlorine compounds released as environmental contaminants from a variety of procedures, including paper and pesticide manufacture. They have been used in the production of plastic packaging since the nineteen-twenties. They do not decompose. They are released by the burning of coal, wood treated with preservatives, the stubble of crops treated with fungicides and insecticides, PCBs, solvents and PVC plastic packaging; the use of leaded petrol (an organochlorine is added to aid the removal of lead into the exhaust fumes); the chlorine bleaching of wood pulp used, for example, to make paper and disposable nappies; the manufacture and burning of chlorinated phenols; and the manufacture of waste metals. In Norway a major source of dioxins and furans is a magnesium smelter. The biggest source of the most toxic of these chemicals is municipal incineration, which contributes about a third of the airborne dioxin in the UK.

The daily dose received by breastfed babies in industrialized countries is about 100 times the guideline adult dose laid down by the UK government. We need to cut down on the chlorine bleaching of wood pulp and on all unnecessary plastic packaging, especially that made from PVC, and it should not be incinerated.

Vegetarians and vegans seem to be less likely to absorb dioxins from the environment than meat-eaters because these toxins tend to concentrate in animal flesh. By the same token, cow's milk usually contains lower levels of dioxins than mother's milk because cows are vegetarians and eat lower down the food chain than women. Nevertheless, in 1989 in the UK cow's milk was found to contain ten times the provisional draft guideline levels of dioxins. Inshore fish are more likely to be polluted with dioxins than varieties of fish caught far out at sea. The World Health Organization and the American Academy of Pediatrics state that the benefits of breastfeeding far outweigh any danger from dioxins and furans.

GUIDELINES ON TOXINS

● So far there is little evidence to suggest any side-effects in breastfed babies from PCBs, dioxins, furans, insecticides or herbicides. Experts are concerned, however, about the rising levels in our food and air, the long-term effects of which are as yet unknown.

● To minimize levels of PCBs, dioxins and furans in your milk, eat less red meat, dairy produce (especially varieties with a high fat content) and other foods high in animal fats. Try to avoid breathing polluted air and using biocides (pesticides and herbicides) at home and – if you can – at work.

● Infant formula contains fairly low levels of insecticides, PCBs, dioxins and furans. The more cow's milk fat is replaced by vegetable fat in the formula, the lower the levels of toxins are likely to be. However, some infant formula is made with cottonseed oil, which may contain traces of pesticides used in cotton production.

VEHICLE EXHAUST POLLUTANTS

Dioxins and non-chlorinated hydrocarbons such as benzene, naphthalene and benzopyrene, are produced by motor vehicles (*see page 37*). These, together with fine particles in diesel fumes, all pollute the air and are potentially cancer-producing, according to American research in 1981.

RADIOACTIVE FALLOUT

Scientists have not been able to prove that strontium 89 or 90 and caesium 137 present in the fall-out from nuclear explosions have affected babies via mother's milk. Radioactivity can enter breast milk, but the amount samples have been found to contain seems to be too small to be a problem.

Levels of radioactivity are much higher in cow's milk. Studies carried out in 1989 into the effects of the Chernobyl disaster in the USSR revealed 300 times more radioactive caesium in cow's milk than in breast milk. Scientists seem unconcerned as yet. However, it is interesting that IBFAN (the International Baby Food Action Network) discovered that a consignment of infant formula from European pasturelands contaminated by radioactive fallout after the Chernobyl disaster was sold to the Philippines without informing purchasers that the milk was affected. If there was no problem, why the need for secrecy? Radioactive cow's milk was passed on to other developing countries: some Polish milk went to Bangladesh; some Dutch milk went to Thailand and the Philippines; and another European consignment went to Ghana. Around this time the safety limit for radioactivity levels in infant formula was reduced by 75 per cent.

HEAVY METALS

Mercury is a heavy metal that can damage babies if it is present in breast milk. Breastfeeding mothers should avoid exposure to mercury (*see pages 37-38*). Lead-poisoning of breastfed babies has occurred in the past when women used creams containing lead to treat sore nipples. Unacceptable levels of lead have been discovered in some processed canned milks. In general mother's milk contains lower lead levels than infant formula and other processed cow's milk. One American study showed lead levels in infant formula resulting in a lead intake nine times higher than the threshold of risk.

Aluminium has been found in far higher quantities in infant formula than in breast milk. Cans of powder are commonly contaminated by aluminium and some have been found to contain 100 times as much as breast milk (*see pages 36-37*).

WORKING & BREASTFEEDING

'Work' here refers to paid or voluntary work either at home or away, as opposed to the work that is done to care for the home and the family. Throughout history, many women have worked, often some distance from their homes. Today, many women all over the world continue to work to provide for their families.

A breastfeeding woman in any country needs to make arrangements for someone to help her care for her baby or child. She should also look into the possibility of having access to her baby while she is working. Canadian researchers found that the main factor contributing to the success of working and breastfeeding was the accessibility of the infant to the mother at her place of work. Other helpful possibilities include giving mothers the options of taking babies to work with them and of taking nursing breaks when they choose.

Canadian researchers found that women whose working times were variable and self-regulated not only started work sooner after their babies were born but also breastfed for longer than women who worked full- or part-time. Full-time work was not necessarily detrimental to the success of combining breastfeeding and work. Not all mothers in the study were able to combine work and breastfeeding, even though they wanted to.

Breastfeeding health workers can be potent role models for other women. Unfortunately, their working conditions often preclude the very activity they are taught to advocate. Dr Natividad Clavano, a paediatrician in Baguio City Hospital in the Philippines, encourages midwives and other nurses to breastfeed their babies on the maternity wards. The breastfeeding rates at this hospital are extremely high.

In some developing countries, such as Pakistan, Sri Lanka and Kenya, breastfeeding is as common among women working outside the home as it is among those who are home-based. However, in Bangladesh breastfeeding is one and a half times more likely in mothers of three- to six-month-old babies who work at home, as in women who work outside the home. In Bogotá, Colombia, in Malaysia, in Nairobi, Kenya, and in the Philippines, breastfeeding duration has been found to be shortened if mothers work. An American study recently concluded that until employers in the USA develop a maternity policy which does not discourage breastfeeding, the recommended minimum six months of breastfeeding will be difficult to achieve for most employed women. Breastfeeding mothers who have a job need information, support and encouragement – and successful role models.

Babies and young children need familiar company and sensitive one-to-one interaction. They can cope well with having more than one mother-figure in their lives, but they do best if the mother-figure caring for them at any one time is well known and makes them feel special and loved.

A breastfeeding working mother has a lot on her plate. She may choose to express milk so this can be given to her baby if necessary, during the hours they are separated. Typical workplace conditions are not in the least conducive to the comfortable and relaxing expression of milk. In fact, they are often dirty and embarrassing. This means that most women choose to express milk for their babies at home, perhaps collecting a little each time they finish feeding their babies themselves.

Some women choose to let their babies have infant formula while they are apart. This is not ideal from the point of view of preventing infection and food sensitivity, but it is better for babies to have some breast milk than none at all, so it is worth continuing to breastfeed when possible.

Many babies who are regularly separated from their working mothers like to spend as much time as possible at the breast when they are together. This means that they want to be at the breast on and off throughout the evening and night, almost as if they are making up for what they have missed during the day. This can be exhausting for the mother, although many learn to live with broken sleep as their babies lie beside them in bed.

I think that one big danger for women who work when they have very young children is that they will underestimate not only their importance to their children, but also the importance to them of being with and breastfeeding their children. The facilities for alternative child-care are so often less than ideal in both rich and poor countries. Moreover, the rewards of working sometimes do not match up to the rewards of being with your young children while they are so dependent.

I would like to see each society give women the option of staying with their young children with no financial hardship, or providing excellent alternative child-care with easy access for breastfeeding if required. Both schemes are expensive.

Breastfeeding women may be exposed at work to dangerous chemicals such as PCBs, insecticides, or jet fuel and it is the responsibility of the employer to find out from a reputable source whether employees are at risk. Both cow's milk and breast milk are subject to pollution from environmental toxins such as agrochemicals, drugs and other preparations.

FACTS ABOUT BOTTLE-FEEDING

By giving their babies infant formula, millions of people have unwittingly entered

BOTTLE-FEEDING HARMS THE ENVIRONMENT:

● Bottle-feeding has an insidious potential effect on world population. If breastfeeding, statistically the most important method of birth control worldwide, becomes less popular, population figures will inevitably rise quickly, adding to the existing threat of a rapidly increasing population (*see page 11*).

● Formula-feeding necessitates the use of vast tracts of land as pasture to raise dairy cows: 10,000 square metres (almost 2.25 acres) for each cow.

● Large amounts of energy are needed to process and transport the milk.

● Bottle-feeding wastes the natural resource of mother's milk and denies babies the intimate relationship that is unique to being nursed at the breast.

● It has been estimated that to boil water to sterilize bottle-feeding equipment and mix up infant formula requires 73 kilogrammes (about 147 pounds) of wood for one baby for one year alone.

● A formula-fed baby of 3 months needs 3 litres (about 5 pints) of water each day for the mixing of feeds and the boiling of bottles and teats (nipples). This does not count the water required to wash and rinse the bottles.

● Valuable natural resources are required to manufacture the cans in which formula milk is packaged.

● For every 3 million bottle-fed babies, 450 million tins of infant formula are used. This makes 70,000 tonnes of discarded metal, which is rarely recycled.

of other animals has been used to rear human young before, but only during this century has the use of cow's milk become so widespread. We have not yet had enough time, or good enough methods, to assert that it is safe in the long-term to bottle-feed a baby with infant formula, even when the conditions are good. We know for sure that bottle-feeding is dangerous when conditions are bad.

Some women choose not to breastfeed; others find they are unable to do so, usually for social reasons, not because they produce insufficient milk. Bottle-feeding has undoubtedly saved the lives of many babies; and most children who are safely bottle-fed grow up apparently healthy. In developed countries and among relatively well-off families in developing countries, bottle-feeding is comparatively safe. But among the poor in developing countries serious health risks are attached to bottle-feeding. For the reasons given above, many of the babies fed in this way end up malnourished and suffer from continual diarrhoea, and many die.

If you decide to bottle-feed take care to prepare feeds hygienically and to dispose of the cans properly. Austrian researchers have found that heating infant formula in microwave ovens can alter certain amino acids in a potentially hazardous way, so avoid using this method of warming up your baby's milk.

ENCOURAGING BREASTFEEDING

Doctors and governments agree that breast is best and they frequently tell women so. But there is no point in merely paying lip-service to breastfeeding. The encouragement to breastfeed must be backed up by practical help. Yet it is probable that millions of women around the world end up bottle-feeding when they would have preferred to breastfeed.

In the UK, for example, in 1985 a large government-funded study of over 7,000 mothers reported that by six weeks after childbirth, one in four of all newly delivered women (or in other words, two out of

themselves and their babies into what has been called the largest uncontrolled clinical experiment there has ever been. The milk five of all the women who started breast-feeding) had stopped breastfeeding sooner than they would have liked. The reasons included poor professional advice. A similar study in 1975 by the same researcher, Jean Martin, looked at the problem of insufficient milk, which was responsible for more than one in two women stopping breastfeeding prematurely at six weeks. Drying-up of milk is the main disorder of breastfeeding in developed countries and, increasingly, in the Third World. This is a preventable and remediable problem. However, according to this study, 94 per cent of these women had been given unhelpful professional advice: for example, to give extra feeds of infant formula or to stop breastfeeding.

In East Germany until 1990 there was no advertising of infant formula and women were given one year's paid leave from work after childbirth, yet few mothers nursed their babies for long, if at all. The figures were similar in Poland. Perhaps women – and their men – were not told about, and could not recognize, the advantages of breastfeeding to themselves and their babies. This may be because there was insufficient skilled help with starting, overcoming the problems and learning how to be breastfeeding parents.

Breastfeeding needs not only promotion but also support and protection if women are to withstand the societal pressures that militate against it. These pressures include aggressive marketing by infant formula companies (*see pages 86-87*) and working conditions which do not facilitate breastfeeding (*see pages 80-81*). Added to these factors is the poor or conflicting advice that mothers receive from certain health professionals. This problem is a major influence on the one in four women in the UK, who stops breastfeeding before she wants to stop (usually because of insufficient milk, a preventable problem – *see page 71*). This problem is also present in developing countries and it kills babies in the Third World.

One solution to the problem of poor pro-fessional advice is more training for health workers in the facilitation of successful breastfeeding and the management of breastfeeding problems. Training is helpful, but it is not the whole answer. Some well educated health workers continue to give bad advice.

THE PSYCHOLOGICAL FACTOR

I would like to ask why it is that some health professionals continue to give advice which makes breastfeeding fail. One possible answer is based on complex psychodynamics, which may be why researchers have shied away from it. Some health professionals may work with mothers and babies for reasons which are unconsciously compelling, though consciously unknown. These reasons could stem from their intense desire for love, acceptance, affirmation and approval, and an underlying yet powerful need to come to terms with emotions dating from their own infancy, which (for some reason connected with their very early infantile experience) were never fully or adequately integrated into their developing personality.

I suggest that the need to keep these potentially painful emotions buried motivates them to separate babies from their mothers' breasts by giving faulty advice: to supplement breastfeeding with infant formula, for example, or to feed to a schedule. The bottle of infant formula symbolizes their need to avoid the emotional turmoil that the intimacy of the breastfeeding relationship would stir up at the conscious or unconscious level. The bottle makes them feel better. The needs of the mother and baby are secondary.

Fear is one such emotion and, while it may have an obvious trigger, its roots are buried deep in the helper's psyche. The helper may, for example, be aware of his or her ignorance about breastfeeding and fear loss of face; be afraid of witnessing the intense intimacy and sexuality of breastfeeding; be afraid of not being liked if he or she does not suggest the most apparently easy option; be afraid of being emotionally or physically involved; be afraid of confronting problems; or be afraid of the emotional effects of relinquishing control. If the reasons which underlie a difficult emotion, such as fear, are not acknowledged, the chance of an empowering, enabling relationship with the breastfeeding woman is effectively cancelled out.

The idea that some health workers need their patients to be ill (to 'fail') and base their relationships with their patients on an abuse of power is not a new one. I have simply applied it to the breastfeeding situation and widened it to include helpers other than doctors.

The best helpers may be those who are most open to the development of self-awareness. They are the ones most likely to enable parents to express their real feelings about breastfeeding. Perhaps all health professionals concerned with breastfeeding should have the chance to learn about themselves in a professionally facilitated and ongoing growth or awareness group, or in one-to-one 'therapy'. This would be a necessary part of in-service training. Talk therapy alone may not be enough because the emotions in question arise from a pre-verbal stage of their development. Unless particular health workers are given the opportunity to recognize, accept and work on their unresolved emotional pain and neediness, they may never be able fully to help breastfeeding mothers.

WHEN TO WEAN

In the UK women are encouraged to breast-feed their babies for a minimum of four to six months. This seems to me to suggest in a back-to-front way that there is no point in continuing beyond this time, simply because doctors have not proved that there is any great benefit in breastfeeding the older baby. This leads many mothers to believe that health professionals do not approve of breastfeeding for as long as they and their babies wish.

Start giving your baby solid foods some time between three and six months. Some babies let their mothers know when they wish to try something a little more solid by taking pieces of food out of their hands and sucking them. You can continue to breast-feed during these months, as you gradually introduce your baby to a variety of other foods and drinks. To avoid allergy and food sensitivity it is sensible to introduce potentially problematical foods relatively later.

I would like to see women as it were, 'given permission' to have more confidence in breastfeeding by the insertion of another clause in some of the professional and governmental literature on infant feeding. This clause would state that mothers and babies should go on with the nursing relationship for as long as they wish. The World Health Organization recommends supporting women who breastfeed into the second year after the baby's birth.

Your breast milk is a precious resource and no other food or drink can replace it. Your baby can increase your milk volume (*see page 73*) so as to get more nutrients to meet his or her growing needs. Breast milk continues to help prevent infection, although antibodies are now being made by the baby. Many mothers all over the world continue breastfeeding into their babies' second, third, fourth or fifth year, and are content to let their babies gradually lead the way toward giving up the breast. When you nurse an older baby, you give and receive in a special way, as I found with mine. Breastfeeding your baby is an irreplaceable way of comforting, loving and mothering. Given a free choice, most babies in developed countries would certainly prefer to be breastfed for much longer than the few months some of them currently receive. I know that many mothers would like to breastfeed for longer. UNICEF experts have calculated that every year, 10 million young children in developing countries become malnourished as a direct result of stopping breastfeeding too early, when there is insufficient other food for them.

TRENDS IN INFANT FEEDING

In the past, fashions in developed countries have tended to be exported to developing countries, perhaps partly because they seemed attractive and enviable. This has happened to some extent this century with infant feeding. In the nineteen-forties and -fifties, women in developed countries turned in vast numbers to bottle-feeding. Since then, many of their sisters in the developing countries have decided that bottle-feeding must hold great advantages because these people, who had such choice and opportunity available to them, voted in its favour.

Similarly, in the developed countries the better educated have tended to lead the habits and choices of the less well educated. For example, in the USA and the UK, the more highly educated women first led the trend toward bottle-feeding. As the risks of feeding with formula became more apparent, these women started to return to breastfeeding. The concern in many developing countries is that the educated women will turn to bottle-feeding and that poorer women will rapidly copy them. The current fashion for breastfeeding in developed countries is short-lived. The majority of women who begin by breastfeeding end up bottle-feeding within only a few weeks.

Many people in developing countries move from the country to the cities, often to find work and a better standard of living. One side-effect of such urbanization is a decline in breastfeeding. This is partly due to the break-up of the family support structure and partly due to working conditions, which make it difficult to breastfeed. In Shanghai, for example, there has been a marked decline in breastfeeding as a result of urbanization and women working. Now only one woman in ten nurses her six-month-old baby.

Workers with the World Health Organization (WHO) see large numbers of babies and young children fall ill and die each year as a result of bottle-feeding in unsatisfactory circumstances. All over the world the WHO, national health ministries and charities are trying to prevent any further swing away from breastfeeding, especially in the Third World.

COUPLES & INFANT FEEDING

Many would agree that a woman's partner has a great influence on whether or not she chooses to breastfeed and manages to do so. Her partner is usually the only other adult living in the home. Babies can bring great joy, but they can alter the nature of an adult relationship and create stress. Breastfeeding women need both protection and support. So do bottle-feeding women. But men also need emotional support.

You will not always be able to give each other support, especially if you both feel that your resources for coping are being stretched, as so often happens in families with young children. Some men react to the stresses of parenthood by having an affair, because it helps them to act out unbearable emotional strains. This is a waste of a trusting relationship going through a sticky patch. Relationship difficulties in the first year after childbirth are so common an occurrence as to be almost expected.

If you are to protect and support your partner while she is doing the valuable task of nursing the baby, you need to look after yourself and allow a friend, a relative or a professional helper to give you any extra emotional support and encouragement you may need. Being vulnerable enough to ask for help when it is needed is a very green thing to do.

If women, their babies, their men and society at large are to enjoy the benefits of breastfeeding, all those concerned must promote, protect and support this green way of feeding in an honest and loving way.

THE COST OF FORMULA-FEEDING

Infant feeding is at the heart of an international furore. UNICEF reports that a bottle-fed baby is 25 times more likely to die than a breast-fed one in poor countries. It estimates that 1 million babies die each year as a result of bottle-feeding with infant formula.

Bottle-feeding a six-month old baby may cost one-third to half of the recommended minimum family wage in poor countries – and many people accept less than the statutory minimum because of high unemployment. Consequently, in Indonesia bottle-feeding can cost up to fourth-fifths of the average family's income and in Niger, more than the average weekly wage. The cost prevents many families from buying sufficient quantities for their babies. The unbearable financial strain leads to family break-up, and a mother left without a man often finds it even harder to make ends meet. Legislation in many countries does not provide for nursing breaks at work, so breastfeeding may necessitate giving up a well paid job.

A mother who needs money to feed the rest of her family may be tempted to make infant formula go further by using too little milk powder – the feed looks the same as if it were made with a full measure. The quality, however, is not the same and the practice leads to a baby becoming malnourished and less able to fight off infection.

Water is a scarce resource in many poor countries. Women may have to travel long distances to collect it. It is often of poor quality, dirty and contaminated. Half the world's population cannot get clean water, so formula feeds are frequently made up with polluted water. The large volumes needed to sterilize feeding bottles are a luxury many women cannot afford.

Fuel to make fires to boil water for formula feeds and to sterilize bottles and teats (nipples) is a precious commodity in many countries. When there is not enough fuel, infant formula is prepared with unboiled water and put into unsterilized bottles. It is therefore likely to be contaminated. Infant formula, unlike breast milk, is an ideal breeding-ground for bacteria and other micro-organisms, especially in the warm climate typical of many developing countries. According to the World Health Organization (WHO), 500 million babies suffer from infective diarrhoea every year; 200 million die.

Infant formula uses cow's milk, which has to be imported at high cost into poor countries which have no dairy-farming. Yet women there are turning from breastfeeding to bottle-feeding and imports of formula-feed are rising. To finance them, many developing countries are forced to sell more cash crops to richer countries.

Meanwhile mother's milk, a free resource, is wasted. In Indonesia, mothers produce more than one billion litres of breast milk each year. Replacing this with imported infant formula would cost Indonesians more than US$400 million, so in financial terms alone, mother's milk is one of the country's most precious natural resources.

CODE OF PRACTICE

Controlling the multinational milk formula companies' sophisticated marketing practices is a problem for health agencies and charities concerned with infant health. The *International Code of Marketing of Breast Milk Substitutes* (published by WHO in 1981 to call a halt to the promotion of infant formula) states that there should be no free samples or supplies of infant formula to mothers or institutions; no promotion in hospitals; no unscientific promotion to health workers; no direct consumer promotion; no promotional labels; and clear statements on packaging about the superiority of breastfeeding alongside warnings about the hazards of bottle-feeding.

But by the end of 1989 only 6 countries out of the 118 which voted for the Code had made it law. In some countries, such as the UK, company representatives and the Government have together reduced the International Code to a less powerful national code.

AGGRESSIVE MARKETING

Infant formula is promoted in hospital maternity wards by the supplying of free samples on the grounds that the International Code forbids free supplies to maternity wards for promotional, but not for medical purposes. Representatives say they tell hospital staff to use the milk only for sick babies. Companies have claimed that the distribution of free infant formula is for purely humanitarian reasons. However, in 1986 WHO and UNICEF clarified this section of the Code with a World Health Assembly resolution banning the supply of free infant formula to maternity wards.

The ready availability of free formula in hospitals encourages its use, so problems with breastfeeding are likely to be treated by putting the baby on to the bottle. If a mother is hooked early, the profits a company can make from her baby are greater. Women tend to be brand-loyal, so formula businesses are keen to promote their products to the mothers of newborns. In the UK one in four breastfeeding women is given samples of infant formula on leaving a maternity ward. In my opinion it is hypocritical to teach mothers that it is best to breastfeed, while allowing infant formula companies to influence them, using sophisticated marketing techniques, via health professionals, during the vulnerable post-natal period.

Many milk company sales representatives gain access to maternity hospital staff by using a loophole in the International Code, which allows them to push 'follow-on' milks (for older babies) much more intensively than infant formula. They also promote (often by granting research funds) pre-term infant formula. In Bangladesh doctors are visited once a month by representatives from each infant formula company. Four formula factories are currently being set up there. Dr Cicely Williams, a famous campaigner against the promotion of infant formula, has strongly criticized such marketing activities, having experienced the disastrous effects of bottle-feeding in developing countries.

In 1989, British Paediatric Association members suggested to their Committee that it should refuse funding from formula companies for its annual general meeting. They thought it hypocritical to accept money from formula companies. Moreover, the UK trains many overseas doctors, who, believing that British paediatricians were in the pockets of the formula companies, would feel justified in accepting financial inducements to recommend infant formula. Their suggestion was overruled.

In India, milk formula companies help fund the meetings of the Indian Academy of Pediatrics. By contrast, the tenth annual congress of the Paediatric Society of Brazil was held in Brasilia in 1986 without such funding. Financed by registration fees, UNICEF and the government, it made a net profit of US$25,000 (£15,000). Congratulations, doctors and health department of Brazil, for putting your money where your mouth is!

Chapter Five
CARING FOR YOUR CHILDREN AND YOURSELVES

If there is harmony in the house there is order in the nation and peace in the world.
Confucius

Natural resources are not only fuel, water and earth; the term embraces everything on our planet. People – both children and adults – are also precious natural resources and they need to be conserved and optimized like the others. In this chapter we will consider exactly what babies and young children need from the adults who care for them; and how the practical and emotional needs of parents and other people who care for children can be met.

There have been times in the past when children were considered to be merely miniature adults and little attention was paid to their needs. Some years ago it was acknowledged that young children had special needs and the situation became reversed: there was so much discussion and writing about children's needs, it seemed as if parents had none. Experiments at striking a balance have not always been successful: during the nineteen-fifties, many parents were led to believe that their breastfed babies should go without night feeds within a few weeks of birth; that it was dangerous for parents to have their baby in their bed; that it was all right for babies to cry for long periods; and that young children needed astonishingly early bedtimes. Such measures were often inadvertently dishonest: they met the needs only of parents and not of children.

Here I aim to demystify child and parent care. I attempt to look at the problem squarely, to discover what caring for babies and children is really like; to consider some options; and to explore ways of caring for babies and young children which acknowledge both that they are unique and valuable and that we are too.

THE REALITIES OF PARENTING

In the early years, parents or parent-figures act as role-models for children and hopefully enable them to establish self-esteem. Little parents do to or with their children is irrevocable – most things can be influenced by a child's later experiences – but early patterning is very strong and hard to alter. No-one has perfect children and a parent's aim should perhaps be to bring up ordinary flawed human beings capable of coping with difficulties and asking for and giving help. A positive approach to children is to regard them as if they are on loan as a gift for us to nurture and learn with and from, albeit for a relatively short time. Every young human being has enormous potential and is a precious natural resource.

You may find that the years of caring for children are like being on an emotional roller-coaster. Children make demands on your physical, emotional and creative energy. But parenting can be a delight and also has restorative and enriching qualities which can more than make up for what it takes away. You can grow in maturity, insight, common sense and the ability to love and be loved as you care for your children. And you will learn much about life and its meaning.

THE MOTHER-BABY BOND

The early hours of contact between mother and baby are special. Even after only one hour together most mothers can recognize their own babies by the touch of their hands, even when blindfolded. Breastfeeding is more successful if mother and baby are together for most of the time.

Rooming-in (being in the same room) is not the best way to achieve mother-baby intimacy; babies can feel isolated even when lying in a cot at the foot of their mothers' beds; they are happier if they can be physically close to their mothers, although it is better than having the baby in a separate room.

If your new baby needs special care in an incubator, find out whether this care simply means keeping the baby extra warm. Researchers in South America and the UK have found that a small or unwell baby can readily be kept warm when snuggled close to the mother's breasts inside her clothing. If the baby needs more specialized care, ask whether you and your partner can sometimes remove him or her from the incubator for a cuddle. Even if this is discouraged, you can spend time talking to your baby and learn how to put your hands through the portholes to stroke his or her skin. Babies become accustomed to the sound of their parents' voices during pregnancy and an environment devoid of these familiar sounds may not aid recovery.

FORMING RELATIONSHIPS

A baby experiences many emotions – joy, rage, anxiety and excitement. The way you respond to your baby helps determine how the baby copes with those emotions. In effect, you and your baby form a workshop of two in which you learn about each other (see *illustration page 103*) and your baby learns about life, confidently assuming that you are on his or her side. Because you love and interact with your baby, the baby feels loved. A baby who feels loved learns to love and accept himself or herself. No emotion is too enormous to confront and no feeling has to go underground only to explode years later. Adult self-esteem – the belief that one is valuable and lovable and has a right to be alive – starts here.

Anyone can perform this mothering role for a baby, so the word 'mother' can be replaced with 'mother figure', whether this person is male or female. Babies can relate to many people in their lives and tend to choose a hierarchy of favourites. Given a choice, they prefer to be with the person they like best, generally the one who consistently gives them the most company, physical contact and sensitive attention – the one who knows them best. This person is usually the mother.

CLOSE CONTACT

The differences in baby care between developed and developing countries are enormous, yet they have been the subject of surprisingly little research. Babies in many Third World countries are kept traditionally in close physical contact with their mother or with another family or community member for most of the time, day and night. During the day they are securely held on the mother's back or at her side, usually with a length of material; at night they lie by her side. They do not have to cry because they already have what they need: the breast and close physical contact. The writer Jean Liedloff, who spent two and a half years with the Yequana Indians in the Venezuelan jungle, commented: 'There is a remarkable contrast between the behaviour of Yequana infants in arms and our own infants, most of whose time is spent in physical isolation'. She believes continuous contact ensures the later development of self-reliance, emotional stability, sociability and helpfulness.

In contrast, the majority of babies in developed countries are separated from physical contact most of the time. They sleep alone and they are not carried around all the time when awake. They cry a great deal by comparison with most Third World babies and many of their parents complain of sleep problems. Psychologists stress the importance of 'quality time' – short periods of focussed, one-to-one attention – but it may be that babies need continuous contact as much as or more than short bursts of intense attention during quality time.

As Niles Newton, Professor at the Northwestern University Medical School in Chicago, said: 'The taboo on tenderness that we see so often in the western world does not have to be followed by individual families. Touching and cuddling can be one of the foundations of a warm family life. This does not have to be limited to the daytime hours'. We are currently seeing a huge increase in violent crime, alcoholism, drug addiction and child abuse in the UK and the USA. I think it is not too far-fetched to suggest that the increasingly separatist way in which many babies are cared for could be one important reason.

SLEEP

Even before birth, a baby has an established cycle of activity and rest. When your new baby is about 16 weeks old, his or her longest period of sleep should begin to synchronize with yours. Overall, humans sleep longer at times of fast growth, especially during infancy. However, some parents find that they need more sleep than their young child, which comes as a shock.

Nearly half a baby's sleeping time is spent in REM (Rapid Eye Movement) sleep, when most dreaming occurs. This is more than in an older child or adult, perhaps because a baby has so much to learn. The rest of the sleeping time is spent in drowsy wakefulness, dozing, light sleep, deep sleep or 'slow-wave' sleep: the deepest sleep of all.

After problems with feeding, sleeping difficulties concern parents most. Sleeping problems are nearly always attributed to babies or young children, but they usually belong to the parents. In the developed countries, parents tend to expect time to themselves while their babies sleep. However, babies need less sleep than most people think and want to be with their mothers when they are awake, not left alone.

There are several ways of coping with this mismatching of expectations. One traditional western way has been to 'break the spirit' of wakeful babies, by leaving them to cry in their cots when they wake before the expected feed-time, when they are put to bed after their feed, or when they are supposed to be asleep (according to the parents' timetable) in the evening. In extreme cases, some babies have been tied to their cots or kept in them with a net. It is much more difficult to keep an older child in bed. Fear of physical punishment or being shouted at sometimes submerges children's fear of being alone and awake in bed and makes them stay there, although it does not make them sleep. It is not surprising that children brought up in this way have long-term sleep and other behavioural problems.

Another way to cope with problems is to teach children gradually and firmly, yet gently, to expect to go to bed at a certain time and stay there. This method sometimes fails. Some parents simply accept that their young children prefer to be awake and with them. They may decide to have their baby in bed with them, which certainly makes breastfeeding easier. One snag is that the baby understandably believes that the parents' bed is his or her bed and is reluctant to leave it when they feel the time is right.

Think of your baby's needs as well as your own when it comes to establishing where, how long and when your baby will sleep. Do not force your child to 'sleep' according to your plans. An emotionally cowed child is a sad sight.

If your baby seems weary but cannot get off to sleep, try a lullaby or another lulling noise, such as the low, boring, repetitive sound of a vacuum cleaner. A ride in your car may also help because it combines soothing movement and sound. Research shows that smoking shortens the time an adult spends asleep. It is possible that a smoky atmosphere may make a baby sleep less too.

In my experience, mothers of babies who wake frequently at night tend to stop dreaming because their sleep is interrupted so often. When they manage to sleep for longer periods, they start dreaming again and report that they feel better. Although you can accustom yourself to interrupted sleep, it may be helpful to organize a period of child care during the day so you can have some uninterrupted sleep.

PREVENTING COT DEATH

Sudden Infant Death Syndrome (SIDS, or cot death) is frighteningly common in developed countries: about 10,000 babies die in this way in the USA every year. In the UK the official figure is about 1,700, but it may be as high as 3,000. There are many theories about its cause but none has been proved. If you have your baby with you all the time, day and night, as many mothers do in some parts of the world, I believe you stand a better chance of preventing cot death. Not only can a mother breastfeed frequently (see page 73) but she is constantly aware of her baby's movements and would be more likely to know if the baby were to stop breathing. If this were to happen the mother would be on hand to give immediate simple stimulation: just by picking the baby up, giving a gentle patting on the back or a very gentle shaking, or, if this did not work, giving the baby the kiss of life. It is possible that the stimulation from your body's sounds, movements and electromagnetic field might anyway prevent your baby's breathing and heart from stopping.

A baby may be safer if allowed to sleep with the upper half of the body higher than the lower half. This is the position babies adopt when sleeping in the crook of their mothers' arms, or when carried next to their bodies in a sling. It is not sensible to sleep with your baby if you or your partner is drunk, drugged or very overweight.

COMMUNICATION

You can communicate with your baby by voice, by your body language and eye contact, by smell, by taste and by touch. Many people believe that there is another, unseen method of communication, a kind of extra-sensory perception, between babies and parents, citing the frequency with which love-making is frustrated by the baby waking up at the crucial moment. Some parents are aware of their children even when they are far away. They know if a child is in danger.

Your child quickly learns to sense your moods by observing your body language and by listening to the tone and speed of your voice, even while not understanding the words.

Touching is an important way of communicating. You can soothe and calm your child in the midst of colic or sleeplessness simply by gentle and rhythmic stroking or massage. Many mothers find they do this instinctively; each has her own way.

NURSERY EQUIPMENT

Bringing up a baby in a simple, green way precludes the need for vast amounts of nursery equipment. If you breastfeed, you do not need bottles, teats (nipples), sterilizing equipment or infant formula. All you need is you. If you choose to have your baby in your bed for ease of breastfeeding and untroubled nights, this cuts costs because you do not need to buy a cot, a mattress, sheets, bedcovers, bumpers and bedding clips. The baby can sleep in a carrycot, a buggy or a pram when sleeping without you. Older children can go straight from your bed into their own or that of a sibling.

Second-hand baby equipment is advertised in newspapers' 'for sale' columns, in mothers' newsletters, or on the advertisement boards in shop windows. Cleaned and spruced up, second-hand gear does just as well as new, but check that it is safe before you use it.

Buy items made from recyclable and biodegradable materials whenever possible. Plastic is not yet environmentally friendly (see page 149). Bear in mind that you contribute to world deforestation if you buy furniture made of hardwoods from non-sustainable forests, such as mahogany, iroko, rosewood and teak. Avoid buying second-hand furniture made from untreated foam or PVC, which gives off poisonous fumes if it catches fire. Some second-hand wooden furniture may be covered with paint containing lead. If such paintwork is chipped or flaking, remove it and repaint the furniture with a lead-free variety.

Four out of five UK babies wear disposable nappies, yet cotton terry-towelling nappies are cheaper and less harmful to the environment. As disposables are used only once, the average baby works through an alarming number each year, resulting in the wasteful felling of trees (*right*). In the UK terries cost about £37 plus laundry costs, in comparison with a bill of approximately £1,000 for disposable nappies by the time a child is potty-trained. In the USA a year's supply of disposables costs the equivalent of £360. In Canada the average yearly cost of home-laundered nappies is C$870; a nappy service costs C$1,200; and disposables cost C$2,300.

More information about creating a green home can be found in Chapter 7. Useful guides to baby products are listed in the **Consumer Guide** (*see page 183*).

NAPPIES (DIAPERS)

The advantages to the environment of using nappies made of terry towelling far outweigh the convenience of using disposable nappies (*see illustration right*). A problem with some disposable nappies is that their plastic backing is not biodegradable, making them a major source of environmental pollution and fuelling a potential ecological disaster. Nappies made with biodegradable plastic are now available in the UK and the USA (*see page 183* **Consumer Guide**). The 18 billion disposable nappies sold each year in the USA use 67,500 tons of plastic. The paper used in disposables comes from wood pulp from trees and the plastic from petrol – a non-renewable resource. Thirty million trees are used each year in the manufacture of disposable nappies. One fully grown tree makes 500 nappies, which may last a baby only a few months. The average baby uses up five trees' worth of nappies before being potty-trained.

Disposable nappies constitute up to one-third of a town's domestic rubbish in the USA and the cost of getting rid of such waste is high. In the UK 3.5 billion disposable nappies are used per year. They form 4 per cent of all household waste. Big

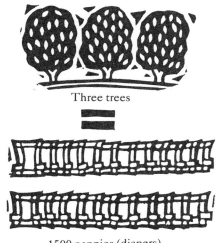

Three trees

=

1500 nappies (diapers)

=

Provision for one baby for one year

✖

The number of nappies (diapers) used in the USA, Canada and Britain.
23.2 billion (thousand million)

2200 sq.km or 850 sq.ml of destroyed forest
and
80 tons of non-biogradable polyethylene

companies are looking at pilot schemes to remedy this problem. One is to recycle the sanitized pulp filling to make cardboard boxes, and the plastic to make rubbish bags. Another involves composting the pulp to make humus for fertilizer.

Many brands of disposable nappy are perfumed or impregnated with unnecessary chemicals which can bring children out in a rash. Chlorine used to bleach cellulose wood pulp produces dangerous dioxins as a by-product of the bleaching process. In the UK 87 per cent of imported paper pulp is bleached with chlorine. These dioxins are released with the factory effluent to poison rivers and seas. All UK nappy manufacturers now use chlorine-free pulp, bleached with peroxide. In some forward-thinking countries, such as Sweden, nappies bleached with chlorine are banned.

Consider using terry towelling nappies most of the time and disposables only when they would be particularly helpful. Boiling, soaking in a salt and lemon solution and drying in he sun will whiten terries. Disposable nappy liners make life with terries easier. Plastic pants are useful to stop a wet nappy from leaking, but they make a rash more likely by keeping air from the skin, and they are non-biodegradable.

Try using Wunderpants, knitted woollen pants designed to be worn over a terry towelling nappy. They are manufactured from Danish wool specially prepared to retain its natural lanolin, making it waterproof. Wunderpants do not need washing every time you change a nappy because the lanolin reacts with the ammonia in the baby's urine to create a soap which neutralizes the ammonia and hence the smell. The Bumkins nappy has a waterproof nylon cover and thick cotton padding. It lasts for 200 washes.

Biobottoms are reusable nappy coverings made in Japan from felted wool. They allow the air to get to the baby's skin more effectively than disposables and they are fully biodegradable when worn out. Biobottoms need to be replaced and washed only every five or so nappy changes. Use them with terry towelling nappies or with fully disposable paper pads which have no plastic layer. Knitted wool or fabric nappy covers are another green alternative to plastic pants.

The **Consumer Guide** (*see page 183*) gives the mail order details of all these products.

NAPPY-FILLING

And still on the subject of nappies, a great many first-time mothers are concerned when their breastfed babies have a bowel motion many times each day. This is perfectly normal. The breastfed baby's 'green bowel' (*see pages 65–66*) is doing a grand job. The formula-fed baby, with a daily or every-other-day bowel motion, is the unusual one. Occasionally a breastfed baby will go for many days without any bowel motion and then pass a large, soft one.

By 16 weeks both breastfed and formula-fed babies have an average of two soiled nappies a day. Formula-fed babies, like breastfed babies, have yellow motions until they are eight weeks old, then the motions of one in three are green. Until you start your breastfed baby on foods and drinks other than breast milk, the bowel motions will not smell unpleasant – they usually smell slightly sweet. The breastfed baby's motions remain softer than those of the formula-fed baby, even after weaning .

CLOTHING

Second-hand clothes, from friends, relatives, mothers' newsletters, 'for sale' columns in local newspapers and charity shops, can save you a small fortune. A little time spent mending and titivating them is always worthwhile. Accept all offers of home-made children's clothes; it is usually most enjoyable to see your child in clothes lovingly made by someone known to the family rather than by an anonymous manufacturer.

When you buy new clothes, choose slightly larger sizes than your baby needs. Children grow out of small sizes quickly.

TOILETRIES

Smoothing sweet-smelling creams on to your baby's skin is enjoyable for both of you, but the experience is marred for some people by discovering that many apparently wholesome creams have been tested on animals for safety. There may be some case to be made for animal-testing during the development of essential new pharmaceutical drugs, but not on toiletries, which are essentially luxury items. It is now possible to buy all kinds of cosmetics and skin preparations that have not been tested on animals. Another possible concern is that some toiletries contain animal products. Again, these are easily avoided in favour of vegetable-based products in most countries. The State of Victoria in Australia has banned animal-testing for cosmetics. The **Consumer Guide** (*see page 183*) lists products and stockists.

TESTING ON ANIMALS

In the UK about 17,000 animals are used each year to test cosmetics and toiletries, to make sure the ingredients are unlikely to harm humans. Many of these tests are duplicated unnecessarily. The British Union for the Abolition of Vivisection (BUAV) has published a list of companies that refrain from testing their products, or the ingredients that go to make them, on animals (*see page 183* **Consumer Guide** for details). There is an EC plan to make all animal testing on cosmetics and toiletries compulsory.

The women's magazine, *Cosmopolitan*, found that 98 per cent of their readers in the UK were opposed to the use of animals to test toiletries and cosmetics; 66 per cent were prepared to volunteer themselves as guinea pigs. One company spokesperson I mentioned this to said that using humans for testing products is expensive and hard to organize. The Center for Alternatives to Animal Testing at Johns Hopkins University in the USA is doing pioneering work to address this problem.

Some of the toiletries that present the greatest threat to laboratory animals, and products to avoid if you are concerned about their safety, are listed below.

Lanolin is sometimes used as a cream to prevent nipple soreness and nappy rash. There have been reports that lanolin can be contaminated with pesticides, because it is extracted from sheep's wool, which may contain traces of the sheep dip used regularly to control parasitic infestations. These pesticides are made to withstand the effects of weather, which means they remain in the lanolin even after the sheep's wool is washed. The amount of pesticide contamination is small and the risk is negligible, but it seems sensible to avoid using lanolin.

Shampoos may be put through the Draize test, in which the product is dripped into rabbits' eyes to see if it causes damage after a certain time (up to seven days) in contact with the eyeball. Shampoos are mild detergents and they sting. The rabbit is usually given no pain relief and cannot get rid of substances by flushing them down the tear ducts. This test is cruel and inhumane – choose a shampoo labelled 'not tested on animals'.

Paper tissues are ideally made from non-chlorine bleached, 100 per cent recycled paper; and cotton wool from hydrogen-peroxide or oxygen bleached cotton.

Toothpaste may be tested on rats and guinea pigs by force-feeding them with the paste until half the animals in the test are dead. This is to find out what scientists call the LD50 – the lethal dose which will kill half the sample. Buy toothpaste from a range not tested on animals.

Titanium dioxide, the pigment used to make toothpaste white, pollutes rivers and seas. Choose a type that is environmentally friendly, such as a gel toothpaste that contains no titanium. Some children are sensitive to the additives, such as colourings and flavourings, found in many toothpastes.

DEAFENING SOUND

Personal stereos are one means of communication that should be kept away from your child's sensitive ears for as long as possible. A young child exposed to high levels of sound from headphones may suffer permanent hearing damage. High-volume sound can snap some of the 30,000 tiny hairs which carry sound in the inner ear. The hearing of a child who uses a personal stereo at high volume every day is likely to be damaged within ten years.

SMOKING

Passive smoking – breathing the air in a room used by smokers – is responsible for a meaningful amount of respiratory illness in children. It also leads to a greater risk of allergy, lung cancer, poor growth, intellectual difficulty, impaired hearing, squint (strabismus, cast, or lazy eye), cot death, heart disease and hyperactivity. There is a higher death rate in children under five years old in smoking families. In China there is said to be a tobacco epidemic, with seven out of ten adult men smoking. Statistics indicate that 50 million of today's children in China will be killed prematurely by smoking. Children who watch their parents smoking tend to pick up the habit, although a few are disgusted by the smell and refuse ever to touch a cigarette.

Smoking kills. It leads to lung cancer, to heart disease, to a great deal of respiratory illness in adult life and to an increased risk of miscarriage, low birth weight, stillbirth and congenital abnormality.

The tobacco industry spends countless millions advertising its products all over the world. In the UK £100 million is spent every year on advertising, promoting and sponsoring to recruit the 300 new smokers needed each day. There is no need to advertise to smokers because they are highly likely to retain their brand loyalty and not give up smoking. The new recruits are needed continually to replace the many smokers who die from tobacco-related illnesses and other causes.

In England 300,000 children aged between 11 and 15 smoke regularly; 180,000 smoke occasionally. In Europe the Greeks are the heaviest smokers, followed by the Swiss. In France, tobacco is the direct cause of 65,000 deaths a year.

CHILDREN & ECOLOGY

Green baby and child care means using the weather and other natural phenomena as a gauge to see how the environment can best be optimized and protected. Whether the climatic changes occurring all over the world are the result of the greenhouse effect or just a normal variation such as the Earth has seen many times before, we still have to adjust to them. These changes are vastly more important and dangerous in certain parts of the world, such as the sub-Sahara in Africa, where climatic changes combined with political upheaval cause thousands to starve.

TOO MUCH SUN

Increasingly more people are being exposed to excessive amounts of sun, perhaps partly because of a thinning of the ozone layer in the outer atmosphere (see page 185). Excessive ultra-violet light damages skin by making it wrinkle prematurely and by increasing the risk of skin cancer. Sun-induced skin cancer can be of the easily treated variety, known as rodent ulcer or basal cell carcinoma; or the more dangerous type, called malignant melanoma. Researchers have found that one or more episodes of blistering sunburn during childhood are a major risk factor in the later development of a melanoma. In the UK 200 people under 40 years of age die each year from a melanoma.

Holidays in hot countries are popular among white-skinned people from cooler climes. While they bask in sunshine, their skin is under attack from rays against which it has little or no natural protection in the form of melanin pigmentation.

It is sensible to protect your child's skin from sunburn. The official recommendation from both the American Academy of

Too much sun can harm a baby's delicate skin (*above left*); too little can cause SAD (Seasonal Affective Disorder) (*above right*). Be aware of the properties of ultra-violet (UV) light: do not put a baby too near a window on sunny days, as some UV light comes through glass – and bear in mind that a baby is not safe from over-exposure, even on overcast days, since up to one-third of UV light can penetrate cloud. When at an outdoor swimming pool or by the sea, protect your baby's skin with clothing and a high Sun Protection Factor (SPF) sun cream before swimming: UV light penetrates water and still has half its potential to cause damage at a depth of 30 cm (7 in). Many surfaces, such as concrete, snow, sand, water and vegetation, reflect UV light, the intensity of which increases with altitude. Your baby's skin is most vulnerable to damage at midday when the burning UVB rays of UV light are most powerful. The most dangerous time in temperate zones is two hours either side of noon (1pm in the UK in the summer). The nearer the equator, the longer the danger time. The ageing UVA rays of UV light are potentially dangerous all day, because they are not filtered out by the atmosphere.

Pediatrics and the American Academy of Dermatology is that protecting the skin from excessive exposure to the sun should begin early. Children can be exposed to too much sun even in temperate climates because they spend more time outdoors and receive three times as much ultraviolet light as the average adult. Their skin cells can be damaged easily and the inbuilt cell memory is imprinted with an early ageing message as a result of this damage.

Ultra-violet light readily penetrates young children's skin. There are three main reasons for this. First, a child's skin is comparatively thin; it achieves adult thickness only in teenage years. Second, babies under six months old are less able to tan. Tanning is a result of melanin pigmentation and is nature's way of protecting against damage. Reduced tanning ability means more chance of burning. Third, a young child's skin reflects only half the UV light reflected by an adult's skin.

Most of us look forward to a holiday, but the reality of a sunshine break with young children is often very different from the expectation. In psychologists' studies, holidays with or without children rate high in the stress stakes. It may be tempting to let the children play in the sun while you relax, but children need care in the sun as much as parents need time to themselves. If you let your child burn, not only will she or he suffer later, but you will feel guilty and disappointed at having the holiday marred by an uncomfortable, perhaps ill child in need of medical attention.

Protect your child's skin from the sun by aiming for gradual, safe tanning without excessive exposure to the sun's damaging rays. If you do this, your child will have healthy, attractive skin with no risk of burning, skin cancer or early ageing.

Natural burning and tanning ability differ from child to child, but all children should wear protective clothing, including a sun-hat, when out in the sunshine. Sunburn goes on developing even when you bring your child in from the sun, so do not try to gauge the degree of sunburn by skin colour. Use a sunscreen cream that protects against both UVB and UVA rays.

Skin-care in the sun is a health issue, not merely a cosmetic one. Children are particularly susceptible to the sun and need their parents to think about skin protection for them. With a positive sunshine strategy, the whole family can enjoy the sun and control its harmful effects.

TOO LITTLE SUN

When the nights are long and the days short, the lack of bright daylight causes a biochemical balance in the hypothalmus, a gland in the brain, which makes some people feel tired, sluggish, hungry and depressed. A few people feel so disrupted in winter that doctors have given their disorder a name: Seasonal Affective Disorder, or SAD. One doctor believes that insufficient calcium in the blood may be a cause of childhood 'growing pains'. Insufficient daylight can result in a vitamin D deficiency, which in turn is responsible for inadequate calcium absorption from the gut. Calcium deficiency could cause the muscles to ache.

If you or your family feel low or flat in the winter, try to spend at least half an hour a day outside, preferably at midday when the light is brightest. Spend a much time as you can outside on sunny days. Sleeping with the curtains open provides you with more daylight in the early hours. Only bright artificial lighting (three times as intense as the brightest domestic lighting) helps SAD sufferers.

One cause of jet lag when travelling between time zones is a disruption of the normal rhythms of melatonin production. Help overcome jet lag by using daylight to reset your body's clock.

The sun's rays enable skin to produce vitamin D, the vitamin essential for healthy bones and the body's calcium balance. Dark-skinned children living far from the equator in temperate climates run the risk of being short of vitamin D and developing rickets, a deficiency disease which makes the bones soften and bend. The risk is greater if these children wear clothes that cover most of the skin, go outside rarely and have a diet which contains little vitamin D. If your child misses out on daily exposure to daylight, make sure that the family diet contains plenty of foods rich in vitamin D (*see pages 52–53*). A vitamin D supplement may be a good idea if your daily meals lack this essential vitamin.

Breastfed babies receive plenty of vitamin D as long as there is enough in the food their mothers eat. Breastfeeding mothers should also take care to spend some time outside every day. If you are breastfeeding and rarely go out or eat foods rich in vitamin D, take a supplement. A bottle-fed baby's formula contains a standard amount of added vitamin D.

COLD COMFORT

Turning up the heating in the home is an expensive and wasteful way of coping with a cold air temperature. It is far more sensible to wear more layers of clothing. Cold air causes some asthmatic children to have an attack, but hot, dry air can make a wheezy child worse by drying the mucus in the breathing passages, making it difficult to shift by coughing. If your child has asthma, make sure the air in your home is warm, yet humidified with a source of water vapour.

Sunshine, wind, rain, atmospheric pressure and humidity levels can alter mood, physical health and well-being. By simply being aware that the weather may be the cause of a bad mood, parents and children can learn to help one another.

Some people feel much better in sunny climates than in temperate ones. High humidity and low atmospheric pressure make some feel lethargic and unwell, and changes in pressure can cause restlessness. Strong winds are known to induce mood changes and a condition called 'wind-madness' in countries that endure long-lasting winds, such as the mistral in France, at certain times of the year.

GOING OUT WITH A BABY

Going out to public places with a baby is easier if those places make the infants and parents feel welcome. Some restaurants do this, providing high chairs and small meals for children. Some stores such as Toys R Us, Children's World and the Scandinavian IKEA provide rooms both for fathers and babies and mothers and babies. They also provide diminutive lavatories for small behinds. A few supermarkets make shopping easier for parents and children by allowing ready access to lavatories.

Baby slings make getting about with a baby much easier than a push chair. They have also done much to improve the lot of western babies, who generally have limited physical contact with their parents, unlike many babies in traditional societies who are carried everywhere by their mothers. If you carry your baby around in a sling you know by the baby's movements when he or she wants to feed, sleep or wee.

PHYSICAL PUNISHMENT

A surprising number of parents smack their young children regularly. Many use it as an outlet for anger; one in two mothers lashes out only when tense or irritated.

Some parents use physical punishment because they know no better way to teach their child how to behave. Some believe that smacking will make the child good. Others smack because they are overwhelmed by their problems. A few people smack in a considered way because they believe that to spare the rod spoils the child.

In the UK, nine out of ten parents believe that it is acceptable to smack their children. Mothers are more likely to smack than fathers, presumably because they are with their children for longer periods of time. A study found that more than three out of five mothers sometimes smack their one-year-old babies. Among the families of professional workers, however, physical punishment is unusual.

By the time they are four years old, most British children are being smacked at least once a week; by the age of seven smacking becomes slightly less common, especially for girls. Most boys are still smacked once a week. By the age of 16 children are more likely to be troublesome if they grew up being smacked often.

Smacking children is illegal in Austria, Norway, Sweden, Finland and Denmark. In the UK corporal punishment is banned in State schools, but fewer than one in ten parents believe it should be banned within the home.

Young children can be very annoying. They do the same thing over and over again even though they have been told not to. This is because they can learn only gradually how you wish them to behave; few children learn something the first time they are told; they may learn only by experience. Sometimes children misbehave to annoy because this is the only way they can get attention; and any attention – even being smacked – is better than going unnoticed.

Smacking is not usually the best way to stop a child doing whatever it is you dislike. It is definitely not the only way of giving the attention your child may need, neither is it the best way of making your difficult life easier to cope with.

Some children accept the occasional smack as part of life and grow up emotionally healthy and with a good relationship with their parents. Others do not. What happens depends on the individual parent and child, on their relationship in general and on the circumstances.

Many children are much more aware of their feelings about being smacked than they are of the adult's motive. What might seem a small tap meted out in the heat of the moment may be enormously important to your child. However good the intention, however considered the smacking, physical punishment can be emotionally harmful to some children. The physical pain and emotional indignity seem like a betrayal of trust and a disregard for the child as a person.

Wise parents are honest enough to work out whose needs are being met by smacking their children and whether they could be better met in other ways. You can learn more constructive methods of showing your young child what you expect than smacking. Positive reinforcement, for example, encouraging and praising children when they behave as you wish, works much better in the long term than ignoring them when they behave well and only taking any notice when they behave badly. Children brought up with plenty of attention and positive reinforcement tend not to demand attention by behaving in an unacceptable way: they have no need to do so.

If you feel you are getting nowhere with your child, seek information and support from sources such as parenting skills courses and books, health advisers, social workers and friends.

THE PROBLEM OF CHILD ABUSE

Children can be abused in three main ways: physically, emotionally and sexually. Sexual abuse is in fact a combination.

Children who are beaten may have an uncomfortable mixture of emotions. They sometimes cling desperately to their violent parent, because they have no-one else. Sometimes they have no idea that other children are treated differently, so believe that violence is normal. A likely end result is that they will beat their own children because violence tends to breed violence: that is how they have been taught that parents behave.

Others go the opposite way, knowing the pain they suffered, and refuse ever to smack their children. As adults they run the risk of pushing their feelings inward and 'hitting' themselves (instead of their children) in one of a variety of ways, such as addictive or other destructive behaviour resulting from their hurts. Some reject their parents.

People who abuse children were often emotionally deprived, unhappy, over-burdened or rejected when they were children. Psychologists know that child abuse is often an unconscious attempt for adults to meet their own needs – perhaps to express their own rage or hurt. Once some needy parents start to abuse their children, there is a risk that they will do it more and more. Child abuse is not confined to any particular social background; people from all walks of life can hurt their children.

Research has found that adults who are violent to their children are more likely than other adults to have been born prematurely, to have been ill at birth, and to have been separated from their mothers in early infancy; and that three of out five sexually abusing fathers had divorced parents.

UNREALISTIC EXPECTATIONS

Some adults find it hard to cope when their young children need more time and attention than expected. They may have grown up with little idea of what being a parent is really like. They imagine that babies sleep soundly, especially at night; and that they feed well and lie quietly gurgling the rest of the time. The reality that their babies may sometimes be impossible to comfort, may have feeding problems, may demand attention for a large proportion of the day and may wake many times at night can be too much for them, especially if they lack practical, emotional and financial back-up.

It is wrong to believe that a child can be 'spoiled' by being comforted when distressed; an unhappy child at first responds to being left alone by crying more. This can be the final straw for a parent already at breaking point from the stresses of life. A baby left to cry for a long time is in danger of becoming depressed and apathetic.

A common expectation is that children should be good and behave like small, reasonable adults. The reality is that young children need to explore, experiment and find out about life in their own way.

It could help if all parents were encouraged to attend classes in parenting skills, such as the excellent Parent-Link course organized by The Parent Network in the UK (see page 183 Consumer Guide). Ante-natal classes are not enough. It is well known that women and men who attend ante-natal courses are more interested in pregnancy and birth than in preparing for a lifetime of parenting. Perhaps some financial inducement from the State could tempt parents of young children to attend classes in child and parent care.

Parentcraft classes for schoolchildren should do away with trite and unnecessary discussions and demonstrations on nappies and bathing babies and address the more important matters, such as what babies are really like to live with and how the needs of both children and parents can be met.

DEALING WITH ABUSE

Children who have been abused have to be protected from further damage; this means that society at large must take the trouble to notice damage and individuals must be brave enough to intervene or point out the trouble to someone able to help. Splitting up the family to protect the abused child is rarely the best answer, though it might be the easiest and the cheapest. Children need the abuse to stop; the best way of doing this in the long term is for their parents – or other adults (see page 106) to be helped to cope better.

Adults who have abused their children must be prevented from doing further damage. Sometimes just knowing that someone else knows about it prevents further abuse. If the violence, sexual abuse or neglect continues in spite of reasonable intervention the adult must be separated from the child.

If the violent adult is acting out his or her emotional pain and distress and inability to cope with life, the hurting and probably once abused 'child' inside this adult needs the experience of being parented or lovingly cared for. This experience can come as skilled counselling or therapy, which is expensive and time-consuming. Nevertheless, if it saves a child from abuse it is invaluable and in purely economic terms it can repay the initial outlay many times.

Help must also be available for the non-abusing parent. The relationship between the abusing adult and the passive partner may be a co-dependent one, in which both partners need love and attention, look to each other for it, but are unable to help each other. Their child ends up suffering as much as the parents.

TWO PARENTS OR ONE?

Here I consider single, never-married parent families. Single parenting from choice is also considered on pages 8-9; from divorce or separation on page 108. Single parenting due to the death of a partner is not looked at here.

The rise in the number of babies born out of wedlock in western countries has been dramatic. In the UK in 1979 one in ten babies had parents who had not taken a legally recognized vow to stay together. The figure today is one in four. The USA passed this point on the graph some time ago; in Sweden the figure is nearer two out of every five babies born.

The increase in the number of babies born to unmarried mothers in the USA and the UK is greatest in the lower socio-economic groups. This means that in some communities most babies are born to unmarried mothers. The question is whether this matters to anyone other than the statisticians. Cynics might argue that it is not important for several reasons.

First, more than one in three of today's marriages in northern Europe will probably break up. The UK has the highest divorce rate in Europe; Denmark has the second highest divorce rate in Europe – about 160,000 couples divorce each year – and divorce creates most of the single-parent families. In the USA it is estimated that more than half of all new marriages will end in divorce. An unhappy marriage or a difficult divorce can be emotionally destructive to children and may even affect them physically, by causing psychosomatic illness and material deprivation. In the USA a divorced woman's standard of living falls to a quarter of what it was before her divorce. Second, in an age of supposed sexual equality, one parent must be just as capable as two of raising a child, given enough financial support. Many single unmarried mothers (and fathers) do an excellent job of raising children, sometimes better than two parents together. Third, two out of three out-of-wedlock births in the UK are jointly registered by the parents, suggesting that they are living together and are emotionally and practically – if not legally – committed to their child and to each other. And fourth, extended families can surely help replace the loss of a fully committed father.

Looking at these arguments one by one presents a less hopeful picture. Live-in relationships are more likely to break up than legally recognized ones. This can be just as painful to a child as an official divorce. It may be even worse for the mother who may be left with no legally imposable financial support from the father.

Second, it can be difficult for single parents, nine out of ten of whom are women, to bring up a baby. Comparatively few single mothers have plenty of money or a large, supportive family. Most of the one in three without a live-in partner find life a struggle. Their only practical and emotional support is their own family and other women in a similar situation. Even with financial assistance from the State, a single mother probably has little money. If she works, she is likely to take a low-paid job and in the UK will forfeit some of her State benefit if she earns above a certain amount, even though she has to pay for child care. Many single mothers are caught in a trap of poverty, loneliness and low self-esteem.

The single mother often does not have another live-in adult to help with the time-consuming and demanding job of caring for a child. Her children may be tightly controlled, because that is the only way she can cope; or run wild because she opts out of discipline from desperation. Often tight control and episodes of violent unruliness go together. The child does not have another deeply committed adult to relate to and to use as a model for what men – fathers in particular – do in families. This may

mean that girls grow up believing that they will follow in their mothers' footsteps and bring up their children without a man. With no experience of being fathered, they may find it difficult to relate to men.

Boys who grow up without any experience of being fathered may find it difficult to relate to men and to other authority figures. Later, they may believe it unnecessary to make a commitment to a woman before she gets pregnant, or to have a responsible role in the upbringing of their children. Those who feel they have a part to play in raising their children might not know how to because they missed out on years of experience of watching their own father or father-figure. It may be very important to a child's developing self-esteem for his or her father openly (if not legally) at least to acknowledge paternity.

On the third point, that of child registration, one in three babies of unmarried mothers in the UK is not jointly registered, which implies that no committed father is around. One in two illegitimate children is born to a mother living on her own. Having only one readily available parent is usually worse for a child than having two. A live-in father is less likely to remain in contact with his children if the relationship breaks up than a once-married father.

In Sweden the facts are rather different. People are increasingly making their own rules for living together and large numbers of people across all socio-economic groups choose not to marry. Unmarried parents are more likely to be committed to their child than their contemporaries in the UK and the USA. Cohabitation is on the increase in the UK, but ultimately eight out of ten such couples marry.

In a society in which many men do not commit themselves to their family, their own fathers, brothers, uncles and cousins are even less likely to commit themselves as relatives. This makes a mockery of the idea of the extended family being a valuable asset, or of other family males (other than the brothers of the mother) being readily available as role models.

Babies are constantly learning about themselves and their effect on the environment. Mothers are usually the most important part of this process. Every time a mother responds to her baby's movements, smile, gaze or voice (*above*), her baby learns the meaning of the action and that someone in the world is sensitive to his or her needs. A mother naturally copies many of her baby's actions, encouraging the baby to do the same again to provoke her response. Rewarding feedback from her baby motivates a mother to continue.

The American political scientist, Charles Murray, of the New York Manhattan Institute, reported in 1990 that sociologists have found that in communities with high rates of illegitimacy, there is more juvenile delinquency, more violent crime (especially among boys in their late teens) and higher voluntary unemployment. Children are also less likely to benefit from their formal education and more likely to grow up in conditions of social deprivation, poverty and drug and alcohol abuse. It is difficult to improve these matters simple measures, such as introducing better day-care for children and creating more jobs.

Overall, the message sings out loud and clear: babies and young children have a better chance if they start off with two committed parents. They usually get a mother. They need a father.

THE WORKING MOTHER

Psychologists see work as crucial to self-esteem, well-being and physical and mental health. For centuries large numbers of women have worked, but only recently have so many with dependent pre-school children taken on paid work outside the home. The work they do is often part-time and low-paid. The Press has dubbed the nineteen-nineties 'the decade of the working mother', and there has been a great deal of discussion about child care provision for women workers. However, it is important that mothers do not feel they are being pressurized into resuming paid work (or staying at home) by the whims of a State needing (or ceasing to need) women in the work-force.

Employers in the UK are currently persuading women back to work for economic reasons; and increasing numbers of mothers are working because of financial pressure or because they want to. Yet there are publicly supported day-care places for only a few 0 to 2 year olds and 15 per cent of 3 to 4 year olds. In France there are places for 22 per cent of 0 to 2 year olds and 44 per cent of 3 to 4 year olds. Just over 1 in 3 mothers of children under five in the UK works (full- or part-time, at home or away). This is one of the lowest ratios (lowest numbers of working women) in Europe.

I have noticed that in countries with universal day care provision for children and a high proportion of mothers of young children working, the birth rate tends to be low, regardless of the standard of living. In Sweden, where welfare policy in effect discourages the maternal care of pre-school children, the birth rate is 40 per cent below that needed to maintain the population. In urban areas of the USSR it is similarly low. There may be little pleasure or reward for mothers in having children if they see little of them because of work; so they see little reason to have more than one child.

Large, well constructed surveys show that in the USA 21 per cent (one in five) of mothers of pre-school children work part-time and 22 per cent work full-time. By contrast, in West Germany 11 per cent work part-time and 44 per cent full-time.

A cross-national survey in the USA, West Germany, Hungary and the Republic of Ireland found that two out of three adults thought that a working woman can establish as close a relationship with her children as one who does not go out to work. However, a majority believed that a pre-school child whose mother works is likely to suffer as a result. Only in the USA was opinion equally divided on this. There, more than 7 out of 10 married mothers do not work full-time the year round. Working mothers are vociferous in their defence of a career, but the fact is that most women would prefer to stay with their young children for most of the time. If a woman has a

choice, her decision about working will depend on the age of her child. A recent survey for an advertising agency in the UK found that three out of four women aged between 25 and 44 felt wholeheartedly that they would rather be the one looking after young children in the home than the one who goes out to work every day. This matched the views of three out of four adults in a large survey in 1987 by Social and Community Research in the UK. They favoured mothers of children under five being at home. The adults surveyed, however, were both men and women, and it was impossible to separate out the women's views from the published results.

A recent survey of 50,000 working mothers by the American *Family Circle* found that two out of three would prefer to stay at home with their children if it were possible. A survey in the USA by *Child* magazine found that 58 per cent of working mothers resumed work because of financial necessity. It is not easy for women who have no choice but to work, but it can also be difficult for women who do have the option to stay at home. Many mothers of young children have conflicting feelings: they want to go out to work and find it a strain being with children all day every day; yet they enjoy some aspects of being with their children and feel guilty because they think their children need them to be there all the time and might suffer as a result of being left with someone else.

In the *Child* survey seven out of ten working mothers said they would prefer to work part-time, and nearly half the non-working mothers voiced the same opinion. One problem with part-time work is that it tends to be poorly paid and is sometimes shift-based. In many countries part-time workers have few statutory rights.

MOTHER VS. CARETAKERS

Mothers, fathers and other family members may have more inclination and incentive to care for and interact with their own children than non-relatives, but this does not necessarily mean that they will wish to look after the children, although the children might prefer to be with their mothers, given the choice. US researchers have found more insecurity, aggression and non-compliance among children who had over 20 hours a week of non-parental care in their first year. This could be because high-quality day-care is not easily available because of the nature of the families that rely on day-care, or because children under one year need parental care. However, there is increasing evidence that even good substitute care may not be good enough for babies under the age of one year.

It is obviously wrong for an unwilling mother to be closeted with her young child. Going out to work is not her only option, however, if she primarily seeks stimulation and adult company rather than money and career advancement. Involvement in local social events and community work are others.

Working alters the amount of time you spend with your child. In the USSR the woman spends only 20 minutes a day with her child. The concept of quality time has been cited as a valuable way of making up for the loss of time working mothers share with their children. Quality time is the term given to short but intensely interactive time spent together. Quality time at the end of the working day may not, however, suit the child, who needs quality time on demand, and not only when his or her weary mother comes home. Babies and young children need company and physical contact as well as focussed attention. If you

Women who have the option to stay at home (*below right*) sometimes find it a strain to be cooped up with a young child all day every day and some would like to work part-time. Women who have no choice but to work full-time often feel they would like to spend more time with their child (*below left*). In a survey by the American *Child* magazine, seven out of ten working mothers and nearly half the non-working mothers said they would prefer to work part-time.

leave your child with someone, try to choose a person who will give the child as much contact, company and one-to-one attention as he or she needs, so that your child does not have to rely only on your limited time together.

Numerous large surveys suggest that the absence of a mother as she works does not affect the health, development or behaviour of her child over the age of one year. There is no difference in language, educational attainment or the rate of behaviour and emotional disorders.

My own professional observations of young children with working mothers are somewhat different. I have noticed many of them to be quieter, less confident, or more attention-seeking than children who have had the experience of continuity of care. Researchers looking for obvious emotional disorders would probably not consider such differences important.

BENEFITS & DRAWBACKS

From a mother's point of view, working full-time may not be ideal because she misses out on the pleasure and privilege of being with her growing child from day to day, and the satisfaction of knowing she is the person her child most wants to be with. She may relinquish her position as the main emotional, educational and moral guide. It can also be difficult for the working mother to breastfeed, especially as she will inevitably become tired holding down a job, while coping with the child care and tasks that most working mothers face before and after work. Finding reliable substitute child care while she works can be an organizational nightmare. If her job is boring or tiring, a mother may become demoralized and irritable. She may also have to cope with guilt engendered by a society ambivalent toward working mothers.

Nevertheless, many mothers find the benefits of working counter-balance the problems because they enjoy the extra money, the social life with workmates and, if they are lucky, the stimulation and career prospects of the job. Going out to work

each day means a woman is able to avoid the down-times of being at home with young children who can at times be boring, demanding and irritating. Mothers who work are half as likely to become depressed as non-working mothers. From the young child's point of view there is evidence that if a mother is depressed, her absence at work shields her child from the worst effects of her irritability and apathy.

From a baby's point of view, there are drawbacks of having a mother who works away from home. A baby has to learn to cope with the daily pain of parting and the fear of being left with someone who is not the favourite and who may not interact as sensitively as the mother. Breastfeeding babies lose their familiar source of comfort and nourishment. There is the added possibility that a rapid succession of caretakers working for short periods of a few months will unsettle the young child or may even be incapable of meeting his or her physical or emotional needs. Child-minders, nursery nurses, nannies, friends and relatives are human beings and as such are not immune from being inadequate or even abusive to the children in their care, in spite of any training they may have. A small proportion are drawn to child care because of their own unmet needs.

Another possible problem needing attention is that a young child brought up without sufficient one-to-one attention and physical contact with a loving, committed carer may fail to learn caring, nurturing, 'mothering' skills. Boys and girls learn how to care for their own children as they themselves are 'mothered'. In some countries, such as the USSR, most children of working mothers are cared for in nurseries or kindergartens in which there might be only 1 member of staff for up to 20 children. The sort of care it is possible to provide in such circumstances is obviously very different from that of a person who has perhaps only one or two young children to look after. Those lobbying for more nurseries in workplaces should perhaps take into account that the most important thing may be the ratio of staff to children, rather than the mere existence of the nursery.

However, some babies undoubtedly gain from having a working mother because their carers come to the job fresh and eager. A baby may gain from the carer's different personality and outlook, especially if the carer replaces a mother who cannot meet her baby's needs. And the mother who gets great satisfaction from working may be more fun for her baby when they are together.

Only you can figure out the pros and cons to you and your baby of working. It is often difficult to gauge how happy the baby is while you are away because many babies make a fuss as their mothers leave and return, but seem fine in between times. The plaintive wail of a baby reluctant to be left has decided many a mother against returning to work.

ADEQUATE CHILD CARE

The quality of the available child care and the ease of arranging it are often the factors that most influence mothers weighing up the pros and cons of working: a willing and loving grandma, a good child-minder or nanny, or a stimulating and well staffed crèche or nursery makes leaving a child to go to work relatively easy. Poor provision for child care makes life hell for the working mother. Some employers address this problem by providing day-care at the place of work, which is fine for young children but obviously does not suit those of school-age.

Other factors that might influence the decision include maternity and paternity leave, the place of work, the hours spent working, leave provision, the availability of flexitime, job-sharing, tax relief for child care and benefits for part-time working mothers.

In Sweden there is automatic parental leave of 270 days for either father or mother after childbirth. There is also joint State-employer benefit to allow a parent to take time off to care for a sick child. In a recent Gallup Poll six out of ten mothers said that a shortage of affordable child care was the most important factor keeping them at home. In Hungary maternity leave is currently available for mothers until their child is three years of age.

Both the stay-at-home and the working mother sometimes experience feelings of regret, exhaustion and depression. Whoever cares for a child – mother, father, another relative, child-minder, nursery nurse or nanny – can have such feelings. From the green perspective it is imperative that child carers in any society take care of themselves, as well as the children, and that they receive back-up from society.

It is up to each individual, man or woman, parent or not, to share in the process of bringing up children by providing either practical help or emotional support. In this way, it is possible to influence the emotional and physical environment provided by parents for their young children and to make the invaluable job of raising children easier.

GREEN PARENTING

Both parents need to work at their relationship so they can cope with the turbulent emotions that come with children and their care. Children bring joy and opportunity, but also pain, conflict and sometimes heartache. The divorce and separation rates peak in the first year after childbirth. To protect your relationship, try to make time for laughter, creativity, cuddling, hobbies and exercise by sharing and planning your time. The techniques commonly taught to sales and management staff: listening (to oneself and to others); encouragement; affirmation; conflict resolution and other communications skills, are also valuable for couples, both for their relationships with each other and with their children. In the USA and the UK there are marriage-enrichment courses to help couples develop these skills, but they are often short of participants. Many parents in the midst of marital trouble wrongly believe there is no way out or find they cannot be vulnerable enough to ask for and accept professional help.

LEARNING TO LISTEN

Part of meeting one other's needs as man and woman includes learning to listen to one another's feelings. An American marital therapist, Gleam Powell, says that learning to listen is a key to maintaining and improving a relationship. Although the ability to listen sensitively may not come naturally, it can be learned. Individuals feel understood if their partner senses their feelings and successfully communicates an understanding of them. An able listener can helpfully identify hidden feelings by translating body language and other unconscious messages. To listen effectively to others, however, you have to learn to acknowledge your own needs and feelings.

Improved communication skills can save a marriage in which both partners feel needy and unloved. Courses are available in many countries: contact a local adult education college or a counselling service.

SEX

A sexual relationship changes when you have young children. Green parents learn to adapt. Emotional honesty and vulnerability are more helpful than acting out hurt feelings by going elsewhere for sex, or responding to exhaustion by ignoring your partner. Growing in personal awareness at this time helps a relationship stand up to the demands made on it, even if physical sex takes a back seat for a while.

One UK study found that breastfeeding women tend to have less interest in sex than bottle-feeding mothers until their babies are about six months old. This may be because of a dry vagina caused by lower oestrogen levels; a difference in the levels of other hormones; and the fact that their need for physical intimacy is to some extent satisfied by breastfeeding; or tiredness. Relationship problems, perhaps caused by the father's jealousy of the intimacy of the breastfeeding mother and baby, or by a polarization of the woman's dual role into a 'mistress or madonna' conflict, may also interfere with sex.

DIVORCE

The emotional and practical disruption wrought by divorce is damaging to children. In one UK study over one-third of the children of divorced parents were still intensely unhappy five years after the split. They were also more likely than other children to have sleep problems and to do badly at school. In years to come, children of divorcees are more likely to exhibit anti-social behaviour and to have broken marriages.

It has been said that children suffer more if parents in a marriage ridden with conflicts stay together than if they have a quick, clean divorce. However, divorce is seldom quick or clean. Some experts assert that children are as damaged by divorce as they are by their parents' poor relationship. Children frequently blame themselves for the break-up of their parents' relationship and spend hours thinking up ways to get them together again. (*See also page 101*).

Even though most parents remarry, happiness is not guaranteed the second time around. People are likely to make the same mistakes. The rates of emotional and physical ill-health and of death are much higher for the divorced and separated parent than for the married one, especially the man.

DEPRESSION

The causes of depression, a not uncommon factor among mothers of young children, are mainly social (*see also page 106*). In one Finnish study nearly 1 in 12 mothers was depressed. A mother's lowness inevitably influences her child's environment. Researchers have found that four main factors provoke depression among mothers:

1. The absence of an intimate, confiding relationship with a partner makes depression more likely, although a close friend or other confidante may make up for this lack to some extent. Women in the lower socio-economic groups are especially likely to find their relationship with their partner suffers dramatically when they

have children. Rather than focus attention solely on the woman's depression, it might be more helpful for her partner to improve his interactive behaviour by learning about emotional intimacy, perhaps by taking a caring for your children and yourselves-course in listening skills, or joining a self-awareness group.

2. The childhood loss of her own mother through death or separation before the age of 11 can make a woman especially vulnerable to depression.

3. A new mother has to adjust to a completely different lifestyle. Her sense of identity is disrupted and she may mourn her former status, freedom and social contacts as a working woman. One of the necessary tasks of mourning is recognizing and accepting the sadness, anger and other feelings that accompany it, but a new mother may feel guilty at having these feelings and try to suppress them. Difficult, buried feelings, particularly anger, show up as depression because it is nearly impossible to suppress such feelings without keeping all of your emotions out of the way.

4. A woman is more likely to become depressed if she has three or more children under the age of 14 at home, because her workload is so high.

HELPING YOURSELF

As a new mother, you may not yet fit into a new circle of friends and may therefore not have developed a network of supportive relationships. You may also be tired out and disrupted by your baby's sleep patterns. It is usually better to talk about your feelings, to a professional health worker or counsellor if necessary – than to take tranquillizers or anti-depressants. Many women benefit from meeting others in informal social groups, such as mother and baby meetings. Plenty of practical help from partner and friends also helps. A good diet with enough foods rich in zinc, and enough exercise and natural light, are useful to stave off depression.

Caring for yourself helps you to care for your baby more effectively, yet you are precious not only to your baby and your partner but also just because you are you. Being a green parent means learning to look after yourself and to consider yourself the most important part of your baby's environment.

MAKING MASSAGE OILS

Massage with fragrant oil is a wonderful way of communicating loving and caring through touch, and releasing emotional tension locked up in the body. You do not have to be an expert to massage your partner or child: simply stroke the skin rhythmically, sensitively and gently with a 'carrier' oil scented with one or more essential oils.

Buy a 50-millilitre dark glass bottle with a stopper from a chemist or pharmacist. The best carrier oil is grapeseed oil, as it has a good texture and no smell. Sweet almond, sunflower seed and safflower seed are nearly as good. You will find these oils in a good grocer or pharmacy. Wheatgerm oil added to the carrier oil helps prevent rancidity. Lavender, rose and chamomile are safe essential oils to use in a massage oil for children under five.

To make up a massage oil for a child under five, add 10 drops of essential oil (or oils in any combination) to the bottle, with a dropper if you have one. Add 40 millilitres of carrier oil and 10 of wheatgerm oil. Put on the stopper and shake gently to disperse the essential oil. There is a wider choice of essential oils for children over five and adults. Each affects the body differently (*see pages 182-3* **Further Reading**). To make up a massage oil for older children and adults, add 25 drops of essential oil to the bottle, followed by 40 millilitres of carrier oil and 10 of wheatgerm oil.

Chapter Six
FEEDING YOUR CHILDREN

Bread baked without love is a bitter bread,
that feeds but half man's hunger.
Kahlil Gibran

The average family in a developed country expects to find an exciting range of foods from all over the world in the local supermarket, whatever the season. Yet the populations of some of the countries which supply our supermarkets with that rich variety of foods are largely malnourished and at worst starving.

Many developing countries are in areas of climatic extremes, making it expensive and difficult for them to increase agricultural production and to optimize natural resources. To feed, shelter, educate and care for the health of their exploding populations (*see page 11*) demands investment, so developing countries desperately need the income they can generate from agricultural production, yet they do not produce enough food crops to satisfy their own food needs. Large numbers of poor people do not own or rent land and so cannot produce or buy enough food for their families, so infant mortality is high and adult life expectancy low.

It seems grossly unfair that economic associations of rich countries – like the EEC – should have accumulated lakes and mountains of surplus foodstuffs, such as milk, grain and butter, without having so much as formulated plans for their rapid distribution to poorer countries at times of desperate need. But there is worse.

The innovations in methods of agricultural production introduced during the twentieth century have been so successful that they have brought about a 'green revolution'. Foremost among them has been the development of the use of agrochemicals, as a result of which harvests have increased virtually every year. But farmers can no longer keep up with the accelerating growth in world population (*see page 11*); in the 1989–90 season the world and its animals consumed 25 million tonnes of food staples more than farmers produced. Furthermore, according to a study by the US Department of Agriculture, there are signs that the extensive use of agrochemicals might in the long term have the effect of increasing crop losses.

Intensive farming practices such as the spraying of crops, battery egg production and intensive dairy farming have detrimental consequences. Among them are eventual erosion of the soil; a reduction in the resistance to disease of crops and livestock; lower crop yields; a lowering of the underground water tables; the use of large amounts of oil in fuel-based fertilizers; the pollution of water supplies; the contamination of grain, vegetables and fruit with agrochemicals; the contamination and weakening of livestock with veterinary pharmaceutical products, such as antibiotics, anti-helminthics (deworming agents) and growth promoters; and a reduction in the mineral and bacterial content of the soil by over-ploughing, overcropping and not using nitrogen-fixing crops and other traditional farming aids. When such large-scale, agrochemical-based farming practices are copied by a developing country, the land, the crops and the economy eventually suffer.

What, you may ask, has this to do with ordinary parents bringing up their children? Can we help right inequity on such a vast scale?

Vast changes can and do begin at grass roots level. If enough families change their

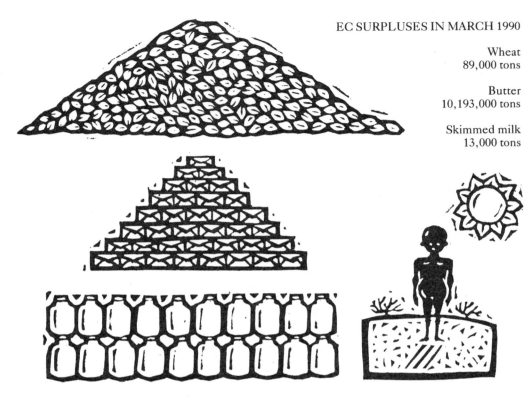

EC SURPLUSES IN MARCH 1990

Wheat
89,000 tons

Butter
10,193,000 tons

Skimmed milk
13,000 tons

European agricultural policy is to store surplus food and drink (*above*). Farmers are paid for their excess produce, which can be set aside for use in emergencies, such as famine.

shopping and eating habits, retail buying practices will change too. More importantly, farming practices will also change, at home and abroad, through example and the sharing of expertise. The way children are fed is important not only to them but also to the billions of other children around the world. All the world's children need our interest and concern.

You can begin this process by eating less meat; buying organic cereals, vegetables and fruit; and buying meat, fish, milk and eggs farmed using humane methods.

EAT LESS MEAT

Cattle are normally fed with grain, vegetables and grass. One hectare (nearly 2 ½ acres) of farmland used for raising beef

produces 20 kilograms (44 pounds) of beef protein. This same hectare, if used to grow wheat, would yield 300 kilograms (661 pounds) of wheat protein. Land is usually much more productive when used for cereals than for meat.

When vegetable food is fed to animals, the protein in the resulting meat weighs far less than the protein in the original vegetable produce. Cattle certainly convert vegetable protein into meat, but at what cost? The amount of vegetable food a cow eats to produce a king-sized hamburger would feed 40 children for one day. Many more people can be fed from arable land than from land used to raise livestock. Ground the size of five football pitches can, in the same amount of time, provide meat to feed two people, maize to feed ten, wheat to feed 24 or soya beans to feed 61. At present 40 per cent of the world's grain is fed to livestock to produce meat for rich people to eat, yet millions starve.

Sheep, pigs and hens can be kept on land unsuitable for agriculture so, in terms of efficiency, their meat can be considered 'greener' than beef.

Any increase from a rise in the number of cows could, they say, contribute to global warming via the greenhouse effect. Scientists say that methane in the emissions of wind from the guts of cows, goats and sheep is being produced in vast amounts. These animals are ruminants – they chew the cud and produce large volumes of wind. Each cow produces 200 grams (7 ounces) of methane a day from the bacterial breakdown of food in the gut. That means the 1,300 million cows in the world produce nearly 100 million tons of methane a year. This is over one-fifth of the annual total global release of methane, an important greenhouse gas (*see page 185* **Glossary**).

A major contribution to the greenhouse effect via an increase in atmospheric carbon dioxide results from the clearing of vast areas of forested land to create pastureland for meat cattle. Trees remove carbon dioxide from the air; grassland does not. Burning felled trees creates large amounts of carbon dioxide. Clearing the rainforest also destroys the natural homelands of traditional tribal peoples. There has been an enormous amount of forest clearance in Central America to satisfy the demand for beef in the USA. It takes 55 square feet (5 square metres) of forest clearance to provide enough grazing to make a single hamburger. This is why many parents in the USA refuse to buy 'forest beef'. Corned beef from previously forested areas of Brazil is still sold widely in the UK. Marks and Spencer plc is one retail outlet that has taken great trouble to ensure that its corned beef does not come from the Amazon basin.

Public and commercial pressure can make a real difference to the rainforests. In 1987 Burger King, one of the largest fast food chains in the USA, stopped its purchase of 70,000 carcasses of beef a year from Costa Rica after pressure from the Rainforest Action Network.

THE ORGANIC CHOICE
ORGANIC FARMING

Organic foods are produced by farmers using largely traditional methods of cultivation. Designed to preserve the natural ecosystems, these strengthen the plants, obviating the need for pesticides and maintaining or improving soil fertility. Organic foods are grown without modern synthetic agrochemicals: fertilizers, pesticides (including organochlorine and organophosphorus compounds), fungicides, soil fumigants and herbicides.

A report of a five-year study of 14 organic farms in the USA, recently published by the US National Academy of Sciences, stated: 'Well-managed alternative farms use less synthetic chemicals, fertilizers, pesticides and antibiotics, without necessarily decreasing and, in some cases, increasing, per-acre crop yields and the productivity of livestock systems... wider adoption of proven alternative systems would result in ever greater economic benefits to farmers and environmental gains for the nation'. The US Department of Agriculture welcomed the report's findings and a representative stated that his department would endeavour to 'put US farming on an eco-sensitive basis'. Yields from organic farms tend to be less, yet one farm in the study achieved corn yields 32 per cent higher than the local average and soya bean yields 40 per cent higher. The farmers can sell organic produce at relatively higher prices.

The US Fertilizer Institute denounced the report as 'an insult to American agriculture and to the consumer'. And the UK Ministry of Agriculture, Fisheries and Food estimates that without pesticides, some 30 per cent of world crops would be lost before harvest. Nevertheless, in view of the many disadvantages and, indeed, failures, of chemical-dominated intensive farming, it would seem that further experimentation with organic farming methods can only benefit the environment of the developed countries and the public health of their populations. Research is also needed to investigate whether the principles of organic farming might be of more use than agrochemical-based principles to those developing countries investigating ways of increasing yields.

Organic farming methods include mixed planting (sowing a variety of crops rather than devoting large acreages to one crop) and non-chemical methods to control pests, such as introducing natural predators, to keep them at tolerable levels. Organic farmers use natural fertilizers, such as raked-in crops of buckwheat, red clover or grazing rye, seaweed, mineral salts and manure. These replenish valuable soil bacteria and fungi, which help crops absorb nutrients from the soil, and create humus, which encourages worms.

They improve the soil in other ways – by growing grass, clover and deep-rooted crops, such as alfalfa, burnet, chicory and rib grass. Ploughed-in grass creates humus, a crumbly material which improves the structure of topsoil, improves drainage in wet soil, improves water-holding qualities in dry weather and makes soil less liable to erosion or hardening. Clover fertilizes the soil by extracting nitrogen from the air and concentrating it in nodules on its roots. Deep-rooted crops bring up trace elements (minerals useful to plants, and to their human consumers) from the subsoil. Organic farmers rotate crops and protect the soil from erosion, a problem suffered by many large-scale, chemical-based farms, by planting hedges or trees as wind barriers; by mulching (protecting the soil against drying out by spreading a layer of organic material on top of it); by not burning off stubble; and by turning the soil over as little as possible. They probably grow more varieties of a crop, which helps protect it from being wiped out by disease.

BUYING ORGANIC PRODUCE

A product can usually be labelled 'organic' only if no agrochemicals have been used on the land on which it was grown or grazed for at least two years. Organic farming does not damage the environment or the habitats of the local wildlife.

Organic foods may not look perfect: they are sometimes blemished, misshapen and relatively small, but you know they are free from agrochemical residues and that the land they come from is well cared for. They also taste good and they may contain more trace elements essential for health. In a sense, by eating organic food, you have more control over what your family eats. In the UK at present organic farms account for less than 1 per cent of arable land and organic produce represents only 1 per cent of total sales. In the USA fewer than 5 per cent of farmers use organic methods. Nevertheless, in 1989 five supermarket chains in the USA and Canada pledged to stop selling all fresh fruit and vegetables sprayed with carcinogenic chemicals. In West Germany, where there is a more established interest in organic food, the sales are about 10 per cent. The aim of the Soil Association in the UK is that 20 per cent of agriculture should be organic by the end of the millennium.

In the UK, organic produce is usually relatively expensive. This is not the fault of the organic farmers, who unfortunately do not receive the government subsidies enjoyed by chemical farmers. Most organic produce is imported. Demand outstrips supply and 75 per cent is sold in supermarkets. Try to find a local source of cheaper organic produce, such as a market stallholder or a Women's Institute stallholder from whom you can buy directly, thus cutting out distribution costs. The UK Soil Association (*see page 183* **Consumer Guide**) has a list of organic suppliers. On the East Coast of the USA the supermarket chain, Bread and Circus, caters for an organic market. These examples indicate that years of experimentation mean that organic methods of farming now offer a practical and economically viable alternative to intensive chemical farming. Perhaps what farmers now need are financial incentives from government to make the transition from chemical to organic farming.

MEAT

Organic farmers produce meat, eggs, milk and fish from animals reared humanely, without the drugs and other devices used in intensive farming by farmers and vets on factory farms (*see page 119* **Factory Farming**). They give their animals enough daylight and space to move; allow them to exercise every day; give them clean water; keep them on suitable land; move them to new grazing regularly to avoid the build-up of parasitic worms on the land; substitute potentially dangerous pesticides with harmless ones; do not mutilate them; avoid inhumane transport; and use alternative remedies instead of drugs whenever they can.

Pigs are not kept in intensive systems on organic farms. They are not tethered or 'constant-crated' (housed in a cage in which they cannot turn around). There is no tail-cutting or castration of piglets. They are kept outside to allow rooting (digging for food), or in a light place bedded in straw for comfort. Calves and lambs are suckled naturally and calves are kept outdoors except in very cold weather. There is no market trading of young calves. Poultry are kept at free-range outdoors, not reared in batteries or barns, their wings are not clipped and they are not otherwise mutilated. Abattoirs are carefully monitored.

Because of these methods the animals live in far better conditions and their meat tastes better. It is interesting that the fat in organically farmed meat contains relatively more unsaturated fatty acids than the fat in meat farmed intensively. Animals farmed intensively are fatter because of the type of food they are given and because they have little exercise. Organic meat is currently more expensive than meat from animals reared by intensive farming methods; in one UK supermarket chain its price is one-third higher. Fish, venison and game birds can be farmed in humane ways, using methods which are not based on cramped conditions and the routine use of drugs. The diet is similar to that available in the wild.

EGGS

Free-range, or organically farmed, eggs have naturally yellow yolks, due to the varied diet the hens get from scratching in the ground. Battery egg yolks are coloured a deep yellow by an additive in chicken feed. (*See also page 120* **Salmonella**.)

RAW MILK

Fresh, raw, unpasteurized milk is called 'green top' milk in the UK because it has a green foil cap, but not all 'green-top' milk comes from organic farms. Some people object to the routine pasteurization of milk (heating in order to sterilize) on the grounds that it alters the taste and the nature of the constituents. The alteration (denaturing) of fats gives pasteurized milk its particular taste.

Raw milk contains vitamin B2 (riboflavin), the amino acid lysine and certain digestive enzymes and friendly bacteria, none of which are present in pasteurized milk. There is also a 10 per cent loss of vitamins B1, B6, B12 and folic acid, and a 25 per cent loss of vitamin C, when raw milk is pasteurized.

Although it is unlikely to occur in clean dairies, bacterial contamination can be a hazard in unpasteurized milk, so buy yours from a dairy with high standards of hygiene and a herd known to be free from tuberculosis and brucellosis (the label will state that it is 'TT accredited'). Some of the royal family in the UK drink freshly collected, unpasteurized milk from well run, clean organic farms with TB and brucellin-tested cows. Government legislation in the UK will make it necessary from April 1991 for raw milk to carry a label warning that harmful bacteria might be present. Yet many other foods are greater potential causes of health problems. The answer to bacterial contamination is not to ban raw milk – as was recently proposed in the UK – but to monitor its bacterial count better and more often. The introduction in the UK of a bonus incentive scheme for milk of low bacterial counts produced an unprecedented response from dairy farmers, most of whom are now producing clean milk.

There are currently about 2,000 producers of unpasteurized milk in the UK and they have a reputation for producing the cleanest, best-tasting milk in the country. Raw milk from cows, goats or sheep is widely drunk in Africa and India, where there is only a very low incidence of heart attacks, although TB is endemic in those countries. The point has been made that it was only after the mass pasteurization of milk in the UK from around 1922 that the heart attack rate soared. Research is currently in progress in Japan to establish a link, if any. Research suggests that atopic milk allergy (causing asthma, eczema and hay fever) is less likely if you drink raw milk than if you drink pasteurized milk. Raw milk is also given as part of dietary treatment to cancer patients in Switzerland.

RETAILERS

Major retailers in the UK are now gradually going green and taking an interest in supplying organic food. Safeway and Sainsbury led the field but Tesco, Gateway, Asda, Marks and Spencer plc and the Co-op are following suit. If you cannot get organic food locally, lobby your local supermarket manager and talk to the owners of local shops and market stalls. Retailers soon respond to demand. In the meantime, wash or scrub fruit and vegetables as well as you can to remove surface traces of pesticides. Remove the outer leaves of leafy vegetables. Nine out of ten lettuces have been sprayed and residues tend to be concentrated in the outer leaves.

AGROCHEMICALS

The registration and use of agrochemicals are controlled by statutory bodies. Yet every so often another agrochemical is withdrawn from the market amid fears that it could be harmful to health if residual traces in foods are consumed repeatedly over long periods. Almost 40 per cent of pesticides have been linked by published research to one or more adverse effects.

The most vulnerable to this danger are thought to be pregnant women, the very young, the ill and the unduly sensitive. Recently, for example, the insecticide, cyhexatin, and a herbicide, dinoseb, were banned in the UK, suspected of causing birth defects.

Traces of DDT have been found in foods such as cabbages and Brussels sprouts, even though DDT was officially withdrawn from use in the UK in October 1984. Chinese rabbits and some lambs in New Zealand have recently been found to be contaminated. Exportation of lambs at risk from DDT contamination has been halted.

It has been estimated that in the Third World some 10,000 agricultural workers die each year as a result of the improper use of such pesticides. Many are illiterate and cannot read a label; others do not realize the need for protective masks and clothing, even if they could get them. A Canadian Federal study of 70,000 farmers in Saskatchewan in 1989 found that those using the herbicide 2,4-D were more likely to die from lymphoma (a cancer of the lymphatic system). A study of children with a particular type of leukaemia (acute non-lymphoblastic) published in the same year found that people who use pesticides at work may put their unborn children at risk of developing this disease. Agrochemicals can be overused, by mixing, by spraying too near the harvest date, or simply by inadvertent repeated spraying of one piece of land. Much tighter control of the application of pesticides is needed in most countries.

Consumer and environmental groups, such as the Natural Resources Defense Council in the USA and Parents for Safe Food, the Pesticides Trust, the London Food Commission and Friends of the Earth in the UK, have begun publicizing the fast-growing use of potentially dangerous agrochemicals on food crops. They have been successful in securing the withdrawal of daminozide (trade name Alar), the ripening spray used on apples and some other fruit which is suspected of producing a potentially carcinogenic by-product (UDMH) when apples are cooked, processed or juiced. This by-product was discovered to be 240 times as toxic as the level set for Alar by the Environment Protection Agency in the USA.

But the chemicals paraquat, 2,4,5-T, lindane and dieldrin are still used in the UK, even though they are banned or severely restricted in countries such as the USA, Sweden, Denmark and West Germany. The herbicide 2,4,5-T is contaminated with dioxin (*see page 79*). In the past few years residues of lindane have been found in peanut butter, infant formula, processed infant food based on cereal, meat, dairy and fish ingredients, lamb, pork, chicken, eggs, milk, cheese, cream, artichokes, aubergines, cabbage, celery, lettuce, beans grapes and herbal teas. Lindane has been identified by the US Environmental Protection Agency as a carcinogen and it can damage nerve tissue in young children. Dieldrin residues have been found in infant food based on meat, dairy and fish ingredients, beef products, chicken, milk, cheese, cream and cherries.

Agrochemicals sprayed on to soil, on to growing or harvested produce and into transport containers do not always disappear from food or break down before it is eaten. Pesticide residues in food have been suspected of causing cancer and food allergy. Tests on animals support this hypothesis, but direct links in humans are harder to establish.

The effects of long-term consumption of pesticides are not clear, as the research is difficult to carry out. One method is to use experimental animals to find out to what level of the chemical they can be exposed daily with no observable effect. This is known as the 'no effect' level. The 'acceptable daily limit' for humans is worked out from this and is at least 100 times less. It is an estimate of the levels to which humans can be exposed every day of their lives without any significant effect resulting. The Maximum Residue Level (MRL) is a figure legally set down for a wide range of pesticides in the UK. It is an offence for pesticide residues in food to exceed these levels. The EC is trying to harmonize MRLs on as many as possible.

Official sources say that 97 to 99 per cent of all vegetables and fruits in the UK are sprayed with a pesticide. Pesticide residues have been found in virtually all types of food, including fruit, vegetables, meat, bread, grain products, pulses, nuts and honey. In the UK, surveys by the Association of Public Analysts have shown that nearly a third of all cereals, fruit, vegetables and meat contain pesticide residues. One per cent of these foods contain residues in excess of the official limit.

Lemons are often coated with fungicide and wax to prevent deterioration and improve appearance. Buy unwaxed lemons from Tesco or Safeway in the UK, or discard the peel.

Pesticides and fungicides are used on both growing and stored grain. In 1987, 11 out of 12 wholemeal infant rusks contained pesticide residues. The levels, however, were nearly all within official safety limits. One recent study found that seven out of ten loaves contained organophosphate pesticide residues and one in ten contained residues of more than one pesticide.

Food imported into the UK usually contains higher levels of residues than are found in home-grown food. These residues are impossible to measure accurately because they become bonded with the grain. Only a fraction of permitted pesticides are tested for at present.

The British Agrochemicals Association points out that when pesticide residues are present in food they occur on average at a level about 10,000 times less than the pesticides produced naturally by the food crop as a prevention against or in response to pests. However, the Association of Public Analysts in the UK reported in 1985 that artificial pesticide residue levels in 1.3 per cent of foods analyzed exceeded the official maximum. Tests by Friends of the Earth and Parents For Safe Food found levels of breakdown products of some fungicides higher than the maximum limits recommended by the World Health Organization in apples, pears, carrots, potatoes and tomato-derived products.

The US Environmental Protection Agency has warned that the breakdown products of certain agricultural fungicides (including maneb, mancozeb and zineb) remaining in our food could be associated with cancer. These fungicides are sprayed on to crops such as potatoes, lettuce, pears, tomatoes, blackcurrants and apples, to stop them going mouldy. The biggest risk is said to be from foods heated during processing, such as apple juice and tomato ketchup, juice and paste. It is important not to forget that toxins from untreated fungus allowed to grow in food before or after harvesting can be dangerous too.

The agrochemical tecnazene is used to stop potatoes sprouting. Even organic potatoes are treated. The UK's recommended safe dose guidelines exceed those of the World Health Organization by three times. The UK Department of Agriculture claims the WHO guidelines are inaccurate and that UK standards (five parts per million) are indeed safe. There is a question mark over whether tecnazene can cause cancer and there is some evidence that it can cause allergic reactions.

Experts say that there is little evidence that the proper use of agrochemicals is bad for the health of most consumers in the UK. All 300 pesticides used in the UK have been officially approved, although not all have been fully tested for safety. The eight major supermarket chains in the UK do their own residue-testing on produce sold. The basic government message is that agrochemical use is under control and that the levels of residue found in our food are not dangerous. However, some pressure groups are lobbying for the suspension of many of these chemicals until they are proven safe, and for the elimination of unnecessary and possibly dangerous agrochemicals in children's food.

One major manufacturer of processed baby food, H.J. Heinz Co. Ltd., has stated

THE DIRTY DOZEN

Modern farming methods are currently under the public microscope. Reports of high levels of agrochemical usage have fuelled concern over food safety. The Pesticide Action Network International, organized by a coalition of citizens' groups around the world, has targeted 12 of the most dangerous agrochemicals and is pressing for international regulatory action. This 'dirty dozen' comprises: the pesticides DDT, lindane (gamma benzene hexachloride), dieldrin, aldrin and endrin, chlordane/heptachlor, pentachlorophenol, campheclor, parathion, ethylene dibromide and chlordimeform; the herbicides paraquat and 2,4,5-T. These chemicals have been banned by many countries as unsafe; yet they are still being widely sold and used in many developing countries because of irresponsible marketing.

its intention not to use any ingredients treated with certain pesticides.

Plants encouraged by artificial fertilizers to grow too big too soon are more susceptible to viral, bacterial and fungal diseases. They are more attractive to insects because they are big and succulent. The chemical farmer uses yet more agrochemicals to treat diseased crops. Similarly, expensive fertilizer becomes increasingly essential to maintain yields from heavily cropped farmland which is never allowed to recover, becoming depleted of humus, soil bacteria and minerals. Pests such as insects gradually become resistant to pesticides. According to Vandana Shiva, Director of the Research Foundation for Science, Technology and Natural Resource Policy in Dehradun, India, 'Pesticides, far from controlling pests, are actually prescriptions for fostering them'.

Farmers are encouraged by the sales representatives of the big agrochemical companies to buy their products. Sales by the British Agrochemicals Industry in 1989 totalled over £1,088 million, of which herbicides represented half and fungicides a quarter. Agrochemicals account for up to four-fifths of the cost of growing wheat. Some oil-based fertilizers are not only expensive but also a drain on the world's oil reserves. In the UK over 1 per cent of total energy consumption goes into their manufacture.

Agrochemicals endanger the life and health of many species of wildlife (such as otters and some varieties of birds and butterflies), of domestic pets which stray on to recently sprayed farmland (*see page 134*), and of people, since they can enter the human body through breathing, through the skin and through food. In India, the use of pesticides has destroyed many of the fish which formerly lived in paddy fields and which contributed to the workers' diets. There is no acceptable way of determining safe levels in foods because some people, especially young children, are more vulnerable than others; and because combinations of these chemicals or their breakdown

products may have very different effects from contamination with a single chemical.

It seems to me that the use of pesticides creates more problems than it set out to solve. Parents and other consumers need to press for much more control of pesticide registration, application and monitoring food for traces; for subsidies to be in favour of organic farming, not agrochemical-based farming; and for the wider availability of organic food. All consumer protection costs should be borne by the manufacturers of pesticides.

FACTORY FARMING

The main motives of the factory farmer are high production and profit. Cramped and unnatural conditions for livestock are coupled with the routine use of drugs to prevent the diseases inherent in poor living conditions and to increase yield. Although official committees of experts police the registration and use of these drugs, many are not routinely assayed in food because tests are too expensive and time-consuming. Occasionally, drugs used for years are withdrawn because of new fears about their safety to human consumers. In 1986, for example, the EC banned all hormone growth promoters. In 1988 it called for an international ban. There is concern that hormones are being given to animals illegally and that we continue to eat meat from countries where such hormones have not yet been banned. American beef is banned in the UK because of the use of growth hormones in the USA.

One hormone growth promoter, bovine somatotrophin (BST), has managed to slip through the EC ban. It is currently being tested secretly throughout Europe as a milk booster, increasing milk yield by up to one-fifth in three out of five cows. In Austria a plant for its large-scale production is already in action. The aim of using BST is to produce more milk from fewer cows, keeping production the same but making it cheaper. The use of BST would bring down the price of milk, but it would necessitate the continuous veterinary monitoring of cows and the use of computer management to control the fine balance between the amounts of growth hormone given, food eaten and milk produced by each cow. The US Congress has estimated that if BST were authorized, only farms with herds of more than 50 cows could keep going. This would put a third of dairy farmers out of business. In Europe, one in two dairy farms might be in a similar economic situation.

There are many reasons why there is a public outcry over BST. The public has become cynical over the use of drugs and other chemicals anywhere in the chain of food production. Drug company arguments that any BST in milk is destroyed by enzymes in the human gut are viewed with suspicion by some people. Not all peptide hormones are destroyed in this way and some people produce only very small amounts of these gut enzymes. It is feared that the nutritional content of milk will be altered by BST, leading, for instance, to lower levels of protein and orotic acid and to a higher fat content. There are also concerns over the safety of the biotechnology used in production and the welfare of the cows (fortnightly injections, increased embryo loss, lowered immunity, more mastitis, more lameness and loss of condition). The EC has called for a delay while more safety studies are undertaken before deciding to ban or approve BST.

UK farmers were recently cautioned against giving certain antibiotic sulpha drugs too near slaughter. One such drug had been associated with cancer in laboratory rats and mice. One in ten pig kidneys tested had levels above the maximum acceptable limit.

The pesticides from sheep dip can enter meat. Dipping to prevent scab (caused by mites) is compulsory in some countries, yet is not necessarily effective, and it is cruel.

SALMONELLA

Many herds of animals have been exposed to numerous antibiotics for such a long time that disease-producing micro-organisms are becoming resistant to treatment. Recently, for instance, experts recognized that salmonella infection is outwitting their attempts to keep it at bay in poultry and eggs. There is now thought to be a growing threat to the prevention and treatment of salmonella infections in humans, because of antibiotic resistance in these bacteria which has developed through the overuse of antibiotics in livestock. Salmonella is even more likely to occur in the crowded and inhumane conditions in which many poultry are kept. Such conditions mean that the farmer makes more money in spite of the high loss of animals due to disease and the high cost of providing veterinary treatment for infections and other problems. In the UK, measures to protect the consumer from salmonella in poultry and eggs include killing infected birds, banning egg sales from infected flocks and imposing much tighter controls over their feed.

Factory farmers attempting to reduce gut infections caused by unhealthy living conditions and the over-use of antibiotics are now turning to supplements of probiotics. These mixtures of friendly bowel bacteria replicate the normal balance of micro-organisms in the gut and promote the growth of normal bowel micro-organisms.

'MAD COW' DISEASE

This unpleasant condition (also called bovine spongiform encephalopathy or BSE), thought to be passed on by an abnormal form of cell protein called prion protein, is a fatal disease which causes the nerves to degenerate. It is similar to scrapie in sheep and to Creutzfeldt-Jakob dementia in humans (a speedily progressive disease in which the brain is eaten away and becomes spongey in appearance). It is believed that the practice, introduced only a few years ago, of allowing meat products to be put into feed for cows – which are herbivorous animals – may be responsible for the outbreak of the disease. Mad cow disease has an incubation period of many years. So far it has occurred only in the UK and in the Republic of Ireland, there are currently 400 new cases a week and half the herds in the UK are affected. In 1990 several countries banned the import of British beef, including West Germany, the USA and US military bases in the UK.

The question is whether humans who eat beef might be affected in any way. The answer is unknown and difficult to ascertain, but most experts believe it unlikely. (It is known that vegetarians and people living in countries unvisited by mad cow disease can contract Creutzfeldt-Jakob dementia.)

In 1988 the feeding of animal protein to cattle was banned and soya beans and fish meal were substituted as a food supplement to promote milk yield. Infected cows were ordered to be slaughtered and burned; the sale of milk from herds with infected cows was banned; and the sale of certain beef offal for human consumption was also prohibited. However, infected carcasses are still fed to pigs and poultry, and calves are still delivered from infected cows prior to slaughter, although no-one knows yet whether the disease can be passed from cow to cow or from cow to unborn calf. Nor do we know whether the BSE agent is present in the milk and milk products (such as infant formula) of infected cows, including the cows incubating the disease.

Clearly, it is essential to devise a test for infection in cows before they develop any evidence of illness. Until more is known about this disease it is advisable to buy meat from animals raised on BSE-free organic farms. Sausages, meat pies and pâtés may be better avoided unless the meat is known to come from unaffected herds.

WHAT IS SAFE TO EAT?

It would not be surprising if you were to think that nothing is safe, given the amount of publicity and scaremongering over food controversies in the popular press. But life goes on and so does the public's determination to know exactly what is put into food and water and not to be controlled or manipulated for the sake of profit or power. Because food and water are basic to life, not only are they precious but in a sense they are sacred as well. Fear, anxiety, anger and protectiveness about the condition of our food are understandable. Food adulteration and pollution are not new problems. They usually result from laziness, greed or an attempt to make food stretch further, last longer or look fresher and more appetizing.

The veiled public mistrust of official food and farming regulatory bodies stems partly from previous abuses of trust throughout the world. Official bodies, like academic bodies, are inevitably subject to economic and commercial pressure. A tendency has been to allow food adulteration to continue until the practice is proven dangerous, instead of demanding that it be verified safe before its application. People want more openness and public accountability from the official bodies empowered to protect them and this is beginning to happen. In the UK, for example, the Ministry of Agriculture, Fisheries and Food (MAFF) stated 'As much information as is practicable is made available as promptly as possible to demonstrate the extent of consumer protection available through food surveillance'. MAFF has working parties on many aspects of food contamination, from food additives to naturally occurring toxicants in food, all of them in communication with a central steering group on food surveillance.

COOKING LEAVES THE KITCHEN

Modern ovens are better than ever, yet people do less cooking and food preparation. The average number of meals cooked in a British household today is two-thirds of the number cooked 50 years ago. This is a remarkably speedy decrease in terms of social change. Instead, more people eat out, buy a takeaway or have a ready-prepared meal from the supermarket. This is partly because our lives are so busy and we have grown accustomed to the ease of other people processing food for us.

Working mothers and fathers have little time to spend cleaning, preparing and cooking food for the family. It is far easier to open a tin and heat the contents or to pop a frozen ready-prepared meal into the microwave oven or cooker.

We have distanced ourselves from our food by abdicating responsibility for much of its preparation. We may save time but we lose control over what we eat and become alienated from our food. More insidiously, we distance ourselves from whoever is growing and preparing our food. We also lose touch with our environment. Food manufacturers come between us and our food in much the same way that bottles come between formula-fed babies and the milk in their mothers' breasts.

Preparing fruit, vegetables, grains, meat and fish connects us with the earth, sun, rain, sky, wind, trees, fields and animals. Our awareness of our reliance on the living flora and fauna of this planet is heightened. We can enjoy the colours, shapes and textures of the various foods as we prepare them. Convenience foods are here to stay, however, and routine food preparation and cooking are things of the past in the daily lives of many families.

Children who grow up eating convenience foods have less opportunity to learn about the environment through the experience of watching parents preparing food at home. The compromise between wanting the ease and speed of commercially processed food and the satisfaction and other benefits of home-prepared food, is to use convenience food only when necessary and to take a positive delight in home food preparation when we can.

HOME-GROWN FOOD

Perhaps, you might argue, it would be even better if we all grew our own food. It is an interesting proposal. Many people enjoy growing their own food crops in a kitchen garden, an allotment, or in tubs, pots and window boxes. However, many of us prefer to do other things with our time and few have enough land to be self-sufficient. In many parts of the East the idea would be laughable because of the size of the population relative to the land available. In developed countries hunting and fishing for food are becoming almost impossible for ordinary people and even rural families are unlikely to have their own livestock.

Things are different in the rural areas of many developing countries, where families are much more likely to rely on valuable domestic livestock as a meaningful contribution to their diet.

PROCESSED FOOD

Food that has been commercially processed is popular but usually expensive, because you pay not only for all the ingredients but also for their processing, packaging, storage, transportation, advertising and marketing. The food industry in the UK spends £4.5 million a year on advertising to persuade people to buy their products. Baby food is an important part of the market. The average baby eats £200 worth of tinned, bottled or packeted food each year.

PACKAGING

Some methods of packaging are greener than others. In the UK 1 in 50 samples of canned food was recently found to contain more than the recommended amount of tin. Tin can cause irritation of the stomach lining. Exposure to the air of an opened can allows metal to leach into the food, especially if the food is acidic, such as some fruits and vegetables. Once a can is opened, transfer its contents to another container.

Fruit juice is sometimes packaged in cardboard cartons lined with aluminium or polychlorine, both of which could theoretically leach into the juice. Traces of dioxin and furan (*see page 79*) had migrated from plastic-coated, bleached paper cartons into milk in nearly half the samples tested in the USA. Meat, poultry, egg and fast food containers should be produced without the use of CFCs (*see pages 185–187* **Glossary**).

Packaging should be biodegradable, should not waste precious natural resources and should not harm the food or the consumer's health. If possible, choose food as free from packaging as possible. The UK supermarket chains, Tesco, Safeway and J. Sainsbury, have shown a commitment to the environment. Sainsbury's stores, for example, recently introduced low-CFC polystyrene trays for meat. They return cardboard packaging to be recycled and are experimenting to see whether it makes sense to collect old plastic packaging materials and recycle them into carry-out bags. Both J. Sainsbury and Safeway went green before it became fashionable to do so. When you go shopping, take a strong basket or bag with you rather than use yet another new plastic carrier bag. Even those plastic bags that are bio- or photodegradable (that is, will break down due to the action of bacteria or light) and said to rot do so only very slowly.

If you buy packs of cans linked by plastic ring-pulls, be sure to cut up the ring-pulls before discarding them, because animals have been known to eat them or get caught up in them. Only photodegradable ring-pulls will be legally permitted in the USA from 1991.

Environment-responsible labelling is potentially a great help to the shopper if it informs the shopper accurately and does not merely help the manufacturer sell more goods. The labelling of organic food is particularly difficult because of the lack of an agreed definition of organic farming.

PROCESSING FOOD

Food manufacturers make certain demands of farmers in terms of yield and appearance which tend to favour agrochemical-based farming. Once they have the raw materials they use a mixture of familiar domestic techniques (on a factory scale) and additional unfamiliar ones to make the food look, taste or feel better, go further for the money or have a longer shelf life both in the retail outlet and in the home. Transporting food to shops is cheapest if done infrequently and in bulk. One feature common to many processed foods is their overemphasis on animal or hydrogenated vegetable fat, sugar, white flour and additives. Some provide little in the way of real nourishment and are known as 'junk' foods. They tend to be high in empty calories and the fats have usually been processed in a way which means they lose their essential fatty acids (*see pages 185–187* **Glossary**).

REFINING

The refining of natural foods is one of the most worrying aspects of commercial food processing from a green point of view. Refined white flour, for instance, is devoid of the outer layers of the grain and is used in a wide variety of processed foods, including the obvious (bread, cakes, breakfast cereal, pastry and biscuits) and the less apparent (soups, sauces, desserts, coating for fish fingers, and so on). There are important health benefits from eating the whole of the grain because fibre, vitamins and minerals are lost in the refining process. In the UK, four token nutrients are added to refined white flour: calcium, two B vitamins and an iron compound. Vitamin E is lost during refining and is not returned; nor is fibre. It is unlikely that these token additions perform as well in the body as the removed natural nutrients. Preservatives and bleach are added to white flour during processing. Pesticide residues may be present in flour of any colour and are present in higher amounts in wholegrains and products made from them. Green parents should study labels carefully and choose wholegrain (and preferably organic) bread and flour. Foods made with refined white or brown flour and white sugar are best reserved for occasional use. When natural sugar is refined it loses B vitamins and trace elements such as zinc, manganese, chromium, selenium and cobalt.

ADDITIVES

Food additives are used to aid the manufacturing process. They often replace spices, fruits and other ingredients that might vary in quality from crop to crop, be unavailable or expensive, or deteriorate during processing and storage. They are also used to enhance the taste, texture, colour and general appearance of food. The banning of additives varies from one country to another. For instance, 50 food colourants are permitted in the UK, 19 in Norway, 31 in Sweden and 32 in Austria. In the UK levels of food colourants must be below the maximum permitted level. Some additives have been shown to provoke asthma and urticaria (nettle-rash) in some children. One in three colourants permitted in the UK provokes symptoms of intolerance in susceptible people. Azo dyes are present in a surprising number of processed foods.

The additives that are most commonly implicated in causing adverse reactions are: the azo dyes, particularly tartrazine (E102), sunset yellow (E110), carmoisine (E122) and amaranth (E123). Amaranth has been banned in the USA since 1976. A study carried out in the UK in 1990 showed that these colours could also lead to hyperactivity in a small percentage of children, possibly because they have a specific inability to handle these substances. Tartrazine has been shown to reduce zinc levels in all children, but more so in those who are hyperactive.

Some processed foods are little more than a cocktail of additives and empty calories in the form of white flour, white sugar and processed fat devoid of essential fatty acids. On average we eat about ten grams (about one-third of an ounce) of additives a day, more than the average consumption of many foods, such as fresh oranges. In the UK most low-calorie soft drinks are sweetened with aspartame or saccharin. One can might contain the equivalent of four tablets of saccharin. The World Health Organization recommends a daily intake of no more than 12 tablets of saccharin per day for an adult weighing 9 stone 8 ounces (60 kilograms). You can imagine that a child drinking several cans a day will easily exceed this limit, with possible ill-effects.

> ## BUYING WISELY
>
> From time to time most parents want to buy foods that happen to contain additives. Choose wisely by following these guidelines:
>
> - Read labels.
>
> - Choose brands with the fewest additives.
>
> - Follow storage advice on packets.
>
> - Avoid the more suspect additives: the azo dyes, preservatives E210, E211, E220, E250 and E251, antioxidants E320 and E321 and the flavour enhancer 621.

FOOD SAFETY

The food we give our children helps determine the internal environment of their gut. The number of cases of gastro-enteritis (infective diarrhoea) and food-poisoning from infected food is increasing. Among those most at risk are children. Additive-free food goes off sooner, so needs to be stored more carefully and eaten more quickly than food containing preservatives. Recently there has been much publicity over the listeria infection often found in foods such as cook-chill ready meals, soft ice-cream sold from vans, soft cheeses, meat and prepared salads. However, whether the infection is from listeria, salmonella, staphylococci or other microorganisms, careful and hygienic food preparation can help prevent trouble. If you have a microwave oven, follow the instructions carefully to avoid cold spots in the food.

IRRADIATION

As I write, food irradiation is legal in 34 countries, including the USA, the UK and most of Europe. Potatoes are irradiated to prevent sprouting in virtually every country in the world; Denmark irradiates herbs and spices so as to avoid fumigating them with

continued on page 126

FOOD IRRADIATION

● destroys most contaminating micro-organisms. However, the few that are left multiply faster because the resistance of the food to bacteria and moulds is lowered by irradiation.

● destroys naturally occurring commensal or 'friendly' micro-organisms. The reduced populations cannot build up quickly enough afterwards to counter the spread of the 'baddies'.

● makes food fail to give a bad smell when 'off'. The characteristic smell of infected food (often caused by micro-organisms other than the infecting ones) may not develop unless both the 'baddies' and the 'goodies' multiply after irradiation, so removing an important, natural early warning.

● can produce mutant micro-organisms which might be more infective than the original ones.

● fails to destroy toxins already produced by micro-organisms such as clostridia, or by fungal spores.

● kills insect pests, such as weevils.

● lowers the levels of vitamins B1 and C substantially; A and E less so; and of enzymes and essential fatty acids. Some doctors say these losses are comparable with those in cooking. However, such losses will be combined when irradiated food is cooked. In a child whose diet is already compromised, perhaps through illness or lack of good food, these losses could be important. No-one could remain healthy on a diet of irradiated foods.

● prolongs shelf life. However, during storage there is a further loss of vitamins.

● can change the flavour of food.

● can change the texture of the food.

This is most common in fruit and vegetables and results from chemical changes in the structure of their cellulose cell walls.

● causes chemical changes in certain constituents of food; the altered chemicals could be hazardous to health.

● causes chemical changes in PVC packaging material which could seep into the food and be a cancer risk.

● fools the purchaser, whether the wholesaler, the retailer or the consumer, until there is a good enough test available to detect whether food has been irradiated.

● makes foods radioactive. However, foods contain natural radioactivity. The extra radioactivity induced depends on the amount of radiation given but is much less than the amount already there. It tends to disappear quickly, often before consumption, because of the long-keeping qualities of irradiated food.

● stops potatoes from going green. However, it does not prevent potatoes from producing poisonous solanin in response to light.

● changes the nature of pesticide residues and additives in an as yet unknown way.

● causes lower growth rates and reduced immunity to disease in experimental animals. This may or may not be important for humans.

● produces free radicals (high-energy chemicals), whose effects on health are not as yet totally clear.

● happens twice if, for instance, irradiated ingredients are used to make convenience foods, which are then irradiated.

● can be illegally used to salvage bad food.

chemicals suspected of causing cancer; South Africa irradiates the widest range of produce of any country. Its use is currently the subject of international controversy. It bombards food with doses of ionizing gamma rays up to 50 million times the strength of chest X-rays Those who support the introduction of food irradiation believe that it will reduce not only the large number of cases of food-poisoning and gastro-enteritis spread by infected food, but also the amount of food lost through spoilage. Those opposed are concerned that it is unnecessary and that the health of the consumer might be adversely affected. Many people are bemused by the level of disagreement and consider it preferable to wait until fears are allayed before allowing food to be treated in this way.

There is no such thing as absolute safety. The majority of the world's scientists believe that food irradiation is safe enough to be allowed. It is already in limited use in many countries, including Canada, Israel, Italy, Spain, Denmark, South Africa, The Netherlands, Belgium, Hungary, Norway, the USA, Japan and the USSR.

Not all scientists are sure, however. The Australian government agreed in December 1989 to a three-year moratorium on food irradiation. The European Parliament voted in October 1989 to ban irradiation of food in the EC from the end of 1992, with the exception of dried herbs and spices. Sweden has banned it.

The World Health Organization's assertion that irradiation is safe seems somewhat suspicious because its report was produced jointly with the Food and Agriculture Organization and the International Atomic Energy Association, both organizations having axes to grind.

The USA allows irradiation, but three states have banned it. McDonald's has joined H.J. Heinz, Ralston Purina, Borden Foods, Quaker Oats and Beatrice Hunt-Wesson in pledging not to sell irradiated foods in the USA.

A Consumer Association report published in the UK in November 1989 stated that one in three consumers think irradiation should not be permitted. The National Federation of Women's Institutes, the Institute of Environmental Health Officers, the Guild of Food Writers and the National Federation of Meat Traders are against food irradiation. Only one major supermarket chain, J Sainsbury, has decided to sell irradiated food.

The labelling of irradiated food is not the whole answer to the question of consumer choice. It would be extremely difficult, for instance, to police unpackaged food, such as fruit and vegetables sold in markets. Food served in restaurants would also manage to slip through such a safety net.

DRINKING WATER

Half the world is without enough clean water, which makes safe water one of the most important natural resources and the provision of a local water supply one of the most urgent problems facing developing countries. In developed countries water may be contaminated with lead, nitrates and agrochemicals. It may contain aluminium, chlorine and related chemicals, and fluoride, which are added with the aim of improving the health of the population.

Much of any deterioration in the quality of water takes place after the supply has reached the building, so green parents can take a number of steps towards ensuring safer drinking water. Clean cold water tanks regularly. Replace old lead piping with plastic, if possible, or use a water filter if this would be too expensive. Allow water to run from the tap for a few minutes if you have not drawn any off for several hours. Check the levels of pollutants in your water and use a filter if necessary. Press for further restrictions on the use of pesticides.

Choose your water filter according to the chemicals you wish to remove. You can use a cheap jug filter containing a cartridge of ion exchange resin and/or activated carbon, or you can fit a filter containing one or more of a variety of filtering devices to the cold water supply. Mains-fitted carbon-only *continued on page 128*

WATER POLLUTANTS & ADDITIVES

The provision of potable water in many countries has been one of the greatest triumphs of modern public health measures. However, there are some problems with drinking water in some areas, such as in the UK:

● **Water may contain too much lead** and a high lead intake is associated with various health problems. Lead leaches into water from old lead pipes in domestic plumbing (now illegal) and from solder used to connect pipes. Contamination is most prevalent in Scotland. The United States Environment Protection Agency suggests that lead may be hazardous at lower levels than has been thought.

● **Water may contain too much copper:** Do not drink hot water from copper pipes, more copper dissolves into hot water than cold.

● **Water may contain too many nitrates,** especially in areas of high fertilizer usage. Nitrates are suspected carcinogens, and can cause methaemoglobinaemia (blue baby syndrome), a rare condition in which blood cannot properly carry oxygen, though this is unlikely unless levels are double the EC maximum. The highest nitrate levels are in East Anglia and parts of the East and West Midlands.

● **Water may contain too much aluminium.** Some may be present naturally, but it is also added to make water clearer. A high aluminium intake has been linked with Alzheimer's disease (a pre-senile dementia and the commonest form of senile dementia). Areas in the UK with high natural aluminium are Northumberland, Tyne and Wear, Durham, Devon and Cornwall.

● **Water may contain traces of agrochemicals,** and their effects upon health are largely unknown. Agrochemical contamination of drinking water in some areas of the UK greatly exceeds EC standards. East Anglia, the East Midlands, London and the South East are most at risk.

● **Water may contain too many trihalomethanes,** a group of chemicals linked with cancer, present in proportion to the amount of chlorine used to disinfect water.

● **Water may contain fluoride.** Some experts claim that it has reduced the amount of dental decay in children; others say that levels have been falling in both fluoridated and non-fluoridated areas due to better nutrition. A study carried out in the nineteen-seventies linked fluoride with cancer, but has yet to be substantiated. Excessive fluoride can stain patches of developing teeth white.

filters are not allowed in France and Italy. Jug filters tend to remove only chlorine and larger lead particles, in spite of their claims. Keep filtered water in a cool place because the reduction in chlorine will otherwise allow bacteria to multiply. Do not use water filtered by ion-exchange for preparing a baby's bottles or feeds: the ion-exchange filter swaps calcium for sodium, too much of which can endanger kidney function. More expensive filters vary as to what they remove and some have a slow flow rate. Ask to see verification independently of the company's product claims, before parting with money.

Change the cartridge or filter at least as frequently as the manufacturers recommend. There are serious problems with bacterial growth in some filters, especially the carbon-only type.

FEELINGS ABOUT FOOD

Our emotional relationship with food is an important green issue. Children grow up learning from us how to relate to food because of the environment we make for them in our kitchen. The way people relate to food symbolizes the way they relate to love. Our ability to love both others and ourselves is shaped by our early childhood relationship with our mother and any other carers. As we accept, welcome and allow ourselves to be nourished, encouraged, affirmed and comforted by love, or as we yearn for, never have enough of, control, are controlled by, or reject love, so also do we relate to food. Overeating, bingeing, starving or self-induced vomiting are frequently examples of difficulties with love being symbolized by our relationship to food. Eating disorders are a powerful form of 'acting out' behaviour, a psychological term for the expression of a repressed wish or experience in one's behaviour.

Food and love are similar in many ways: we can store up certain bits of both; quality is more important than quantity and so, like the loaves and fishes, a little can become a lot; we need the right amounts at the right times; if we do not get either when we are

EATING GREEN

A 'green' lifestyle brings good food and mealtimes into the heart of family life. This means feeling better and being healthier. In the USA three out of four people die from disorders such as heart attacks, strokes and certain sorts of cancer, related to diets which are not green. Your children will probably eat the sorts of food you give them now when they grow up, because old habits die hard.

● Base your meals on fresh, whole, organically farmed foods (meat, fish, poultry, eggs, milk, grains, vegetables and fruit) whenever possible.

● Buy fewer commercially processed foods.

● Buy less meat.

● Choose foods wisely to provide a nutritious balance.

● Avoid too much of the wrong sorts of food. This is a waste of your family's health and money.

● Have a loving involvement in some part of the growing, preparation and serving of food if you can.

hungry the need apparently disappears, but we are left wanting; we can crave too much of the wrong sort; various factors can stop us absorbing either one; we can become deficient in either; too much of the wrong sort of love smothers us and too much of the wrong sort of food blocks up our arteries: one prevents the free flow of feelings, the other the free flow of blood.

No wonder that both food and love are such essential parts of a child's environment and therefore such important green issues. As we feed ourselves and our children in the kitchen at home, so do we powerfully demonstrate our feelings towards ourselves and towards them. This is a green issue which has not yet received sufficient attention.

WEANING

In the first five years of life, children gradually switch from a high-fat (50 per cent of food energy), low-fibre start on milk to the family food which, ideally, is high in fibre and relatively low in fat (35 per cent). This change is best done gradually because young children need more energy-dense fats than older children. Milk plays an important part in diet until well into the second year and probably beyond. If your baby is bottle-fed, change from infant formula to full-cream cow's milk at one year.

ENERGY FOODS

A good diet for a young child must provide enough calories for growth. When you start adding foods to your baby's diet, remember that home-prepared baby food is 'often more energy-dense than commercially processed food. Cereals and pulses are more energy-dense than fruit, except bananas. Some wholefoods provide bulk without sufficient calories, so avoid becoming 'muesli belt' parents, who insist that their children eat only wholefoods. Complex carbohydrate foods (such as bread, cereal, rice, pasta, potatoes and other starchy roots and fruits) are usually an important part of diet. Fat can be added to cereal foods to make them more energy-dense.

Encourage your children to eat little and often, a habit they will probably prefer anyway. In the USA this sort of eating is appropriately called 'grazing'. A child's appetite and taste change not only from day to day but also from one season to another. The green parent is sensitive to these changes, meets them in a common-sense way and seeks advice from an appropriate health professional as necessary.

EVERYDAY MEALS

Base everyday meals on foods processed at home to make them suitable for young children. In the UK £150 million a year is spent on commercially processed baby foods. It is much cheaper to make your own, although convenience can be an attraction. Ground rice, for example, is one-sixth of the cost when cooked at home as when bought as jars or cans of 'baby rice'.

Commercial foods intended for babies are free from unnecessary additives. Beware, however, of the high sugar content of some commercially processed infant foods, such as the herbal teas popular in Germany. Buy less refined white flour and sugar and fewer foods made with them (such as biscuits, buns, pastry, desserts, cakes and ice-cream), since refining removes nutrients. Once such foods were precious because they were available only during certain seasons and because of the labour involved in refining them. Then they were eaten only at feast times, but now they can be eaten every day. They are not intrinsically bad, but many families in developed countries eat too many. Paradoxically, many older children and adults are overnourished with calories from sweet, fatty, refined food, yet undernourished with essential nutrients. If children fill up with such foods between meals they may not want nutrient-dense foods at mealtimes. It is better to save refined feast food for out-of-the-ordinary occasions and to use white sugar as a flavouring, rather than as an essential ingredient.

The nutrients in a healthy diet (*see pages 52–53*) help protect you and your children from the effects of traces of pesticides and other environmental toxins. Such toxins can occur naturally. Cow's milk, for example, can be affected by the food cows eat. In Australia some years ago, many children developed goitre (swelling of the thyroid gland in the neck), which was eventually traced back to a particular weed of the brassica family on which a herd of cows had grazed. Peanuts and fruit can contain naturally occurring, poisonous mycotoxins (produced by moulds and other fungi).

THE GREEN GUT

The micro-organisms inside the gut vary with the type of food eaten. Bottle-fed babies, for instance, have different flora inside their gut from breast-fed babies. Formula milk alters the internal environment of the gut and favours the growth of certain micro-organisms associated with ill health. This is one reason why bottle-fed babies suffer from diarrhoea more frequently than breast-fed babies. A diet high in added sugar, white flour and meat, or low in essential nutrients, can also lead to a less healthy population of micro-organisms.

FRUIT AND VEGETABLES

Fresh fruits and vegetables contain plenty of trace elements, vitamins, enzymes, essential fatty acids and other important nutrients. Nuts and seeds are other good sources of nutrients for babies over one year, but grind them finely (to prevent choking) before giving them to a young child. Buy and use vegetables and fruits which are as fresh as possible. Lettuces stored in the fridge lose half their vitamin C in three days. Produce imported from abroad is likely to have been stored a long time, possibly irradiated and treated with more pesticides and fungicides en route.

Cook vegetables and fruits for as short a time as possible to avoid excessive vitamin loss. Steaming and stir-frying are good methods. Be creative with salads to make them attractive and try mixing raw and cooked fruit, vegetables, grains, sprouted seeds and pulses. Salads are nutrient-dense and retain their hormones and enzymes if fresh. Some people believe that raw food has an energy or vitality (the Chinese *ch'i*) that cooking destroys. You cannot make changes overnight but the more you eat green, the easier it is and the better you feel.

VEGETARIAN FOOD

More and more families are becoming vegetarian for health, religious, philosophical, economic, humanitarian and/or green reasons. They share their diet with much of the world's population. In the UK 1 in 30 adults and 1 in 10 teenagers are vegetarian. A further 1 in 12 adults eat no red meat. Vegetarians eat some combination of grains, vegetables (from land or sea), pulses, fruit, nuts, seeds, milk, cheese, yoghurt and eggs. Most vegetarians are lacto-ovo vegetarians: they eat every sort of food except meat, poultry and fish. Lacto-vegetarians eat everything except eggs, meat, poultry and fish. Total vegetarians, including vegans, eat no animal products. Some families are semi-vegetarian and eat everything except red meat.

Vegetarians tend to live longer and be healthier than meat-eaters. They experience less heart disease, high blood pressure, obesity, food-poisoning and cancer, and fewer stomach disorders. A total vegetarian diet should contain a mixture of proteins (*see page 131 under* **Combining proteins**). An ample intake of foods rich in vitamin C helps ensure that enough iron is absorbed from the diet. Some vegetarian children are given insufficient energy-dense foods, such as fat, and can go short of calories, calcium and vitamin D. If you have recently become a vegetarian, especially a total vegetarian, learn from more experienced vegetarians or from a knowledgeable health professional how to choose foods and put together meals to give your family a healthy diet. This is especially important when weaning your baby.

Parents who adhere to religions or philosophies which specify a particular diet (such as Jews, Hindus, Muslims, Sikhs and Buddhists) usually have access to nutritional knowledge and wisdom from older members. Some of the newer philosophies do not have centuries of nutritional wisdom behind them and young children can become malnourished. Zen macrobiotic, Rastafarian and fruitarian diets are not suitable for babies and young children.

Babies in vegetarian families may benefit from vitamin drops containing vitamins A, C and D, especially from the time when weaning begins. A potential but unlikely problem for vegetarian children is a diet which does not give enough energy, protein, iron and vitamin B12. If you wean your child on to a total vegetarian diet it is probably wise to supplement it with vitamin B12. If you are pregnant or breast-feeding and you are a total vegetarian, make sure your diet contains plenty of foods rich in calcium, iron and zinc. Supplements of calcium and vitamins B12 and D are an additional safeguard.

VITAMIN B12

The main sources of this vitamin in the vegetarian diet are milk, cheese and eggs. Boiling milk for any length of time destroys vitamin B12. The vitamin is present in smaller amounts in root vegetables (absorbed from bacteria in the soil), other vegetables (from bacteria), seaweed, yeast and yeast extract. It is sometimes present in beans, bean sprouts, peas, whole wheat, peanuts (groundnuts), sunflower seeds, lettuce, turnip greens and fermented soya bean foods. It is possible that the use of animal manure on farmland may increase the amount of vitamin B12 in produce. The vitamin is found in well water exposed to soil. Cooking destroys some of the vitamin. A lack of vitamin B12 with consequent anaemia in a total vegetarian diet is a theoretical but rare risk, although it is fairly common in some immigrant groups, such as people coming from India to live in the UK.

Recent research suggests that the micro-organisms living in the upper part of the gut (the upper small intestine) can manufacture vitamin B12 if conditions are right. A total vegetarian diet may promote such bacteria, especially if it contains seeds (suitable if crushed for babies over one year old) and sprouted seeds such as mung beans.

VITAMIN D

Vegetarian children may go short of this vitamin, especially in the winter months when they are not getting enough sunlight on their skin, although some vitamin D from the summer sun is stored by the body. In the UK, vegetable margarines and many processed cereals are fortified with vitamin D. Pregnant and breastfeeding vegetarian mothers need sunshine on their skin in addition to vitamin D supplements.

COMBINING PROTEINS

Proteins in food are made up of strings of amino acid molecules. Of the 22 amino acids only eight are essential to our diet. Animal proteins contain all of them; vegetable proteins are 'incomplete', because they do not contain a full complement. Each vegetable protein group has a different and incomplete mix of these essential amino acids. This is why complementary foods need to be mixed together in one meal to give children what their bodies need for growth, development and repair. The protein combination must be eaten at the same time because the body can only utilize all the essential amino acids if they are eaten together. Grains, for example, contain relatively little of the amino acids lysine and isoleucine, but plenty of methionine; whereas pulses, beans, peas and legumes (lentils, chick peas and peanuts) contain plenty of lysine but little methionine and tryptophan.

● Cereal grains complement pulses, legumes (lentils, chick peas and peanuts), potatoes, vegetables, milk and yeast.

● Rice is richer in lysine than wheat.

● Oats have the most adequate amino acid content of all the cereal grains.

● Grains vary in their amino acid composition and it is best to mix them. Baked beans on toast, and rice and lentils, are two examples of complementary vegetable proteins.

● Pulses and legumes complement cereal grains, seeds, nuts and potatoes.

● Dark green leafy vegetables (low in protein but a good source of sulphur-containing amino acids, such as methionine), plus milk, cheese and yoghourt, complement any vegetable protein.

Chapter Seven
CREATING A GREEN HOME

And he who gives a child a home
Builds palaces in kingdom come.
John Masefield

All parents can create a green home environment in which to bring up their children, and it is important to do so. The way you as parents run your home and the equipment and products you buy affect the health and quality of life of you and your children. They also affect other parents and children, not only in your own community but on a national and even on an international scale. This chapter takes a practical look at some domestic green issues.

WHERE YOU LIVE

The places in which we live influence us in many ways. They can affect both our feelings and our physical health. The Chinese link feelings about the landscape with the flow of *ch'i*, the energy which flows in channels throughout the world and through our bodies. This may explain why some people feel more at one with themselves when they live on a hill or on a mountain, while others prefer the shelter of a valley or the wide open space of a plain. Living near trees or water, either running or still, may be right for you. You may prefer to live in an old house which, because it holds memories of generations past, carries with it a sense of continuity with former times. Alternatively, you may like the feeling of moving into a brand new house. It is, for you, a way of starting afresh.

It is worth while analyzing your feelings towards the place in which you live. If you are not particularly happy there, understanding the reason why might help you find a simple solution. For example, depression could result from a lack of exposure to daylight causing SAD (Seasonal Affective Disorder), rather than from living in a dark flat or house. If this is so, spending more time outdoors might help relieve it (*see pages 97-98*). However, perhaps your home really is too gloomy. If so, you could find ways of making it lighter, such as painting the walls white or a pale, light-reflecting colour, lopping overhanging trees, or even enlarging windows or adding new ones. Other examples of how to improve your home are listed on page 136 under **Your home environment**. Even if you cannot immediately do anything about such problems, understanding them will help you choose a more suitable home if you eventually move. By the same token, understanding why you are happy in your home may help you search for the same conditions in any new home.

This is especially important from the point of view of health, since where you live can have an important effect on the health of you and your family. Climate is a major consideration for some families, who may have a definite preference for a hot, warm or cool location, or for a drier or more humid atmosphere. Health can be related to climatic conditions. Some children with asthma, for instance, do better in warm, dry climates.

Enough research has been done in the UK to recommend that families with young children should ideally not live high up in high-rise blocks of flats. The reasons are both practical and social. Carrying small children, shopping and a buggy up many flights of stairs (if there is no lift or when the lift has broken down) is no joke. Children are often kept indoors to play because they cannot easily be watched when they are outside. There may be little or no opportunity to meet neighbours unless you make specific arrangements. This can result in loneliness and isolation, particularly for parents already living far from their own families. These feelings can foster depression and other psychological problems. Families living in flats have more illnesses and their children have more respiratory complaints, according to a study of British service families living in West Germany.

However, in many countries, especially in large cities, most families live in flats. The fact that living in an apartment is the norm may account for the apparent lack of problems, but the customary presence of a live-in porter and/or housekeeper – a concierge – to maintain communal areas, such as lifts, and to both help and keep a friendly eye on the inhabitants, may be an important factor. Somehow caretakers are not quite the same, perhaps because they are more concerned with the fabric of the building than with the people. It might be a good idea for apartment blocks under both private and public ownership, to have a concierge living at a reduced rent on the ground floor by the communal entrance.

You may have little or no control over where you live for any number of reasons. Indeed, being able to choose a home is a luxury envied by homeless couples, four out of five of which in the UK have children. But if you can, avoid living in areas where there is high atmospheric pollution or excessive noise from roads or factories. If you live in an area where it is easy to rent property, or if you are about to buy a house or a flat, carry out a thorough search into its location: problems caused by toxic fumes can occur in houses built over old rubbish tips or toxic waste dumps.

It has been estimated that urban air pollution causes one per cent of lung cancer cases. Road vehicles release hundreds of pollutants, which can have a very detrimental effect on the health of city dwellers. These pollutants contribute towards the formation of photochemical smog, produced by sunlight acting on them, which is dangerous for people with respiratory illnesses. Large quantities of lead, from leaded petrol, can cause damage to the brain and nervous system, and anaemia, and is thought to damage the mental development of children. Carbon monoxide, also found in petrol fumes, is a poison and a suspected carcinogen.

Living in the countryside is not necessarily the way to avoid pollution problems. Agrochemical-based farming could mean that you and your family are exposed to many poisonous chemicals each year. My house is surrounded by agricultural land which is frequently sprayed with a variety of chemicals. A week after a walk along a public footpath through one of these fields, my dog became very ill with large open sores on her tummy and the fronts of her legs. She was too weak to walk, whimpered and had nightmares for several days. Unbeknown to us till the end of that walk, the field had just been sprayed with pesticide.

If you live among cropped fields, ask the farmer to tell you when spraying is going to start so that you can arrange to go out for the day. Droplets drifting in the wind can carry sprays far beyond their intended destination, while vaporization from sprayed fields can be a problem for days, especially if the air is warm and dry.

Ideally, farmers should always notify local inhabitants of intended spraying times and they should also put notices up along public footpaths when fields have been sprayed with noxious chemicals.

THE HAZARDS OF RADIATION

The electromagnetic (EM) spectrum comprises the complete range of EM radiation of energy waves. This encompasses low-frequency radio waves (long, medium and short wavelength and very high-frequency or VHF radio waves); ultra-high frequency (UHF) television waves; microwaves (used for satellite communication, radar and microwave ovens) and infra-red rays. It includes visible light rays from the red end to the blue end of the light spectrum; ultraviolet rays and X-rays. And the high-frequency radioactive gamma rays in natural radioactivity from the sun (cosmic rays, most of which are absorbed by the Earth's atmosphere) are part of the EM spectrum. Gamma rays are emitted by our own bodies, soil, rock, building materials, air, coal and food. They also include radioactivity harnessed or induced from nuclear power and emitted by the testing of nuclear weapons, luminous watches, food irradiation, television sets and VDUs.

However, the word 'radiation' is commonly taken to mean ionizing radiation: X-rays and the radiation from radioactive sources. We are all naturally subject to low levels or doses of background radiation of this sort every day, but exposure to radiation is thought to be a serious risk to health only if the dose received per year is high. There has recently been considerable concern over the relatively high incidence of leukaemia in people living near the nuclear power plant at Sellafield in the UK. The source of the high levels of radioactivity there seems to have been in the water effluent from the plant, which was discharged into the sea. Contaminated mud and sand from the seashore were then transferred inland. It is possible that there might also be a mutagenic effect on the sperms of men who are over-exposed to radioactivity.

Radioactive contamination with the isotopes strontium, plutonium and caesium 137, following the major leak at the nuclear power reactor in Chernobyl in the USSR in 1987, has already caused a high incidence of cancer in children and adults. The most contaminated areas are in Byelorussia.

We are also subject to the microwave radiation from radio and TV broadcasting stations, FM (frequency modulation) towers and radar systems which emit pulsed radiation. In addition, some people are subjected to the electromagnetic fields of high-voltage power lines and radon – natural radiation from the ground in some areas (*see page 136*).

Apart from moving far away from sources, exerting political pressure and using adequate protection if exposed to emissions, we can do little about the effects of many of these sources, but we do have influence in our homes (*see page 148 under* **Electromagnetic radiation**).

ELECTROMAGNETIC FIELDS

There is continuing research into the possibility of health dangers from living under, over, or close to high-voltage power lines (cables) which create electromagnetic (EM) fields of low-frequency, non-ionizing radiation. In considering the effects of these lines, the configuration of their EM fields is probably more important than the strengths of EM fields at various points. The EM fields of telecommunications systems, radio and television transmitters, electrical transformers, subway tracks, early-warning radar systems and military installations have similarly come under suspicion.

The question is whether exposure to such fields increases the risk of leukaemia or of other types of cancer, threatens the immune system in other ways, leads to headaches or affects mental health. One UK study found that migraine was much more common in people living within 500 metres (about 550 yards) of an overhead power line. Research carried out in the USSR, the USA and the UK indicates that people living near such power lines are more prone to non-specific symptoms such as fatigue, palpitation, weakness, eye pain and ear noise. One study has indicated a doubling of the risk of cancer in those living near overhead power cables but such research is notoriously difficult to evaluate. In June 1989 the US Congress Office of Technology Assessment produced a report which said, 'Although as recently as a few years ago, scientists stated that available evidence showed no health risks from power frequency fields, emerging evidence no longer allows a categorical denial that risks exist'. Until more is known it might be prudent to avoid choosing to live near one of the EM field sources listed above if you are about to move. However, this same organization also said that if there are effects on health from exposure to EM fields, they arise mainly from the use of electricity in the home. Household appliances and wiring can produce fields which are comparable in magnitude to those near overhead power lines (*See page 148.*)

North America leads the world in action for home buyers. Florida is the first state in the USA to have established a guide to EM fields; and in Canada, British Columbia Hydro is buying up houses along a new power line from homeowners who fear detrimental effects upon health.

RADIATION FROM UNDERGROUND

In many countries certain disorders are common in specific areas. Epidemiologists – specialists in the incidence, prevalence and clustering of medical conditions – sometimes trace the cause to the local soil, underlying rock, vegetation or climate. For instance, the uranium in the rock underlying parts of the UK emits high levels of naturally radioactive radon gas. These are thought to be associated with an increased risk of cancer. Scientists have estimated that 2,500 deaths from lung cancer are caused by radon each year in the UK. The risk is higher if you also smoke. Cancer of the kidney, melanoma, certain childhood cancers and acute myeloid leukaemia all show a significant correlation with radon exposure in the home too. In Cornwall one in two cases of myeloid leukaemia may be attributed to radon.

The gas seeps into homes through foundations and floor-boards. In the UK about 90,000 households have levels of radon above the level at which the government recommends remedial actions, such as sealing the floor-boards with plastic sheeting, or installing a below-floor extractor fan to channel the gas away from the house. The National Radiological Protection Board (*see pages 183–184* **Consumer Guide**) can advise you on how to find out whether your house is at risk. Average radon levels are much higher in Sweden, Norway and parts of Canada than in the UK.

LOCAL DEFICIENCIES

In the county of Derbyshire in the UK there is little iodine in the soil. People living there used to be prone to a condition called Derbyshire neck, a goitre, or swelling of the thyroid gland in the front of the neck, caused by insufficient iodine in the diet. Now that these people eat vegetables and meat drink milk from farms over a much wider area, and eat iodized salt, they have no increased risk of goitre. However, it is estimated that up to 800 million people throughout the world live in areas with soil deficient in iodine. Among these areas are Zaïre, Nepal and western China. People there are at risk of goitre or other disorders caused by iodine deficiency, such as hypothyroidium (formerly called cretinism; a form of mental retardation combined with short physical stature).

YOUR HOME ENVIRONMENT

Wherever you live, you can adapt the environment inside your home to suit you and your family by altering such variables as colours, temperature, the amount of fresh air circulating, and floor- and wall-coverings. The use of colour in the home can have pronounced psychological effects on the family, both positive and negative. Warm, dark colours can be used to make large rooms look more cosy, to the point where people feel warmer, even though the temperature is not higher. Such colours can also make people feel more secure. Painting walls in a single pale colour or white not only makes a small room appear larger, but also makes it feel cooler in hot weather. Most children like strong, primary colours: bright reds, yellows and blues. Use small amounts of these colours in play areas, kitchens and bedrooms for a cheerful effect. It is important, however, to avoid over-using primary colours: large unbroken areas of red, for example, can be over-stimulating, because red quickens the heart rate and raises the blood pressure. Break up primary colours with neutrals for a calmer effect.

Soft blues and greens can make the pulse rate fall and are used to create a calm atmosphere, so blue is a good colour for a bedroom. You may be fascinated to know that one reason behind the custom of pink for a girl and blue for a boy was that centuries ago the blue dyes, which were the most expensive, were reserved by some families for their prized male children. Soft violet is said to aid imaginative ability and yellow to improve and activate the mind. Pale pink has an obvious quietening effect on adults. Pink paint is used on prison walls to calm and relax violent prisoners quickly in the USA and more recently in Huddersfield Prison's anti-drunk cell in Yorkshire. However, two New Zealand researchers found that pink does not have a tranquillizing effect on children. Instead it arouses them and stimulates their creativity and physical strength. Consider your child's personality when choosing the colour of a bedroom. An excitable child might respond to the calming effect of blues or greens, while a naturally quiet child might be stimulated by warmer, brighter colours such as peach, yellow or pink. When choosing colours for a room, the right shade is crucial if you are to achieve the effect you want. A clear, grass or sea green usually has a restful effect, but a yellowy-green can make people feel ill. A factory manager in the USA found that painting the staff lavatories a nauseous shade of yellowy-green cut down the time people spent chatting in them by an appreciable amount.

But more important to young children than their physical surroundings is the need to grow up feeling and believing that they are important and that they matter to a group of people. Children's paintings or models make wonderful decorations and help the children feel they belong in their home. Putting their work on show encourages them in their creativity and ability to enhance the family's environment. Some of us live far away from our own parents and family. We can help ourselves feel closer to them by putting their photographs on the walls around us.

ENERGY IN THE HOME

Large-scale electricity production in power stations fuelled by coal releases enormous volumes of carbon dioxide into the atmosphere. Electricity generation and vehicle exhaust fumes together contribute 45 per cent of emissions of carbon dioxide caused by human beings. This is a major contributor to the greenhouse effect and acid rain (*see pages 185–187* **Glossary**). Although this problem may seem too great for individuals to combat, it is sensible for each family to work out how to avoid wasting electricity, both because of the greenhouse effect and acid rain, and because it will save them money. The same goes for using other forms of energy, such as oil, gas and wood. Heating domestic space and water uses most energy in cooler countries. An obvious way of saving on heating is to put on extra layers of clothes. A surprising number of people do not think of this solution, but automatically turn the heating on or up. Here are just a few of the many other ways you can cut down:

POWER STATIONS

Choose gas (or hydroelectric energy) in preference to electricity derived from coal and oil, if you can. Power stations fuelled by coal or oil turn only a third of the fossil fuels they use into electricity; the rest is lost as waste heat in the generation of electricity. Along with the waste heat goes an enormous volume of carbon dioxide, which is produced unnecessarily and adds to the greenhouse effect. In several countries, including Denmark, West Germany and the Netherlands, many homes are now heated using this 'waste' heat.

Make sure that your gas boiler and cooker are regularly serviced. Carbon monoxide gas from poorly maintained appliances can cause respiratory infections and asthma if the room ventilation is poor.

INSULATE YOUR HOME

● Loft insulation will make the most difference to the amount of energy used in the home. One quarter of all heat lost from the average house is through the roof. Conversely, roof insulation prevents heat from the sun getting in through the roof during hot summers. However, insulation can cause serious problems in a poorly ventilated building, so seek the advice of a professional.

● Ensure that your hot-water tank is adequately lagged with an 80-millimetre (3-inch) lagging jacket. The cost of such a jacket, around £8 in the UK, is quickly recouped as electricity bills will be reduced. Lag hot-water pipes to prevent heat loss and cold-water pipes to guard against freezing. Use natural lagging materials if possible.

● Double-glazing is not immediately cost-effective but it will gradually make a difference to your fuel bills.

● Draught-proofing measures and underlay, carpets and rugs are useful. Use felt and newspaper under carpet. Stop heat from escaping through the floor by putting aluminium foil, hardboard or softboard under the floor covering.

● Line curtains with thick interlining.

● Cavity wall or external wall insulation can be helpful. Choose glass fibre or mineral wool rather than a plastic insulation, such as urea formaldehyde foam or expanded polystyrene. The manufacture of plastic insulation pollutes the environment and urea formaldehyde foam emits formaldehyde fumes, which can seep through walls for many years (*see page 141*).

IN YOUR KITCHEN

● Keep the fridge and freezer away from the cooker, boiler or radiator; keep them full but not over-full; check their seals; keep the condenser clean of fluff; let food cool completely before putting it in; and open the doors for as little time as you can.

● When buying new, choose an energy-efficient boiler, fridge, freezer, dishwasher, kettle or washing-machine. In the USA such appliances are labelled with details of their energy consumption. Using a dishwasher now uses less energy than washing up by hand. A plastic jug-type kettle uses only three-quarters the energy of a metal one. A toaster is much more efficient than a grill.

● When you buy a new fridge, buy an energy efficient one with a reduced amount of CFCs (chlorofluorocarbons) in the insulation foam of door and walls. When you dispose of your old one, take it to a recognized disposal agency which may be able to draw off the ozone-damaging CFCs which would otherwise escape from the cooling system when the fridge was crushed. In the UK this service is offered by most Electricity Boards and by the freezer food retailers Bejam Freezer Food Centres Limited and Iceland Frozen Foods plc.

● Dry clothes outside when possible. Tumble driers use a lot of electricity.

● Do not use unnecessary electrical gadgets, such as knife-sharpeners and can-openers.

SAVING POWER

● Turn off your TV set with the on-off switch rather than the remote control. A set left at stand-by continues to use a quarter of the electricity it uses when activated. The energy currently wasted each year in the UK through not using the on-off switch costs £12 million.

● **If you are having a new house built,** orientate it so that the main rooms face south to get the heat and light of the sun, and make north-facing windows small. Solar heating panels can be effective. High-standard building techniques and modern building materials make it possible for new buildings to be very heat-efficient. Finland's houses are super-insulated; many countries could benefit from copying them. Architects will advise on ways of conserving energy.

● **Put aluminium foil behind radiators** to reflect heat back into the room.

• **Try not to use batteries.** They are part of many families' way of life but they are not at all energy-efficient. It takes 50 times more energy to manufacture the average battery than it produces in its lifetime. Some batteries are made nowadays without the toxic metals cadmium and mercury. One town in Canada is experimenting with special disposal facilities for batteries. In the UK, the battery companies Memorex UK Limited and Varta Batteries Limited will take back their used, rechargeable batteries to recycle the cadmium.

LIGHTING

• Turn off lights when not in use and switch them on only when you really need them.

• If your dwelling needs to be rewired, have your standard lighting replaced by low-energy lighting circuits.

• Low-energy fluorescent light 'bulbs' or tubes use only one-fifth of the electricity of the ordinary incandescent light bulb. For all the energy produced as light from the ordinary light bulb, 30 times as much is wasted in the conversion of the locked-up coal energy into electricity. It has been estimated that each low-energy light source saves the atmosphere from receiving almost a ton of carbon dioxide. Low-energy fluorescent light sources last five times as long as most ordinary bulbs. The newer fluorescent 'bulbs' or tubes give light of a well balanced colour, do not flicker when turned on and off and light up immediately. However, fluorescent lights create higher electromagnetic fields than incandescent bulbs. They also emit some ultraviolet (UV) light, in increasing quantities as the tubes get older and the inner coating of phosphorus decays. Long-term exposure to UV light may cause skin problems (such as dermatitis) and eye problems. Low levels of microwave and radio wave radiation from fluorescent lights have been tentatively linked with miscarriage and with behaviour disorders in children. The possible glare, noise and flicker from fluorescent lighting can be associated with headaches, eyestrain, difficulty in concentrating and an increased risk of fits in people with epilepsy. A fluorescent light works out much cheaper than incandescent bulbs when you take into account the initial purchase cost, together with the cost of electricity during its life, but the economic advantage lessens if you choose warmer or natural light tubes which are less energy efficient. Researchers at the London Hazards Centre believe that in view of the health problems fluorescent lighting can cause, it is better for people to work under natural or other non-fluorescent lighting. Halogen lights also consume little energy. Nearly two out of three homes in Britain are said to be poorly lit. This can be a problem when it comes to doing close work, such as reading, writing, playing the piano, sewing or typing. Make sure you have daylight from a window, or light from a light fitting, coming over your left shoulder (if you are right-handed) when focussing on close work. Insufficient lighting is also blamed for an increased risk of accidents in the home.

LIGHT THERAPY

Many parents who live a long way from the equator, work indoors and drive everywhere in a car see very little natural light during the week, especially for the three or four winter months. This may be more important than most of us have realized. If you or your children suffer from SAD (Seasonal Affective Disorder or 'winter depression', *see pages 97-8*), try to increase the amount of time you spend outside, especially in the sun, during the winter months. If you still feel low for no apparent cause, you might benefit from light therapy. Studies have shown that light therapy with rows of full-spectrum fluorescent lights can reduce the symptoms of SAD in some people. This is believed to be due more to the brightness of the lighting than to the effect of any specific wavelength in the light. See page 183 **Consumer Guide** for suppliers of low energy and full-spectrum lighting.

WOOD IN YOUR HOME

TROPICAL HARDWOODS

Green families avoid buying new furniture, household equipment or building materials made from tropical hardwoods taken from non-sustainable forests. Cutting down the rainforests is a major problem of the nineties. Avoid mahogany and teak especially, but also rosewood, African walnut, meranti, iroko and others. The tropical rainforests of Sarawak currently help supply Japan with 1 billion pairs of chopsticks a year, with disposable scaffold poles and with plywood boxes for take-away food. Japan accounts for a third of the industrialized nations' consumption of hardwood products. The EC imports another third and the USA 10 per cent. The UK is one of the world's biggest consumers of tropical hardwoods at between 5 and 7 per cent. Some 95 per cent of its imports come from forest-destroying sources. The EC is considering restricting imports of hard woods.

Reduce the danger of polluting the air in your home with a cocktail of poisonous fumes by buying solid-wood furniture, using non-toxic 'organic' paint-strippers and wood preservatives, latex-based adhesives and organic, lead-free paints and varnishes. Old-fashioned, horsehair-stuffed sofas are less of a fire hazard. If you buy foam-filled furniture, buy new to be sure the foam is combustion-modified. The healthiest carpets are hessian-backed and not treated with pesticides.

WOOD PRESERVATIVES

The chemicals used in wood preservatives include toxic fungicides and insecticides which prevent or treat insect or fungal infestations (such as the common furniture beetle – woodworm – or the death watch beetle, or dry or wet rot). Examples of these are lindane (a pesticide, *see also pages 116-117*); tributyltin oxide (TBTO, a fungicide); and PCP (pentachlorophenol, an organochlorine fungicide). These three chemicals are poisons and have been associated in the past with a high death rate among workers at production factories.

They have been banned in many countries, including the USA and West Germany. Another wood-preserving chemical currently under investigation is permethrin.

Wood treated with such chemicals gives off a slow stream of poisonous molecules into the air for years. At present 500 court cases are pending in the UK and 5,000 in West Germany over toxic reactions following wood treatments. Suspected reactions to the long-term inhalation of fumes from certain preservatives include asthma, leukaemia and other cancers. You would be well advised to use alternative, non-toxic wood preservatives on any wood in your home. The Swedes use borax-based wood treatments, instead of toxic preservatives. It is also sensible to consult a professional body on how to modify the environment so as to protect wood from infestation or control any infestation already present. This basically means keeping internal timbers sufficiently dry to prevent insects or fungi from becoming established or from multiplying. (*See page 183* **Consumer Guide** for suppliers and advisers.)

· Ideally wood should be kiln-dried at a temperature high enough to kill woodworm and fungi before being used in buildings. Modern building techniques should meet standards which prevent wet and dry rot from developing.

UREA FORMALDEHYDE RESIN

Particle boards – medium-density fibreboard (MDF) and chipboard – are made with wood fibres or particles bonded together with the synthetic resin urea formaldehyde. Formaldehyde fumes leak or 'outgas' from this resin into the air for years. Sensitivity to formaldehyde has been linked with eye, nose, throat and lung irritation, headaches, depression, memory loss and dizziness. One in five people exposed to formaldehyde may be affected by prolonged or excessive exposure. Particle board bonded with urea formaldehyde resin is banned in Canada and several states in the USA, but it is commonly used in the UK. Use solid wood instead of these boards, or keep rooms with new board very well ventilated. Problems with building materials are not new. It is only a few years since asbestos was found to be potentially lethal.

PAINTS & RELATED PRODUCTS

Most paint is based on petrochemicals. Although modern paints are not as toxic as their forerunners, their manufacture can produce poisonous effluent which pollutes the rivers and seas. Most of the raw materials used in their manufacture are non-reusable. Some emulsions contain fungicides, although ICI have now removed the most toxic, pentachlorophenol (PCP) and lindane, and the USA has banned the use of PCP in inhabited places. PCP can harm the liver and the nervous and immune systems. It has also been linked with cancer. Paint continues to emit chemicals into the air after application, albeit at a very low concentration. The air in our homes can very easily contain a cocktail of low levels of a variety of toxic synthetic substances. Even though the level of any one substance may not be particularly high, the combined effect of many of them may, it is suggested, compromise the body's immune system or even the blood cells.

Only low-level lead paints are now allowed in the USA and the UK, although lead is permitted in paint thinner and undercoat. It is thought that lead-containing dust from old lead paint has contributed to lead toxicity in some children and adults.

Paint thinner or stripper is likely to be based on hydrocarbons or chlorinated hydrocarbons, which are potentially poisonous. They evaporate readily and it is best to use them as quickly as possible and in a well ventilated space.

Breathing in the vapour from adhesives, such as those used to stick down vinyl floor tiles, can endanger a child. Petrol-based adhesives, for instance, produce a toxic vapour. Most others contain hydrocarbons which have been linked with cancer. Children have died from the effects of sniffing certain glues. Use a white latex-based glue whenever possible as this is safer.

Non-toxic 'organic' paints, varnishes, paint thinners, paint strippers and adhesives are available in many countries (*see page 183* **Consumer Guide**) and are the green choice for families doing up their homes. These 'organic' DIY materials were developed in West Germany. They are based on plant and mineral raw materials, so their manufacture does not pollute the environment and makes allergic reactions less likely. 'Organic' paints are made from natural ingredients such as beeswax soap and orange peel oil; they are free from fungicides and chemical additives. Pleasant to use, they emit only the aroma of essential oils and natural plant extracts. They cost generally double the price of conventional paints, but may spread further. 'Organic' paint thinners are also made from natural ingredients, such as citrus peel, and give off only a pleasant, natural fragrance. Instead of using wallpaper, you could try decorating walls by stencilling, or by using special effects with paint such as rag rolling, stippling or spongeing, or even painting a mural or laying a collage directly on to the wall.

FOAM

Furniture with polyurethane foam-filled cushions or padding is a fire hazard. It burns rapidly and gives off poisonous gases as it does so. Avoid buying second-hand furniture of this type unless it contains combustion-modified foam – now legally required in the UK in new furniture. This does not ignite so readily and gives you the chance to put the fire out or to get out of the house before being affected by the gases. Old-fashioned horsehair stuffing, which smoulders slowly, giving off smoke but not poisonous fumes, is better than both.

CARPETS

Carpet backed with polyurethane foam gives off an irritating vapour containing dibutyl hydroxytoluene. Your expensive new woollen carpet may contain toxic insecticides, such as permethrin or mitin FF. Choose 'organic' carpets backed with hessian and bound with 'organic' adhesives which do not contain urea formaldehyde resin (*see page 141*). Any synthetic flooring, whether vinyl tiles or man-made carpet, is likely to be derived from oil, a non-renewable resource. Such flooring is not biodegradable and may release toxins when burnt.

PLASTICS

These are ideally best avoided in the home. Their manufacture uses oil reserves and can pollute the environment. Most do not biodegrade and their incineration produces dangerous chemicals, such as dioxin. Plastics in your home include many building materials (plastic roof tiles, imitation boarding and wall insulation); vinyl wallpapers and shelving; furniture; textiles such as acrylic and poly-cotton; and cheap kitchen items, such as bowls. All of these have natural, non-toxic alternatives. Polyvinyl chloride (PVC), a plastic commonly found in the home, emits low levels of vinyl chloride. This has caused cancer in people who work in plastics factories. It seems unnecessary to add toxic chemicals to the air in your home. For more on plastics see page 150.

BIO-HOMES

In the USA builders have developed techniques to combat the chemical pollution of indoor air. They use airtight vapour barriers to prevent vaporized pollutants in the building materials of the fabric of the house from entering the air inside. However, other ecologically-minded builders point out that it is preferable not to use potentially-toxic building materials in the first place, especially as alternatives are available; and that vapour barriers prevent the natural 'breathing' or diffusion of air through porous brick, stone, timber and plaster. Some builders make sure that oil is washed off any steel used in construction. Substitute materials are found for particle boards, wood treated with poisonous pesticides, foam-backed carpets, PVC floor tiles

and potentially toxic glues and cements. The same policy is being applied in West Germany: ecologically aware West Germans call their products 'bio-homes'. But such efforts are pointless if the homeowner then fills this organic shell with toxic fumes from products brought in .

WASHING POWDERS & LIQUIDS

About half of a typical detergent washing powder consists of a builder or 'filler'. Substances such as optical brighteners, surfactants, enzymes, perfumes and colourings may be added.

Phosphates also act as 'builders': they stop the powder from caking; prevent dirt from settling back on to the fabric; and precipitate out calcium and magnesium ions from the water to soften it and prevent scum formation. They can be an environmental hazard if they enter rivers and lakes, because they act as plant fertilizers and start off a process known as eutrophication in which certain algae flourish, blot out the

Many of the products illustrated (*above*) are expensive and unnecessary, as well environmentally harmful. Many kitchen and bathroom cleaners are based on petrochemicals. Most 'green' cleaners are based on a mixture of a vegetable oil, chalk and a mild acid (such as citric acid or vinegar). Try washing soda (sodium carbonate) instead: it is an excellent de-greaser.

light and so kill fish and other plant life. Zeolites are a green alternative.

In Sweden, phosphates are removed from water at sewage plants. In the UK sewage treatment seems to be eliminating phosphates in most areas. They are banned in Switzerland, the Netherlands and in USA. They have been removed from commercial laundry washing liquid in the UK, but are still present in all powders except the products marketed as being free from phosphates. The unnecessary production of cadmium, a poisonous by-product of phosphate manufacture, is another reason for going green on washing powders. Green washing powders score on many environmentally friendly counts, but not all. Some of them, for instance, are based on petrochemicals rather than on vegetable oils.

Soaps were traditionally used for laundering, but they have become unpopular in the UK as an increasing proportion of domestic water now comes from rivers. River water is harder than water from the underground water table and it forms a scum when soap reacts with its calcium and magnesium ions. Make washing scum-free by softening your water with sodium carbonate and bicarbonate, then using a soap-based product.

Surfactants separate dirt from clothes and hold it in the water. They also create foam. They are the main cleaning agents in detergents and are derived from petrochemicals, so they deplete the world's oil reserves. An EC directive states that all surfactants must be at least 80 per cent biodegradable because of the harm the foam can do to the rivers, lakes and seas. The important question is how biodegradable the foam is and how quickly it breaks down. Vegetable oil-based surfactants are between 95 per cent and 100 per cent biodegradable, which is better than most others. These green products rely on renewable resources, not on petrol, and tend to break down quickly.

Optical brighteners (fluorescent whitening agents), enzymes, perfumes and dyes in washing powders can cause dermatitis. Some of the chemicals used to treat textiles can also cause dermatitis, so wash new clothes before your child wears them. Cotton, for instance, is usually treated with a moth-repellant and easy-care fabric is treated with formaldehyde (*see page 141*).

OVEN CLEANERS

Try using a paste of baking soda (sodium bicarbonate) and water instead of an aerosol cleaner with propellants which damage the environment. A 'knitted' stainless steel pad used with hot water and washing soda has revolutionized my (infreqent) oven cleanings. Some oven cleaners contain caustic soda (sodium hydroxide), which can irritate skin and eyes.

WASHING-UP LIQUIDS

Contrary to much received wisdom, all washing-up liquids are free from phosphates. Under EC legislation the liquids must be biodegradable. Most contain some surfactants which make the foam (*see opposite under* **Washing powders and liquids**). Some green brands are sold in environmentally friendly containers which do not release poisonous fumes when incinerated. Buy a product with a small hole in the nozzle so that you squirt less into the water.

BLEACH

There is concern that the by-products of the processing and breakdown of chlorine bleach could include toxic organochlorines. Use a bleach free from chlorine made from hydrogen peroxide instead: there are now several on the market. Nappies come up well with lemon juice and salt added to the washing water, especially if they are then dried in the sun. Vinegar will bleach stains in the toilet bowl.

DISINFECTANTS

Disinfectants are widely over-used and usually unnecessary in the home. Some of them contain potentially poisonous cresol. Use a borax solution, a strong infusion of thyme leaves, or one of the commercial green products if you need to disinfect.

TOILET FRESHENERS

Solid toilet blocks and blue water cleaners for the lavatory bowl kill all bacteria there. But – and you may be surprised at this – the sewage works need domestic sewage bacteria in order to function. An obsession with disinfecting the loo is unnecessary. Some toilet freshener blocks and liquids contain paradichlorobenzene, a persistent environmental pollutant which could be harmful to wildlife. Environmentally friendly toilet cleaners are available in the UK (*see page 183*, **Consumer Guide**). Ecover manufactures a toilet cleaner which kills harmful bacteria but retains essential friendly bacteria.

AIR FRESHENERS

These are a source of pollution of the air in the home with unnecessary and possibly even harmful chemicals. They mask or deaden our sense of smell and some of their ingredients are suspect. Several perfuming agents, including artificial lemon (limonene) and imidazoline, have been linked with cancer in experiments with laboratory animals. You could use a pot pourri of naturally fragrant plant material instead, refreshing it every so often with a few drops of essential oil. But the best air fresheners are plants.

Fascinating recent research concludes that some house plants can improve the quality of the air in the house by absorbing toxic chemicals from it. One such substance is formaldehyde, which escapes from items containing synthetic resin, such as chipboard, and from rotting fruit, wallpaper, fabric and carpet finishes, urea formaldehyde cavity wall insulating foam, and many glues, detergents and kitchen and bathroom cleaners. Plants also absorb carbon monoxide and carbon dioxide from the air. Too high a concentration of these gases can make you feel sleepy and apathetic. The most environmentally friendly plants are the coconut palm, the weeping fig (*Ficus benjamina*), dracaena, spathiphyllum, gerbera, spider plants and chrysanthemums. The presence of such plants in a room may help reduce the risk of sick building syndrome (*see page 159*).

AEROSOLS

The propellants used in aerosol dispensers can harm the ozone layer whether they are the more dangerous CFCs or hydrocarbons. It is better to use dispensers with a pump or trigger action, with no propellants. The Americans banned CFCs in 1978 and all Australian aerosol sprays are now free from CFCs. Aerosols formerly contributed as much as two-fifths of Australia's total CFC emissions.

HOME DRY-CLEANING

Home dry-cleaning products, such as suede and leather protectors and car interior cleaners, contain the solvent 1,1,1-trichloroethane (also known as methyl chloroform) which, like CFCs, can damage the ozone layer. Learn how to remove stains with traditional remedies instead. Eucalyptus oil rubbed on to tar, oil or grass stains loosens them miraculously before washing. Lard will get rid of tar too. A solution of borax (one part to eight parts of water) helps remove mildew, urine, blood, chocolate and mud. Let it dry before you wash the treated item. Glycerine removes grass stains well.

Each of the two chemicals used most commonly in commercial dry-cleaning has an ecological question mark against its name. Perchloroethylene (Per) has been found as a contaminant in drinking-water, possibly because of bad disposal methods. The symbol for this on clothing labels is a letter P in a circle. Long-term exposure (for instance of dry-cleaning workers in premises with inadequate ventilation) can lead to nerve disorders and damage to the lungs and kidneys. The other solvent, known as R113 (and also as CFC 113 and Arklone), is a chlorofluorocarbon (CFC) and a danger to the ozone layer. The amount released by the dry-cleaning industry represents half of one per cent of the world's CFC output, a considerable contribution. Avoid buying clothes which need to be cleaned with R113. The symbol for this on clothing labels is a letter F, circled. Many garments labelled 'dry-clean only' can be washed. Consult a handbook on fabric care.

DOMESTIC PEST CONTROL

Pest control is sometimes essential, particularly in warm, humid climates. Mosquitoes, ants, slugs, silver fish, moths, cockroaches, woodworm and death watch beetles can be difficult to live with, but the chemicals used to control pests can be hazardous to your family's health. Here are some alternatives:

FLIES

It seems silly to expose your family to constant levels of toxic chemicals in the air (such as those from dichlorvos in fly killer strips) when alternatives, such as fly swatters, citrus fruit peel, cloves and mint are harmless to humans and can be just as effective.

ANTS

Use dried mint, chilli powder or borax to kill ants, instead of a poisonous ant-killing product containing lindane or chlordane. These are persistent poisons which have been linked with cancer. Chlordane, a suspected carcinogen, is widely used in the UK, despite an EC prohibition directive.

MOTHS

Use cedar wood oil, lavender oil or camphor instead of mothballs, which contain a poison, paradichlorobenzene.

MOSQUITOES

Oil of pennyroyal diluted in vegetable oil repels mosquitos. Test a small patch of skin for sensitivity before applying it. Do not use it if you are or might be pregnant, however. It could be absorbed through your skin and might damage your baby.

GARDEN PESTS

Use non-toxic methods of pest control in the garden, when possible. One study revealed six times as much leukaemia in children living in homes where toxic biocides (pesticides and weedkillers) were used. Garden plants become more pest-resistant when strong and healthy. Organic gardening techniques (*see page 179*) foster pest-resistance, although they do not preclude pest infestation. Begin by improving the soil with well rotted domestic compost, manure and old-fashioned fertilizers, such as bonemeal, dried blood, hoof and horn, rock potash and seaweed in meal or liquid form. Crop rotation prevents the soil in the vegetable garden becoming exhausted and needing chemical fertilizers.

Encourage natural predators. Hoe between vegetables and plants to bring insects to the surface for birds to eat. Attract ladybirds and hoverflies (which live on aphids) by growing herbs, marigolds and poached egg plants. Frogs, toads and hedgehogs prey on insects; attract them by leaving parts of your garden wild or by making a pond.

Grow companion plants (such as garlic and chives next to roses, and onions next to carrots) to deter slugs, ants and aphids.

Use safe pesticides. Diluted soft soap solution can be used to attack greenfly and blackfly; bowls of beer to entice slugs; pyrethrum (from chrysanthemums), an infusion of crushed basil leaves or marigolds, or potassium permanganate solution, may all be used to combat powdery mildew; urine can be used as a wash for fruit trees; and Bordeaux mixture for blight and fungal diseases. Weeds can be controlled by regular hoeing and mulches. Difficult weeds can be treated with ammonium sulphate.

Avoid using captan (a fungicide often used as a seed dressing or a rooting powder); lindane; and the weedkillers or herbicides paraquat, 2,4-D and 2,4,5-T (*see pages 116-7*). The latter is banned in India, the USA, Sweden, Norway and the USSR. All are potentially hazardous to health.

PETS

If your domestic pet has fleas, be wary of using pesticides in the form of sprays, shampoos and flea collars. Those which work are necessarily toxic and include lindane, dichlorvos and carbaryl. If you do use them you must follow the instructions carefully and keep the products out of the way of children. Treat your pet outside and stand upwind to avoid breathing in vapour or dust.

Better than pesticides are green methods of pest control. Regular combing with a fine-toothed comb helps keep the flea population in your pet's coat down. Squash the fleas or drown them. Vacuum your carpets and upholstery thoroughly and very often with a really powerful vacuum cleaner, to

SAFE PEST CONTROL

The most important thing about using chemical methods of pest control is to use them safely. Theoretically, all chemicals used as pesticides are officially approved, but this does not mean that they are not very toxic, especially if used incorrectly, so use them only if there is no other solution. If you do use them, follow the golden rules:

- Follow the instructions carefully.

- Avoid direct skin contact by using a scoop or by wearing gloves and other protective clothing. If some does get on your skin, wash it off quickly and thoroughly with plenty of running water, then soap.

- Avoid breathing vapour by standing upwind if you are using the product outside. If you are treating a pet, keep its head upwind too.

- Keep children and pets away while you are using pesticides; store them in a safe place well out of reach of either.

- Keep pesticides away from food.

- Never store pesticides in unlabelled containers in which they could be mistaken for food or drink.

- Bear in mind that anti-fouling paint for boats contains a pesticide.

- Avoid using slow-release flykiller strips or blocks containing dichlorvos. This has been associated with cancer in the USA and is classified by the World Health Organization as highly hazardous.

remove fleas and their eggs, and burn the collected debris or put it into a sealed bag. Most flea collars contain chemicals which are better avoided for daily exposure and should not be used on puppies and kittens. Choose a herbal collar containing oil of pennyroyal and eucalyptus. Shampoo with a preparation containing mint, citronella or eucalyptus to repel the fleas. Give your pet some fresh, raw garlic mashed in its food every few days, if you can. Chemicals in garlic are exuded from the body and act as a natural insect repellant.

AIR TRAVELLERS

Passengers entering certain countries are sprayed in the plane with pesticide to prevent insects hazardous to crops or health from entering the country. People flying from India to Australia, for example, are sprayed three times: first with 2 per cent permethrin; second with 2 per cent permethrin plus 2 per cent di-phenothrin; and again with 2 per cent permethrin. Permethrin is said to have low toxicity in humans, although it has been linked with cancer in animals. However, some people may unknowingly be particularly sensitive. If you find spraying unacceptable, or if you or your children suffer from asthma or other allergic reactions, tell the cabin crew. According to the World Health Organization you do not have to be sprayed if this would be detrimental to your health. To give yourself the best chance of co-operation, however, it would be best to inform the airline early – when you book your ticket or even before.

TESTING & LABELLING

Two last thoughts on household products: many new products are tested on animals, but in one British survey nine out of ten people were against such testing. Many consumers are concerned with the publicity over the environmental dangers that are inherent in products they use daily. They want honest and explicit labelling of products. Many countries (such as Canada, Germany and Japan) are working towards better systems or already have them. Ideally, the label should show details of the energy consumed in making the product, the raw materials used, whether it has been tested on animals, the product life and the waste it produces. 'Environmentally friendly' labels are often misleading.

ELECTROMAGNETIC RADIATION

In most homes in developed countries there exist electromagnetic fields (*see page 135 under* **The Hazards of Radiation**) derived from extra-low-frequency AC electrical wiring and appliances. There is increasing speculation and controversy among doctors and physicists about the possible health risks from the (mostly non-ionizing) radiation in these EM fields. Some people seem to be particularly sensitive to them, but everyone is affected to a

---

REDUCING RADIATION

Until more is known, here are some measures you can take to minimize exposure to domestic EM fields:

● Modern television sets emit extremely low levels of ionizing radiation compared with the natural levels in our homes. However, you may wish to choose a low-radiation set when you replace your old one (*see page 183* **Consumer Guide** for manufacturers).

● Discourage your child from sitting within 6 feet (2 metres) of a television.

● If your young child plays computer games, buy a remote controller so she or he can sit away from the VDU or TV screen.

● Turn off electrical appliances, including the TV, when not in use.

● Do not allow your child to sleep on or under an electric blanket. Use one if you wish to warm the bedclothes, but switch it off and remove it before the child goes to bed.

● Use electrical appliances less often.

---

greater or lesser degree. Research produces conflicting evidence, but two studies in Denver in the USA reported twice as much childhood leukaemia in homes in which EM fields were higher than average. One showed that high appliance use leading to strong EM fields was associated with an increased risk of all cancers in children.

Using a VDU screen has been linked (so far inconclusively) with miscarriage and birth defects (*see pages 43-4*), as well as with headaches, eye and wrist strain and fatigue. The strength of the field produced by each source decreases rapidly the further you distance yourself from it. Television screens are the same as VDUs in all essentials. It is not known whether any possible risk results from long-term exposure to EM fields, or from intermittent exposure to high EM fields.

The Earth has its own magnetic field from pole to pole. A popular old wives' tale is that people sleep better if their body is aligned with the magnetic north-south axis, with their head pointing to the north.

RECYCLING WASTE

It makes every sense to recycle waste if by doing so natural resources can be saved. Generations have always recycled second-hand items by accepting, buying, passing on or selling clothes, toys, household and baby equipment and furniture. In the UK car boot sales, jumble sales and charity shops selling second-hand goods are all popular. A card in a local shop window or an advertisement in the local paper is another way of recycling as is passing on children's clothes and equipment to other families.

Many people are interested in helping to reclaim basic materials. Here are some guidelines:

NATURAL FIBRES

Cotton and wool clothing and textiles are valuable because they can be recycled into items such as donkey jackets and roofing felt. Oxfam collects unwearable second-hand clothing from their shops in the UK and sells it for recycling.

METALS

Aluminium has been collected, melted down and reused for a long time. Tin and iron can be recycled. It takes 95 per cent

less energy to make a can from recycled aluminium as compared with raw aluminium. Nearly all food cans and half the drinks cans are made from steel in the UK, so great savings can be made by recycling. Cans made of mixed metal (tin-plated steel, perhaps with aluminium ring-pull tops) must be separated first. You can test cans with a magnet: aluminium will not be attracted.

PAPER

Paper can be recycled and used to manufacture newsprint, cardboard and other packaging, toilet paper and kitchen paper and other types. Some high-quality papers, such as office letterheads, have long been made of recycled offcuts. The recycling of paper is especially vulnerable to market forces, which sometimes make it economically unviable. For example, recycled paper of the quality required to print this book is more expensive than unrecycled stock of the same quality: perhaps as much as £900 to £1,000 per ton as compared with

Market forces largely determine the feasibility and success of any reclamation scheme. The ease and practicality of collection is another factor. Recycling extends the useful life of a raw material but at present only a fraction of the waste that could be is being recycled. The illustration (*above*) shows some of the few items that are now recycled on a large scale.

some £800 to £960 per ton for unrecycled stock (paper prices fluctuate enormously). Recycled board for use as covers is much more expensive and unavailable in the quality required for use as book covers. These price differentials are partly due to the high cost of recycling, but also partly due to the relatively limited demand at present. Sources are listed in the **Consumer Guide** (*see pages 183–4*).

If you use recycled paper products, choose those which are not bleached with chlorine as this process releases dioxins from the factory into rivers. Fruit juice should be bought in bottles rather than in cardboard cartons lined with aluminium and plastic, which are impossible to separate for recycling.

PROBLEM PLASTICS

Most plastics are made from oil, a precious natural resource. Plastic is increasingly used for packaging. In the UK it comprises 20 per cent of dustbin contents by volume. France produces 5 billion PVC bottles each year, 3 billion for water and 2 billion for oil and vinegar. PVC is virtually indestructible and the bottles are becoming a serious problem. This could be overcome by legislation making manufacturers take back empty bottles, as they do in Denmark and Germany, or by using glass bottles.

Many of the plastics that are said to be biodegradable (destroyed by the action of bacteria) or photodegradable (destroyed by light) do not decompose fully. Most biodegradable plastic is simply plastic injected with starch. A recently developed plastic is said to be completely biodegradable but is at present extremely expensive.

Several types of plastic can be recycled, but in practice rarely are. One reason is that there are too many different types and they have to be separated out first. Labelling would be a help here. The Body Shop aims to code all of its plastic products by 1991 in order to aid the process of identifying and sorting. Some supermarkets are also beginning to label plastic products and introduce plastic bottle banks.

Some states of the USA are trying to ban plastic packaging. You can help by not buying any disposable item made of plastic and by not using flimsy plastic carrier bags for your shopping. Never burn plastic in the house or outside as the fumes may contain dioxin (*see page 79*) and hydrogen fluoride, both of which chemicals are very poisonous and dangerous.

GLASS

The greenest option for glass bottles is for them to be returned and reused. Recycling is the next best. Bottles have been recycled for a long time, but glass objects must be separated into different colours for recycling. Bottle banks, now fairly common in many industrialized countries, have made the recycling of glass more attractive. In the Netherlands there is one bank for every 1,300 people, but in the UK only one for every 16,000. Only one in seven bottles and jars are recycled in the UK, compared with over one in two in the Netherlands. In Oregon, USA, non-returnable bottles are banned.

KITCHEN WASTE

Food scraps can be composted and used as a fertilizer and soil improver if you have a garden. It might be possible for whole communities to have a joint composting plant. Some communities are leading the way with ambitious waste-collection schemes, in which families are invited to participate. Ontario is a leader in Canada; Wiesbaden and other small towns in West Germany; Malmö in Sweden; and Sheffield and Cardiff in the UK. Methods include local banks for bottles, paper and cans, and door-to-door collection of separated waste in bags or compartmentalized boxes. Perhaps the most successful scheme of this type in Europe is in Neunkirchen, Austria. Householders receive two heavy-duty boxes. One is for dry waste (paper, tins, glass), the other for wet waste (potato peelings, tea bags, and so on). The dry waste is sorted into component parts and reused where possible. The wet waste is composted down and used in agriculture or in the householder's own garden. Austria recycles two-thirds of its total household and commercial waste.

In a growing number of German towns the sorting of domestic rubbish before collection is enforceable by law. Many people are becoming dissatisfied with methods of waste disposal which threaten the environment. Incineration, for example, adds to the greenhouse effect and pollutes the air. Its only redeeming feature is that waste heat from the process can be used to heat homes, as it is in Malmö, Sweden, in Edmonton, Canada, and in Shef-

POISONOUS PLANTS

The plants in the illustration (*left*) are poisonous. Remove them or put them out of reach if they are house plants; fence them off if they are valued garden plants. Explain to older children which part of the plant is dangerous and why. The Christmas cherry (1) is a poisonous house-plant. All parts are toxic and can cause nausea, abdominal pain and drowsiness if ingested. The house-plant dumbcane (2) has a poisonous stem which can cause burning sensations and irritation of the mouth, lips and tongue if bitten. The poinsettia (3) is a houseplant with poisonous leaves and sap, which causes blistering of the skin and gastroenteritis if it comes into contact with the mouth. Rhubarb (4) has highly toxic leaf blades, which can cause vomiting and sometimes even death when only small quantities are eaten. Laburnum (5) has attractive but toxic pods and seeds. The results of poisoning are vomiting, nervous symptoms, convulsions, coma and even death. Daffodil bulbs (6) can cause gastroenteritis, trembling and convulsions if swallowed.

Other poisonous plants include aconite, arum lily, broom (pods and seeds), bryony berries, cotoneaster berries, daphne berries, deadly nightshade berries, foxglove, young leaves and unripe fruit of hemlock, holly berries, honeysuckle berries, ivy berries, laurel leaves and berries, lupin pods and seeds, mountain ash berries, oleander, potato fruits and green tubers, pyracantha berries, rhododendron leaves, yew berries and some mushrooms and toadstools.

field in the UK. A UK company, Secondary Resources of Chipping Norton, reclaims domestic waste. Its modern technology enables it to sift out metals, plastic and glass. Eight per cent of the waste is tipped and the remainder is converted to refuse-derived fuel (RDF) and organic humus. Dumping rubbish on landfill sites causes ugly eyesores which will last for generations. Biodegradable rubbish can take many years to rot and a large proportion of rubbish is not biodegradable at all.

Dumping lets illegally dumped poisonous chemicals seep into the underground water table and can lead to explosions from methane gas, a by-product of rotting organic material. In the UK half of all the domestic waste dumped could have been recycled. You can buy one of 51 regional recycling information directories in the UK if you wish to help improve on this figure but are not sure how. Before you take waste to a collection point, calculate the amount of energy that will be used in making the journey. If the collection point is not reasonably near your home, you many find that the trip wastes more energy than the recycling process saves. Take larger loads there more infrequently, or save up waste until you are making a trip near to the collection point.

AUTOMOBILES

Vehicles on the roads are a major cause of atmospheric pollution and a major contributor to the greenhouse effect and to the photochemical smogs that can occur in hot, sunny, still conditions. Ozone levels in photochemical smogs are high and health hazards include susceptibility to infections, lung disease and irritation of the eyes. Seventy per cent of the lead in our bodies comes from the air we breathe. The British Lung Foundation recommends that pedestrians, cyclists and those working in the open in cities should wear anti-pollutant masks. The number of cars on the road is soaring: as I write there are said to be 500 million in the world. We have to find ways of cutting down on the damage they do.

When you replace your car, buy one with a catalytic converter to take some of the poisonous fumes (carbon monoxide, hydrocarbons and nitrous oxides) out of the exhaust gases. These will soon be compulsory on new cars in member countries of the EC. However, these do nothing to reduce the vast amounts of carbon dioxide produced by car exhausts. Only a reduction in the fuel used will do that. Buy a car which is energy-efficient (perhaps with a 'lean-burn' engine) and has a low petrol consumption so that it goes a long way for each unit of petrol bought. Drive at energy-efficient speeds (check with the manufacturer if you do not know what these are for your car). Learn to drive without undue revving up and acceleration, which waste fuel. In Budapest in Hungary, which has serious problems with air pollution from factories and cars, traffic lights tell drivers to turn off their car engines while they wait. Have your car serviced and tuned regularly and consider cutting down its use by walking or cycling more, by sharing car journeys (for example to school, work and shops), and by using public transport when appropriate. In the UK, the London borough of Sutton pays mileage expenses to council staff who cycle to work. Sutton has the title 'London's Greenest Borough'.

Buy unleaded petrol for cars that will run on it. In the UK the consumption of unleaded petrol rose from 3 to 28 per cent in 1989. In the USSR leaded petrol is to be discontinued by 1995. However, unleaded petrol has snags: in the UK (unlike in the USA and the rest of Europe) it has increased levels of potentially carcinogenic benzene. It is hoped that the petrol companies will soon be able to correct this drawback. Unleaded petrol is also slightly less efficient than leaded petrol and therefore produces more carbon dioxide (a greenhouse gas) for the same road coverage. Air-conditioning systems in cars currently contain CFCs. Du Pont, the world's largest manufacturer of CFCs, is testing a new coolant in Australia which is as much as 98 per cent CFC-free. Leaky automobile air-conditioners are some of the worst CFC polluters in Australia.

For years Sweden has tested carbon dioxide levels in vehicle exhaust emissions. The UK is to do the same as part of the MoT test. At present 63 per cent of cars, vans and motorcycles do not come up to EC standards for pollution, but regular testing should bring carbon dioxide emissions down by 4 per cent.

'GREEN' BUSINESS

The purpose of business is to make money, making it tempting for the profit motive to take precedence over green issues. If you use a bank, an insurance company or a building society, or if you have money invested in any other business interest, check that your money is not being used in any way which could endanger the environment or the people in it. Write to the central office of your bank, for instance, to ask what their policies are. If you are a shareholder, attend meetings and lobby for change, if necessary, or place your money elsewhere. If you have your own business, look at its raw materials, its waste, its energy consumption, its pollution, its cars and its safety record.

Environmental awareness in business and other organizations can be influenced by the employees as well as by the shareholders or other owners. Whether your work place is at home or away, and whether you are employed full- or part-time, consider joining a union. To date, West German trades unions have the best record of action on environmental issues, but virtually all trade unions in Europe, the USA and Australia have someone with responsibility for environmental issues and much useful research into safety and health in the workplace has been carried out by the major unions. Thus, trades unions can and should be lobbied to influence environmental policies concerning both employees and products.

The Valdez principles are guidelines that have been drawn up by concerned investors and environmentalists. In a nutshell, they call for the sustainable use of natural resources; the wise use of energy; the minimization of waste; and compensation for environmental damage. They also call for the disclosure of any damage; having at least one environmentalist on a company's board of control; and carrying out an annual environmental audit. Clearly, being green is not something you do only at home. One survey of top business executives in the UK found that pressure from their partners at home had made nearly half of them switch to environmentally friendly policies.

You can do great things for the benefit of the wider environment, as well as for your family's home environment, if you do your bit in a small way.

SAFETY IN THE HOME

The safety of your child's environment is a vital green issue. Think through your home room by room to identify possible hazards and do something about them before your child has an accident; then memorize the preventive measures listed below:

BASIC SAFETY MEASURES:

FIRE:

● Put a secure fireguard in front of any open fire.

● Position a paraffin heater where it cannot be knocked over; never move it when lit.

● Use a cooker guard (similar to a fireguard) on the hob; and turn all pan handles in when cooking.

● Keep your child well clear when handling hot pans and dishes.

● Do not leave a young child in the kitchen when food is cooking on the cooker hob.

● Install smoke alarms. Buy a fire extinguisher or a blanket.

● Keep the temperature of the running hot water below that which could accidentally scald a child.

continued overleaf

- Keep matches and lighters out of reach.

- Do not let children play unsupervised near a bonfire.

ELECTRICITY:

- Teach young, inquisitive children not to poke anything into electricity sockets. Fit socket covers.

- Turn off appliances at the socket when not in use and remove the plugs.

- Earth appliances with a three-core cable.

- Do not overload a circuit by plugging too many appliances into a socket or an adapter into an adapter.

- Service appliances as necessary.

- Do not put flexes under carpets or rugs or leave them trailing. You can buy curly flexes for kettles, irons and other small appliances.

- Do not leave a young child in a room alone with a hot appliance, such as a kettle or an iron.

- Toys operated from the mains electricity are best reserved for older children who have respect for electricity.

- Electric blankets are not safe in children's beds: a child might wet the bed or spill drinks. If you use one to warm the bed, disconnect it before the child goes to bed.

- Do not obstruct the vent-holes of a convector heater.

- Never use electrical appliances in the bathroom except for a shaver with its own socket. Have pull cords for lights instead of wall switches.

- Do not encourage a young child to experiment with electrical kitchen appliances.

- Beware of batteries. Tiny ones can be swallowed or pushed into the nose or ear. Batteries can leak if they are wrongly used; for example, if old and new ones, or batteries of different types, are mixed in an appliance; or if batteries, especially dead ones, are left in equipment that is not much used. Do not throw exhausted batteries on to a fire as this can make them explode. Supervise a child replacing batteries in a toy to make sure they are fitted correctly and to ensure that leakage will not occur.

KITCHEN:

- Fit safety catches to low cupboards.

- Keep knives and plastic bags out of reach.

- Secure a tablecloth to the table with clips to prevent a young child from pulling it off and risking a scald or other injury.

- Keep hot drinks, teapots and dishes out of reach.

- Use a non-slip flooring if possible and always mop up floor spills quickly.

- Keep household chemicals out of reach.

- Never put household chemicals into unlabelled containers.

- Do not let children play with a pet's bowl, bedding, or litter tray, from which they could get worms.

HALLS, STAIRS, LANDING:

- Guard stairs with a safety gate if your child is crawling or learning to walk.

- Check that any carpet is well fixed and not frayed.

- Put a non-slip backing under a rug at the bottom of the stairs.

- Never carry anything else at the same time as you carry your child on the stairs.

- Do not carry a child on the stairs if you are wearing socks or tights, sloppy shoes or slippers, or a long dressing-gown.

- Never leave things lying on the stairs.

LIVING-ROOM:

- Do not put a mirror over a fire. A child will be drawn to it.

- Check the room for hazardous objects, such as sewing scissors, record sleeves, trailing house plants and heavy ornaments.

- Choose non-poisonous indoor plants (*see page 151*).

BATHROOM:

• Put medicines in a locked cupboard and keep them in labelled, child-resistant containers.

• Do not keep old medicines. Give them to your pharmacist for disposal.

• Use non-slip flooring.

• Keep scissors and razors out of reach.

• Never leave a young child alone in the bath, even for a very short time.

DOORS, GATES, WINDOWS:

• Make sure your front gate (or your front door if you have no gate) is secure.

• Replace non-safety glass in doors with laminated, toughened or wire-reinforced (shatter-proof) glass.

• Fit safety locks on windows so when they are opened the gap is too small to climb through.

• Check that a balcony railing is safe.

GARDEN:

• Never leave electrical equipment unattended.

• Store garden chemicals out of reach.

• Take special care when using garden tools with a young child around.

• Cover a septic tank securely. Fence a pond or cover with wire netting if your young child plays in the garden alone.

• Never let a young child play in a paddling-pool unsupervised.

• If you have a swimming pool, fence it securely and lock the gate when not in use. Never leave a child alone near or in a pool.

• Check bicycles, swings and other equipment for safety regularly. Tighten up the screws on swings: they work loose.

• Supervise young children on swings and other large play equipment.

• Fix garden ornaments in place with concrete.

• Avoid poisonous plants (*see page 151*).

• Discourage your child from playing with mushrooms and toadstools.

• Never let children play unsupervised when a bonfire is burning.

• Never let young children light fireworks or approach fireworks as you light them.

SHEDS & GARAGES:

• Keep all chemicals and tools safely out of reach.

• Keep your child out of the way when doing any DIY projects.

• Never let a child near a jacked-up car.

• Always check that your child is out of the way when you reverse or drive off.

• Double-check for young fingers before shutting the car door or boot.

ROAD SAFETY:

• Teach your child to respect traffic.

• Keep a toddler's hand held securely anywhere near a road.

• Never push a pram or a pushchair into the road until it is absolutely safe.

• Do not carry a baby on your lap in the car.

• Use a robust carrycot restraint or a special baby seat for a baby weighing up to 10 kilograms (22 pounds). Babies under nine months are safest in rear-facing seats.

• Put a bigger child under 18 kg (40 lb) on a booster seat and secure with a seat belt.

• Allow a young child in the back of a car only; babies in backward-facing seats at the front.

AND ON HOLIDAY ...:

• Take water-purifying tablets abroad if necessary.

• Never leave a young child unsupervised near the water's edge.

• Hold inflatable water toys, such as boats, on a line.

• Always put a life-jacket on your child in a boat, or tie him or her to part of the boat.

• Check baby equipment for safety.

Chapter Eight
YOUR HEALTH

Love is the medicine for the healing of the world.
Karl Menninger

'Your health!' was the toast used in my family when I was a child. During the seventeenth century, men used to honour an attractive woman by raising their glasses to the lady's name. This custom was known as a toast because they hoped that the name of the lady they honoured would flavour their drink like the piece of spiced toast often added to drinks in those days as a flavouring. The health of the body, mind and spirit can likewise flavour our lives. Whether the taste is of spice, sugar, salt or something bitter is very much a green issue. We are a valuable natural resource, but we must be healthy to function at our best. Our health deserves to be promoted, protected and supported; not ignored, drained and let down. Tragically, in poor countries one child dies of a preventable disease (such as diarrhoea or measles) every two seconds. There is tremendous inequity of health and opportunity in the world and it is largely caused by the greed of those people who already have enough.

Health means living in a state of ever-changing compatibility with ourselves, with each other and with our environment. It also means learning from ill health. Healthy people listen to the messages from their body, mind and spirit that say change is necessary for comfort, stability, healing and harmony. Most of the time you can help your child remain healthy yourself (*see pages 164-167*). But sometimes you will need to ask another, more skilled person to help you interpret the messages you hear, see, feel, smell and otherwise sense. This is the basis of the ancient Chinese system of medicine based on preventive health measures.

POOR HOUSING

Most of the great advances in public health in industrialized countries during the last century have resulted from improvements in living conditions. People had so de-spoiled their environment that cramped, dark, damp housing with dirty water, air and poor sewage facilities had taken their toll on health. Respiratory problems and infections of various sorts were rife and lives too often ended early and abruptly.

By now, most developed countries have put many of their housing problems right. However, many places remain where parents struggle to bring up children in horrible conditions which they are powerless to alter alone. We owe it to one another to improve unacceptable housing. It is also important to maintain the fabric of good housing. The constant process of repairing your home and protecting it from damage through ageing and exposure to the elements is a very real service, not only to your family but also to the community, helping it conserve its housing stock.

DIRTY AIR

OUTDOORS

Many municipal authorities are doing their best to control pollution from traffic fumes and factory and domestic smoke. This is not working everywhere, however, and some families have no choice but to breathe smog-filled air heavy with toxic chemicals and with poisonous ozone, created by the action of sunlight on pollutants in the air. Children who breathe dirty air risk developing lung infections and wheezing. They are also more at risk than adults from the lead poisoning caused by inhaling traffic fumes, because children's guts absorb lead more efficiently than adults'.

The air, ground and water of many areas in East Europe are heavily polluted. In Hungary, for example, 60 per cent of the air pollution stems from industry, 30 per cent from traffic (much of it from the crowds of two-stroke car engines), and 10 per cent from the domestic burning of the pungent brown coal called lignite. In Krakow in Poland, pollution is so bad that one in ten children have chronic bronchitis, asthma is common, cancer is four times as common as in western Europe, the rates of premature birth, congenital malformation and miscarriage are high and average life expectancy is six to eight years shorter than in western Europe. Tourists are warned to stay only three days because the air and water are so unhealthy.

Many developed countries have taken measures to clean up their traffic fumes. In the USA, for example, catalytic converters are compulsory. The Swedes are now fitting particulate filters to heavy vehicles to trap the diesel soot responsible for so much asthma, bronchitis and perhaps also cancer.

Dirty air is not only a feature of some industrial towns. Air from polluted areas, such as parts of East Germany, can travel thousands of miles to fall as acid rain on unspoilt areas, such as the Swedish forests. Country dwellers may also breathe unacceptably high levels of toxic agrochemicals from adjacent or upwind farmland (*see pages 116-119*).

Carbon monoxide (CO) is a poisonous gas. Most of us are exposed to it to varying degrees every day. The chart (*below*) shows that the majority of carbon monoxide in the air in large cities comes from the exhaust fumes of vehicles running on leaded petrol. Exposure to CO makes the blood less efficient in carrying oxygen. People with heart disease or breathing disorders may find that their conditions worsen; and sleepiness, unconsciousness or even death can be caused by exposure to CO.

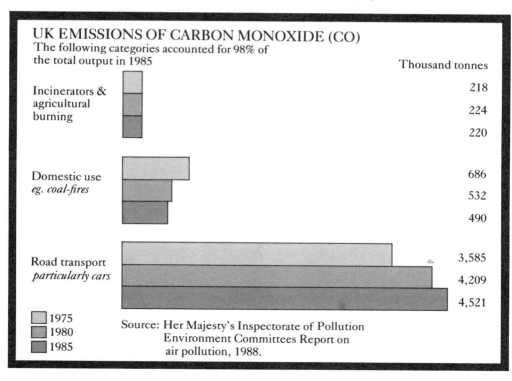

UK EMISSIONS OF CARBON MONOXIDE (CO)
The following categories accounted for 98% of the total output in 1985

Thousand tonnes

Incinerators & agricultural burning	
	218
	224
	220

Domestic use *eg. coal-fires*	
	686
	532
	490

Road transport *particularly cars*	
	3,585
	4,209
	4,521

1975
1980
1985

Source: Her Majesty's Inspectorate of Pollution Environment Committees Report on air pollution, 1988.

INDOORS

Pollution can also affect the air in the home, although most people are unaware of any ill effects. Those who spend most time at home – usually mothers, children and the elderly – are most at risk. Many spend four-fifths of their time indoors. Radon gas, which seeps up through the floors of houses from underlying rock (*see page 136*) is a problem in some areas. Researchers are investigating an association between radon in the home and a raised risk of cancer.

Carbon monoxide from car exhausts (*see page 37*), a faulty heater, a smoky fire or cigarette smoke can lead to unacceptably dirty air. Smoke from fires and cigarettes also pollutes the air with nitrogen dioxide. Carbon monoxide is fatal in high concentrations, while high levels of nitrogen dioxide have been linked with a possible increase in respiratory infections. Inhaling cigarette smoke can cause respiratory infections and eventually lung cancer. If you smoke, your child in effect smokes too, albeit involuntarily. This 'passive' smoking carries health risks similar to those of active smoking.

Before its dangers were understood asbestos was used in building, and it is still found in some homes. Asbestos is a naturally occurring substance composed of tiny fibrils; inhaling these can lead to lung cancer or a malignant growth in the lining of the lungs called a mesothelioma. Asbestos used in the construction of a building is not a major health hazard as long as it remains intact, but there is a risk to health if the building becomes damaged or decayed and the asbestos is disturbed. Its removal must be handled extremely carefully, as it can be a major risk.

Formaldehyde has many possible sources, including building materials (*see page 141*). It irritates the mucous membranes of the eyes, ears, nose, throat and lungs and may be carcinogenic.

The excreta of the minute house dust mite can cause allergies, asthma, runny

The sick building syndrome is a collection of vague symptoms which has been reported by some office workers in particular buildings, usually modern ones, which are air-conditioned, centrally heated, and contain mainly synthetic wall and floor coverings and furniture, together with much electronic equipment. The syndrome includes irritation of the mucous membranes of the eyes, nose, throat, ears and lungs, headaches, fatigue and nausea. The causes are not entirely clear but there seems to be no reason to suppose that a similar problem should not exist in certain homes. The remedies depicted above include using natural materials for furniture and wall- and floor-coverings, turning off electrical appliances when not in use, humidifying dry air, improving ventilation, wearing leather-soled shoes and adopting a no-smoking policy. House plants absorb toxic fumes from the air.

nose and eczema. Mattresses are the most likely mite habitat. Covering an allergic child's mattress with a polyurethane-coated fabric, Ventflex, (*see page 183–184* **Consumer Guide**), will reduce symptoms, according to recent research. Bacteria and fungi in dust and mould can be associated with both allergy and infection. Do not buy over-the-counter preparations to kill these organisms. Ask your doctor about eradication.

You can cut down on indoor air pollution and improve the quality of the air in your home simply by increasing the ventilation. Double-glazing, cavity wall insulation, draught-proofing and loft insulation (*see pages 137–138*) save fuel but also cut down the rate of air exchange. This means that air pollutants are less diluted by fresh incoming air. It is especially important that any form of heating or cooking in the home that uses gas, oil, coal or wood should be well vented. Dampness should be treated, as it encourages the presence of mites and mould.

SENSITIVITY TO CHEMICALS

One newly recognized problem is that of the chemically sensitive person. Everything is made up of chemicals, but the ones responsible for this condition are volatile, manufactured chemicals, especially those made from petrochemicals. A cocktail of volatile chemicals in the air is thought to overload or stress the immune system of chemically sensitive people, so that it fails and they become ill. They develop diseases of the skin, lungs and nervous system and end up unable to withstand even low levels of any one of these chemicals.

It is possible that many more people than we realize have symptoms as a result of low-level exposure to volatile chemicals. There certainly seems to be a great deal of unexplained illness in many children, such as eczema, asthma and a constantly runny nose. Volatile chemicals enter our homes from a variety of sources: building materials such as pressed particle board in the very fabric of a house (*see page 141*); household paints; foam-backed carpets; the glue used to stick plastic tiles to the floor; insulating foam and foam-filled furniture; fabric coatings and household chemicals.

Chemical sensitivity may not only result from the air we breathe. Pollutants can also enter our bodies from food and water. Statisticians have worked out that three out of four of all cancers are caused by food, smoke and chemicals in the environment. Clinical ecologists maintain that we need to look at every aspect of potential pollution when assessing environmental effects on health. It is possible that the combined effect of all the pollutants to which we are exposed may be greater than the sum of the individual ones. In other words, combinations of pollutants may be more poisonous than you would expect through knowing what is in the mixture.

HEALTHY FOOD & WATER

Our food can be polluted as it grows or during its processing. Such contamination can change the internal environment of our bodies. Added to the list of generally invisible polluting substances discussed in detail in Chapter 6 are nickel (from stainless steel pans) and plasticizers (from cling film). The scale of food contamination by such pollutants is not to be underestimated: air pollutants precipitating on to soil result in 60 per cent of the food in and around Krakow, for example, being unfit for human consumption.

Too much or too little food can both have disastrous consequences. Every year sees over 500 million people undernourished and 40 million dead from hunger-related diseases or starvation. The environment, or rather their fellow human beings, have failed them. Large numbers of people fall ill or die prematurely every year from diseases related to the long-term consumption of an over-large or otherwise unhealthy diet. Their environment has provided well for them but they have failed to make good use of the bounty of the harvest. We do not yet know whether the food our children eat affects their chances of contracting food-related disorders, such as heart disease, in adult life. But it seems likely, if only because eating patterns for life are established in childhood.

SYMPTOMS

Symptoms of contamination by pollutants are many and complex. For example, symptoms of agricultural poisoning as a result of exposure via the lungs (perhaps from drifting spray) or skin (from a spillage) can appear quickly. Poisoning via traces in food usually takes longer. Poisoning from pesticides has been linked with asthma, headaches, coughing, fever, abdominal pain, behaviour disorders, leukaemia and other cancers, fits, dermatitis, birth defects, high blood pressure and even multiple sclerosis. One in 200 cases of cancer in the USA may be caused by pesticides. Dr William Rea, Director of the Environmental Health Center in Dallas, USA, and Professor of Environmental Medicine at the University of Surrey, England, says that pesticides can severely disturb the immune system, hence their ability to cause cancer. Of the 400 or so pesticides used in the UK, 40 per cent have been linked with one of the following: cancer, birth defects, genetic mutations, infertility or irritant reactions.

HEALTH HELPERS

Over the last two decades there has been a great deal of interest in alternative therapies, such as homeopathy, acupuncture, herbalism, naturopathy, aromatherapy, hydrotherapy and massage, including shiatsu. Counselling is increasingly being used by people suffering from psychosomatic and other emotional problems. This is currently limited mostly to adults, but family or child therapy is sometimes used.

The popularity of alternative therapies is partly due to the time and attention given to the patient. In the UK, consultations with general practitioners frequently last only three to five minutes. Furthermore, maintaining health is often a greater priority for alternative therapists than for many doctors, who still tend to be primarily concerned with diagnosing and treating illness.

Brief, focussed medical diagnosis and advice has an important role, but the facts are that two out of three people consulting a doctor have symptoms that are fairly vague and often psychosomatic or environmentally induced. Approximately eight out of ten conditions will get better by themselves or are beyond cure. A brief consultation has little chance of being fundamentally useful, or of helping to right the balance of health in the majority of cases. Helping parents and their children achieve and maintain health usually takes more than that. It may involve a time-consuming look at their environment, including the relationships within the family; it might need a determination to help right social injustice; it might involve a look at the reasons for making unhealthy choices in the way in which they live; or it might necessitate an on-going, supportive and loving relationship with an affirming and encouraging helper.

The condescending attitudes of some health professionals have contributed to the current dissatisfaction with orthodox western medicine. Helping people to health involves working with them so that they can better recognize and trust their body's signals of impending illness. It also involves listening to them more skilfully and lovingly and encouraging them to become more confident in their own common sense and ability to heal themselves and perhaps others. One important healing factor in any illness is faith in the chosen treatment. Children are good at picking up such confidence from their parents.

Good health workers or healers, whether involved in orthodox or complementary therapies, never stop learning. They continue to polish their skills and learn from their experiences and those of others; to learn from and with their patients; to care for people more often than cure them; to have the humility to be aware of and work on their own problems, rather than fool themselves that only others have health problems; to recognize the privilege and

No single system of medicine is foolproof or necessarily the most useful for the treatment of any disease or condition. Experts in the same field often disagree about how best to treat a condition, but orthodox medicine and the complementary (or 'alternative') therapies – osteopathy, homeopathy, acupuncture, naturopathy, aromatherapy massage, the Alexander technique and other techniques illustrated *above*, can indeed complement each other well. Increasing numbers of doctors are now becoming interested in the methods and techniques used in complementary therapies. Some are incorporating them into their medical practice or referring their patients to known practitioners.

opportunity of being invited to walk with someone at a time of need; and to know that healing involves a recognition of the emotional and spiritual dimensions of life.

In summary, both helper and helped need to have realistic expectations of what treatment can and cannot do. This sort of health care is green because it optimizes the resources of both.

A recent survey carried out by the Consumers' Association in the UK found that most patients had serious doubts about the competence and honesty of their doctors. By contrast, a MORI poll of over 1,400 people in the UK in 1989 found that 75 per cent of men and of women were satisfied with their doctor. The word 'doctor' comes from the Latin for 'teacher'. A useful aphorism comes to mind here. It is, 'The good teacher is the one who is always learning'.

KNOWING WHO TO CONSULT

With the plethora of helpers, both orthodox and complementary, in many developed countries today, it can be confusing and difficult for a parent requiring help with a child's problems to know who to consult. We know that some of the drugs and other treatments of orthodox medicine can do harm, causing iatrogenic (doctor-induced) illness. According to the US Office of Technology Assessment, only one in five medical procedures have been demonstrated scientifically to be safe and beneficial. It is also fair to say that the codes of practice, the years of training, the reporting of adverse effects from drugs, and the system of referral for second opinion when necessary, are very good safeguards. However, orthodox medicine can do little for most of the common problems of childhood and it ignores some completely.

As a parent you may feel that the burden of responsibility for your child's health is great and you may be afraid of doing the wrong thing. I suggest you always consider consulting a doctor qualified in orthodox western medicine first. This should ensure that no serious problem is missed. You can then go on to consult a complementary therapist, as well your own doctor. Some doctors are trained as practitioners in complementary therapies, most commonly homeopathy, herbalism and acupuncture. They perhaps combine the best of both worlds. Both orthodox doctors and practitioners of complementary therapies should refer patients to each other if they think their own treatments are inappropriate. In the UK the Institute for Complementary Medicine (*see pages 183–184* **Consumer Guide**) maintains a register of trained practitioners in complementary therapies. Training for the different therapies varies greatly but many of their professional bodies have (or are working towards) effective registration schemes.

PHARMACEUTICAL REMEDIES

Much modern orthodox medical care is drug-based. Most pharmaceutical drugs owe their origin to the active principles in plant extracts. Some are synthetic copies of these plant principles, while others are synthetically constructed relatives. Plants in our environment have given us some vital tools in the treatment of illness. Four-fifths of the world's population rely on plants for their medicines. Aspirin from willow bark, vincristine (used to treat leukaemia) from the periwinkle and steroids from the yam are just three examples.

The destruction of the rainforests is an enormous threat to the discovery of new medicines. The process of cutting down millions of acres of tropical rainforest means that almost one in four of all plant species face extinction within the next 40 years. There are many thousands of untested plants in this habitat which, research chemists believe, could yield exciting new drugs, but if their habitat disappears, so does the hope of finding new cures. American scientists are currently studying thousands of plants in the hope of finding more cures for cancer.

Herbalists believe that it is better to give an extract of a plant rather than a synthetic copy of what is thought to be the active ingredient. It may be that something in the plant – perhaps its 'essence' or life-force – is missing in a synthetic copy. There is a commercial problem, however, with this green approach for the drug companies which effectively dominate the medicines market. Drug companies cannot hold a patent on a natural plant extract. They have to alter it in some way to make it patentable and this makes it more expensive. A patented drug must be thoroughly tested (on animals as well as in other ways) before release, and then it has to be marketed either to the public, to pharmacists as an over-the-counter preparation, or to doctors. In the UK the pharmaceutical industry spends £30,000 a year on direct or indirect advertising to each doctor.

The pharmaceutical industry has undoubtedly done a great deal of good in creating and improving drugs, but certain companies sometimes behave unethically, despite their image. In the Third World, for instance, antibiotics are promoted (and are often available over the counter) for the treatment of diarrhoea. Many babies have died from this unnecessary treatment for a condition which can be cured by oral rehydration therapy (giving a simple but precisely mixed drink of water, sugar and salt), and prevented by breastfeeding and the provision of clean water (*see page 128*).

Both pharmaceutical drugs and herbal

remedies or products can have side-effects. It is better to use them only under professional guidance, unless you are familiar with them or unless there are clear instructions for their use with children on the packaging. For example, Aspirin should not be given to children under the age of 12 because of the remote possibility of causing Reye's syndrome (brain and liver damage). Some herbs used in remedies to treat eczema have recently been shown to cause liver damage. However, some pharmaceutical preparations have been proved to be both safe and helpful as long as they are used properly.

There is every reason to include a selection of both herbal and pharmaceutical remedies for common childhood ailments in your green medicine cupboard, although none should be used for any reason other than an essential one. Any medicine, whether plant extract or synthetic analogue or derivative, is a potential stress on the body's mechanism for coping with illness, if all it does is take the symptom away, rather than deal with the cause. This extra stress could add to any other chemical pollution of the child's environment. On the other hand, homeopathic remedies aim to stimulate the body's own healing mechanisms into treating the cause of illness.

SOME COMMON AILMENTS

If you consult both a doctor and a complementary therapist about your child's symptoms, you will get two sets of advice. This is a common problem for green parents and perhaps one good reason why many prefer to stick to one trusted adviser rather than exposing themselves to several. The plan of action with any problem is first to look for the cause and to treat it if possible; and second, to treat any unpleasant symptoms. If there are two recommended treatments, you will need some way of deciding which to choose and of establishing whether or not you can combine both. I will now examine a few common ailments and discuss various approaches from a green perspective.

MINOR CUTS & BRUISES

Clean with plenty of warm water and with antispectic solution (containing chlorhexidine and cetrimide) if dirty. Dry and apply witch hazel to promote healing. Cover a large cut or graze with a sterile dressing. A small cut is better left uncovered. Go to a casualty department if the cut needs stitching or further cleaning.

COLDS

The orthodox medical advice is either to do nothing because there is no recognized treatment for viral infections, or to treat the symptoms. Most doctors prefer parents to treat the symptoms of minor coughs and colds themselves. There are plenty of green options. Among them are the many homeopathic remedies chosen according to the basic disposition of the child and to the nature of the catarrh and other symptoms. There are also many herbal remedies: an infusion of elderflower or peppermint; the (carefully supervised) inhalation of vapour from a bowl of hot water with a few drops of eucalyptus, hyssop or cinnamon oil; a few drops of cinnamon oil in a hot bath rubbed into the temples and chest several times a day. Other well known treatments include adding crushed, raw garlic to food; pads of first a hot and then a cold flannel placed on the forehead or the back of the neck; gentle face massage; and zinc and castor oil cream rubbed into the skin round the nose to prevent soreness. You can make a refreshing drink with freshly squeezed orange and lemon juice, to which you add pounded or liquidized peel to take advantage of its bioflavonoids, which aid the action of vitamin C. Other, more general remedies are rest; keeping the child in air that is warm but not too dry (which might dry the catarrh and make it difficult to shift); avoiding refined foods and ensuring your child's diet is healthy.

Some children seem to have frequent coughs and colds. Possible reasons include being run down due to an unhealthy diet and a lack of fresh air, exercise and sun-

To treat earache gently, place a warm, covered hot water bottle on the pillow on the side of the affected ear and let your child lie with the bottle (not too hot) against the ear (*top*). Alternatively, lie your child on one side, with the affected ear uppermost, to encourage the catarrh to drain down to the back of the throat, then pour a few drops of oil that has been warmed but is not too hot into the ear (*centre*). Do this several times a day. Any variety of cooking oil can be used. Let your child stay in this position for a few minutes. The warm oil may loosen or thin the catarrh the other side of the ear-drum, in the middle ear, and ease its departure down the Eustachian tube. However, if the ear is discharging pus, do not use this method because oil could enter the middle ear via the perforated ear-drum. A discharge could mean that the drum had already burst, and the earache should be relieved. If your doctor recommends antibiotics, give your child some live yoghourt every day (*above*) to help counter the detrimental effects of antibiotics on the friendly micro-organisms in the gut.

light; continued exposure to environmental pollutants (*see pages 157-161*); or acute or long-term emotional stress.

EARACHE

Earache is sometimes caused in children by infection spreading along the Eustachian tubes, which run from the back of the throat into the middle ear cavities. An infection of the middle ear is called otitis media and is particularly likely to occur in babies under one year old. Doctors commonly treat it with antibiotics in an attempt to kill off the infecting organisms. Opinion is divided, however, as to whether the routine use of antibiotics is really helpful. It is possible that the underlying cause may be an allergy which has caused the lining of the Eustachian tube or tubes to become inflamed and swollen.

One recent international study carried out by doctors in Australia, Belgium, Israel, the Netherlands, New Zealand, Canada, Switzerland, the UK and the USA found that children who were given antibiotics had a slower rate of recovery than children who were not. A Dutch study found that there was no difference in outcome whether a child was treated with antibiotics; with a myringotomy (a surgical puncture of the ear-drum to allow infected catarrh to come out); antibiotics and a myringotomy; or a placebo (an inactive medication). Clearly there is plenty of room for green treatments, but whether many parents faced with a distressed child screaming with earache in the middle of the night should or could resist the temptation to call a doctor is debatable.

If your child has earache you can use all the green remedies described above for colds. The inhalation and the oil rubs may be particularly helpful. Several of these remedies, as well as the top two home remedies illustrated (*opposite*) encourage the inflamed mucous membrane lining of the Eustachian tube to shrink, making it easier for the dammed up and possibly infected and thick catarrh to find its way down the tube.

COLIC

Colic in young babies is frequently unexplained. Causes include hunger, and sensitivity to infant formula and to traces of substances, such as onions, beans, cabbage or alcohol, in mother's milk. Check with your doctor that there is no serious cause. The chiropractic technique of gentle spine manipulation proved very successful in 94 per cent of colicky babies treated in one Danish study, but seek professional advice; this is not something to try at home yourself. A variety of green remedies will help alleviate your baby's distress. For example you can massage the baby's tummy gently (*see opposite; see also page 109* for a recipe for massage oil). Others are listed on page 77 and below:

● If your baby is breastfed, have something nutritious to eat between each feed, or about every two hours if your baby is at the breast for much of the early evening. Avoid foods to which you are sensitive.

● Use a form of contraception other than the contraceptive Pill while breastfeeding.

● Hold your baby and keep moving.

● Try massaging the baby's tummy or spine gently.

● Give a teaspoonful of an infusion of dill, matricaria (German chamomile) or fennel after a feed. Pour boiling water on to three ounces (84 grams) of fresh herb or one ounce (28 grams) of dried herb in a teapot; let it stand for ten minutes, strain, cool and use.

● Try alternately placing a warm, then a cold flannel on your baby's tummy and repeat several times.

● Simply being there in the hour of need is helpful.

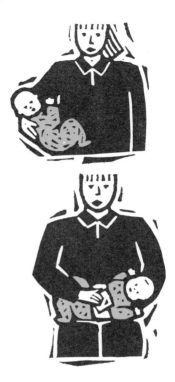

Soothe a colicky baby by massage. Warm some massage oil by immersing the bottle in warm water for a few minutes. Put your baby on a warm towel on your lap, then gently and slowly make clockwise circles all round the baby's tummy with your hand.

SORE THROAT

Three out of five sore throats are caused by viruses. Antibiotics can attack only very few viruses, yet some doctors routinely prescribe them (usually penicillin) for sore throats. This is because it is difficult without considerable experience (monitored by bacteriological tests carried out in a pathology laboratory) to distinguish accurately at first consultation between ordinary sore throats, which will cause no harm in the long term, and sore throats caused by bacteria known as group A β-haemolytic streptococci. These bacteria can lead in some sensitive children to immunological problems such as scarlet fever, rheumatic fever or nephritis (inflammation of the kidneys).

In one large study, carefully carried out

in the USA, penicillin failed to provide any significant relief of symptoms from group A β-haemolytic streptococcal sore throats; and two British studies provided no evidence that penicillin was a protection against the immunological consequences of this type of sore throat. Given that the use of penicillin carries side-effects such as diarrhoea and allergy, there seems to be relatively little benefit in giving it, even if the infection is suspected of being caused by group A β-haemolytic streptococci.

Nevertheless, some doctors, worried by a few cases of septicaemia (blood poisoning) and toxic shock (collapse due to poisoning with bacterial toxins) which have followed infection with these particular bacteria, choose to protect everyone with penicillin even though it is unnecessary for all but a few.

Whether or not your doctor prescribes antibiotics, you can do your bit at home with the green remedies discussed here. In addition, be sure to keep your child's throat warm and try to keep him or her cool if there is any sign of a fever. Try not to let a baby cry, and discourage older children from too much talking.

NITS & HEADLICE

Nits, the eggs of headlice, are about 2 millimetres long, cigar-shaped and pearly white. They are generally found stuck to hairs about 1 centimetre (half an inch) from the scalp. Adult lice look a little like mosquitoes. For a long time now headlice have been treated with pesticide lotions and shampoos. The three pesticides approved for this use in the UK are the organochlorine lindane (trade names Lorexane and Quellada, see page 117), malathion (trade names Prioderm and Suleo-M), and carbaryl (trade names Carylderm and Suleo-C).

These pesticides are extremely toxic substances. Some children are very sensitive to them and develop symptoms after very low exposure. Over-exposure can lead to symptoms as severe as convulsions and vomiting. Claims that lindane can cause cancer, kidney damage, allergy, and symptoms of nerve damage such as fits and insomnia, are currently being investigated. In most cases these problems are thought to have been caused by misuse or over-use. Lindane is the least often recommended of the three, but only because head lice are becoming resistant to it, not because of its toxicity. Ever more toxic pesticides are needed to kill the resistant 'superlice' and chemists are concerned that the level of toxicity of these pesticides to humans, even with only one or two applications at widely spaced intervals, will be too high.

Pesticides for the control of head lice should be treated with great respect. Do not, for instance, use a nit lotion or shampoo on your child's hair in the bath. Toxic chemicals can enter the body via the scalp, but stand an even better chance if applied to the whole body, as they would be in a bath. A worrying factor about nit lotions is that they are left on the scalp and hair overnight, so pesticides will inevitably be absorbed through the scalp. This amounts to chemical pollution of your child's body.

The traditional and green way of treating nits is by grooming your child's hair regularly. Lots of mammals enjoy grooming the coats of their young. This does not mean washing hair more often. In fact, clean hair seems to be more attractive to lice than dirty hair. Go through your child's hair with a fine-toothed comb (a 'nit comb') every month or so as a precaution. Dip the comb in hot vinegar to help unstick the nits from the hairs. The comb will reveal any adult lice which you can crush or drown in a bowl of water. You must use the comb every day for ten days if you find a louse because the louse eggs (the nits) take up to ten days to hatch. By day ten all the existing nits should have hatched and your child's head will be clear.

Some insects dislike the smell of garlic in body secretions. I have no scientific proof for this suggestion but if your child attends a nursery class or a playgroup, or if you have an older child who might bring lice home from school, it might be worth adding a clove of crushed raw garlic every day to his or her food. The snag with this is that the smell might repel other children too. In the UK parents can be fined up to £50 for failing to eradicate head lice, but this does not mean that they are legally required to use a possibly toxic treatment.

IMMUNIZATION

Immunization is a fascinating green issue. This branch of orthodox medicine has been or is responsible for controlling nine major infections: smallpox, diphtheria, tetanus, yellow fever, pertussis (whooping cough), polio, measles, mumps and rubella, or German measles. It can also protect temporarily against several more, such as typhoid and cholera. It works in one of two basic ways. In one, a small number of inactivated or attenuated (weakened) micro-organisms which cause disease – bacteria or viruses – are introduced into the body. The immune system then produces antibodies to deal with them. These stay in the body, ready to multiply and deal with any virulent micro-organisms which may subsequently attack the body. In the other way, ready-formed antibodies are injected into the body to give short-term protection.

The area of infection is fascinating. Many living things manage to co-exist in harmony and without threat for long periods, although they may use each other. However, infection threatens people's health and sometimes their lives. If a life-threatening infection is allowed to spread unchecked by immunization or the isolation of infected people in a community, it is quite capable of wiping out large numbers. This has happened with the introduction of measles to the people of the Brazilian rainforest. Yet some peoples escape infection completely or are only mildly affected and develop their own immunity. The basic level of immunity in a community is known as 'herd immunity'.

There is a fine ecological balance between people and disease-producing micro-organisms. People know they are more likely to succumb to infection if they are already run down and unwell, but this is not always the case, as a perfectly healthy person can be struck down with a life-threatening infectious disease. Micro-organisms do not always respect health.

Immunization is one of the great success stories of modern medicine. Smallpox is eradicated worldwide and poliomyelitis has been virtually eradicated from the western hemisphere. It is confidently expected that in 1990 four out of five children in the world will be immunized against common childhood infections. This is the result of a vast amount of hard work at the international, the national and the grass roots level. It will also save millions of lives. Currently 8,000 children die each year from measles, tetanus and whooping cough, all preventable diseases. Health workers are using the research-based technology of modern medicine to trick potentially infectious bacteria and viruses. There are, however, some worries.

The World Health Organization aims to increase massively the number of children immunized by the end of the millennium. When the control of an infection reaches a certain stage, the risk of a child who has not been immunized contracting that infection is diminished. Parents in a green family then come up against a difficult decision: whether to submit their child to immunization, with its tiny but real chance of side-effects, but with the probability of protecting not only their child but also the community; or whether they are justified in taking advantage of the immunity of the rest of the community to protect their child. In effect, the decision comes down to a choice between what is best for their child and what is best for everyone else's children. From a green point of view – that of loving one's neighbour as oneself – the latter might be the preferred choice.

In the USA and in some provinces of Canada, a child is legally required to have been immunized before starting school. Attendance at school is compulsory, so the USA consequently achieves very high levels of immunization and a reduction of

90 per cent or more in the occurrence of diseases preventable by vaccination. The results are good but the methods may be questionable. It is surely preferable to have a child immunized through free choice and not by any sort of manipulation or coercion. After all, medical procedures have not always proved safe in the long-term; and enforcement of a medical procedure smacks of a brave new world in which people are the pawns of an authoritarian (and always potentially misguided) overclass. If the benefits of immunization are so great, education must be the preferred tool to encourage people to have their children immunized.

Some doctors fear that any immunization might prejudice the health of a child. Homeopaths link certain long-term health problems with immunization. Theirs is a gentle and thoughtful discipline, so they may have a point. Certainly, many people with access to the best of medical care prefer to consult a homeopath. Whether homeopathy could protect an Amazon tribe against the ravages of incoming infections or not is another matter.

A breastfed baby's gut is the site of action of maternal antibodies against polio and other gastro-intestinal infections. Maternal antibodies can also be taken up by the gut wall and passed to the mucous membrane lining of the lungs. Immunization can be ineffective in a breastfed baby or in a baby who is still protected by antibodies received from the mother across the placenta before birth. The 'age-window' between a decrease in maternal antibody protection and the acquisition of infection is very small. Continuing research into this and other factors means that immunization schedules are constantly changing and differ from one country to another. It may be that built into every baby is a series of optimum times for immunization against each disease. So far, however, immunization schedules have been based on probability.

Researchers are currently working on vaccines against chicken pox and infection with viruses responsible for lung infections: the respiratory syncitial virus, rotavirus and *Haemophilus influenzae* type B.

Consider your own immune status when it comes to polio immunization. A baby who has been immunized against polio will shed live polio virus in the bowel motions for about three weeks. If you have not been immunized against polio, you should avoid changing nappies during this period.

ASSESSING A CHILD'S HEALTH

A regular green health assessment can help a family to better health. A physically and mentally healthy child grows well, but not at an even rate. Growth is faster in summer in most children and can be interrupted by episodes of illness. A healthy child is not often unwell with minor infections and other problems. Take a look at your children and the sort of life they lead, and try to decide whether they are eating a healthy diet with few pollutants and having enough exercise, rest, fresh air and sunlight. Think about their environment, both inside and outside your home.

Consider whether your family has enough laughter, games and fun, enough loved and loving friends and enough shared curiosity and learning. Do you dance, make music or tell stories to each other, or is all your entertainment passive – from the TV, the radio, a cassette player or books? Do you hug each other? Hugs can keep people well. Are you able to recognize, express and accept feelings in each other? Do you think your children feel loved? This will be essential to their ability to love themselves and others in the future.

Do you as parents make time for awareness of your spiritual dimension and your communion with a 'higher power' or 'God', whoever or whatever you perceive him or her to be? Children readily pick up their parents' openness to something beyond themselves. Moreover, research in the USA showed that attending Christian church service, at least one a month, was associated with a halving of the rate of divorce (*see pages 180–181*).

Chapter Nine
LEADING YOUR CHILD THE GREEN WAY

Many eyes go through the meadow, but few see the flowers in it.
Ralph Waldo Emerson

Cultural values have always been handed down from parents to children, and green babies will ideally grow up to become green parents themselves. It is a mistake, however, to assume that your philosophy will automatically be adopted by your children with little effort on your part. Leading your children the green way involves two closely interrelated processes: leading through example; and teaching environmental awareness. Children learn by the apprentice system. They usually grow up modelling themselves on their parents' way of thinking, feeling and behaving. Children brought up in a green way by parents and other people who believe them to be valuable and irreplaceable, and who care for the environment, for themselves and for other people, naturally grow up with a concern for the environment and the people in it. Green parents can build on this by actively teaching their children about the need for conservation of the world's natural resources and the nurturing and optimizing of the environment.

Green education is more about the process of learning than about knowing facts. The way children are helped to learn makes as deep an impression as what they are told. The process affects them at the level of the heart or gut: the emotional level. Head-learning alone is not always real learning. If the process is right, the goal of a loving concern for the environment, other people and oneself follows naturally, as does an openness to the spiritual dimension of life.

It is unlikely that you can teach your children a genuine concern for the environment, or indeed for themselves, unless you bring them up in a green way. The love and care children feel for the environment and the people in it stem from their experience of being loved and treated as valuable people with exciting potential. If they feel loved and lovable they can give love, both to other people and to the environment, and will grow up with genuine self-esteem. The first few years are the sensitive period for learning these essential abilities. However, people who do not have the chance to learn them in early childhood can do so later with varying degrees of ease, provided that the opportunities for learning to love through being loved come their way, and that they can recognize, accept and use them. Some people describe learning to feel loved and lovable from their partner, from a close friend or from God who, many people believe, works through other people. Love is the main resource we as humans have to give to and take from each other.

PARENTS HAVE NEEDS TOO

It is difficult, if not impossible, to give your children what you do not have, or not to give what you do have. That is where the ability to love others through the experience of having been loved and having learned to love yourself comes in. You also need to have experienced tolerance, encouragement, praise, playfulness, fairness, security, approval and acceptance if you are to give them easily to your children. You may not have enough experience of these qualities to give them to yourself automatically, but you could ask for what you need from your partner or a close friend, or you could work on yourself with the aid of books or self-awareness courses, or with the help of a counsellor. Encouragement and affirmation, for example, can be acquired skills.

Simply expressing your needs to others may help, although some people find this very difficult, expecting others to know in a magical way. Their underlying belief is, 'If they really loved me, they would know what I want'. If people live with hostility, ridicule and shame emanating either from within themselves (and stemming from their own childhood) or from someone else, they will pass it on to their children unless they can find a constructive way of recognizing and dealing with it.

As in any movement there will inevitably be a few people in the green movement whose greenness results from unresolved emotional problems. Being green could be a way of 'acting out': a psychological term meaning 'the unconscious expression in one's behaviour of a compulsive outward repressed wish or emotion'. Psychiatrists explain that some of our wishes or experiences are unacceptable because they are so painful. In childhood such pains can be hidden (repressed) by the unconscious. In the teenage years or in adulthood these unconscious hurts are sometimes sublimated, by being unconsciously turned into strongly held views or campaigning behaviour. Such views and behaviour may (or may not) be socially acceptable and valued, but they can be a smokescreen, used unwittingly, to hide emotional pain from the owner. Being green could, therefore, represent a need to work through difficult feelings. Some examples might help make this clearer.

A concern with conserving resources can be fuelled by a real and justifiable fear that shortages will become worse. Could another cause be that some people feel very needy and greedy at an unconscious level, however much they have? Things become very important to them. These feelings could stem from never having been given enough time and attention as young children. They might be angry unconsciously at not having had enough, or fearful of further loss.

An interest in pollution can stem from a rational concern about air, food and water becoming less safe. Could it also be that some people are blaming others for pollution as an unconscious projection of their own desire to pollute, dirty or spoil their surroundings? One of the ways in which some upset toddlers express feelings of anger, hurt, jealousy or fear is by soiling their pants. That soon becomes unacceptable and the feelings may go underground, only to surface in another form later.

As parents we can usefully look at our own motivations for wanting to teach our children about the environment or to bring them up in a green way. If we feel excessively strongly about either, we may be acting out our hidden and painful feelings. Acting-out behaviour is not at all green. Hidden feelings of any sort are a natural resource which can, with patience and time, be accepted and used in a positive and genuine way. If we fail to make an effort to understand ourselves or to be understood, our children are likely to grow up unable to accept and use their difficult and painful feelings too. That is not the way to raise a green baby.

THE ESSENCE OF YOUR CHILD

One of the great pleasures of bringing up children is discovering what makes each child tick. To what drumbeat will she dance through life? What will be his song? Will he be allowed to tell his own tale? What is her essence – the 'Amy-ness' of Amy – her uniqueness, the vital spark or source that is in her and that is her? Green education centres on a continual process of recognizing, greeting, encouraging, affirming and so leading out that special essence which makes a child different from any other who has ever lived.

Children need to be believed in. To do that you need to be able to recognize, greet and affirm your essential 'you-ness' too. That comes from being loved and feeling special and uniquely valuable yourself.

All children possess the seven basic types of 'intelligence' or talent illustrated (*above*) to some degree, argues an American professor of education, Dr. Howard Gardener. They are: linguistic ability (use of words); logical-mathematical ability (reasoning); musical ability; spatial ability (understanding and use of space and of relationships of objects in space); kinaesthetic ability (ease of movement); interpersonal ability (understanding and relating to others); and intrapersonal ability (self-awareness and understanding). You can encourage your children in each of these areas as they grow. Perhaps you could also consider how they relate to you. Which are you best at? Which could do with polishing? Can you acknowledge yourself as a valuable person with a unique combination of abilities?

Adults who feel positive about themselves in this way can enable their children to feel the same way. The relationship becomes what Martin Buber, the Austrian philosopher, called an 'I-thou' one, with two human beings recognizing and accepting the true essence of each other. The child whose essence is valued learns trust rather than suspicion, and self-confidence rather than self-doubt. This is how every child, regardless of capability at an intellectual or physical level, can be a success. No-one else can be more successful than she is at being her and he is at being him. You are the person entrusted with the task of helping them realize their own potential.

THE FASCINATION OF LEARNING

As a green parent you help your children to learn by breathing life and enthusiasm into them. You become an 'animateur', a person who awakens the essence or soul of a person. You put the heart into your children's education. Green education means understanding what your children need in order to learn, rather than teaching what you believe children should learn at that age. Rather than always being in front of your children, metaphorically, you can lead by walking alongside. You can share a sense of wonder and joy in the colours of a rainbow, the clarity of a dewdrop, the exuberance of birdsong, the feel of wet sand underfoot, the taste of honey and the smell of baking bread. You can delight in a cuddle, or in the sensuality and even spirituality of breastfeeding or massaging your young child. You can share with your children the fun of being king of the castle, of hiding behind a tree, of being tiny like a curled-up mouse or big and fierce like a roaring lion. The more learning opportunities of every sort you help your children take, the more their brains will develop to accommodate this learning. Learning is just as much about sensing the world around – both seen and unseen – as it is about learning to speak, read and write.

Sometimes you will lead from behind, letting your child guide both of you in the direction in which she needs to be going. Sometimes you may hold your child's hand to give comfort or strength, or to share your feelings of togetherness. An older child may occasionally hold your hand to let you know that he understands how you are feeling, even if he cannot put it into words. Wise parents accept and delight in the knowledge that they can learn from and with their children. Learning is not just something you do as a child but throughout your life.

Some parents find it difficult even to contemplate learning from their children. At a deep level this may stem from a need to prove themselves and an inner lack of confidence. Perhaps as children their learning ability was never affirmed and valued. It is never too late to change and it is much easier if they as parents can learn to encourage themselves or to ask for encouragement and affirmation from someone close.

DISCIPLINE

Children learn most easily if they feel safe. This is where discipline comes in. The word carries overtones of harshness and correction, yet it stems from the Latin word meaning 'teaching'. Constructive discipline is about enabling children to learn through making them feel safe. Children can be frightened of themselves, their strong feelings and sometimes uncontrollable behaviour. Angry or upset children who are allowed to behave destructively or unkindly are afraid deep down of this aspect of themselves and do not learn how to direct the difficult feelings into more constructive outlets.

Green discipline is not about stamping out difficult feelings or behaviour (*see pages 99–100*); its aim is to make it clear that it is the behaviour that is unacceptable, not the feelings or the child. It is about offering a choice of alternative ways to behave which are not destructive or unkind. It is also about recognizing the feelings that lie behind the child's behaviour, letting the child know that you realize they are there and accept them, and considering whether the situation that led to those feelings might be better managed in a different way. Accepting a child's difficult feelings is an important task for parents. Through your acceptance, the child learns to cope with these feelings rather than to be frightened of them or to repress them. It is a good idea always to carry around this thought:

Your child learns via many complementary channels: through his or her own experience, imagination and recreation; through following your example; and through having someone to listen.

LEARNING BY EXAMPLE

Children learn by using the people round them as models or patterns. Your behaviour, the way in which you run your house, cope with life, demonstrate your feelings, interact with others, celebrate and express your views are all naturally absorbed through every pore of your child's body. This is the reason why the way you bring up your child will probably be the way your grandchild is brought up. Your child will soak up your concern and feelings for green issues and the steps you take to respond to the environment and the people in it (including yourself).

It is never late to start. You can begin with something simple, such as collecting milk bottle tops and giving them to a local collection point. You can take your used bottles to a bottle bank when you go shopping; turn off lights in rooms you are not using; and start walking instead of going everywhere in the car. If going green is a recent decision, you and your child can learn together, which is more exciting than doing it alone. It is really a case of practising what you preach. Even better, just practise, do not preach. Actions speak louder than words and useful communication is far more about what we do and how we do it than about what we say.

Children also pick up attitudes from the people they live with. A child who is constantly ridiculed or put down will grow up with low self-esteem and an aptitude for spotting the negative side of people; a child who is constantly criticised learns to condemn; and a child who lives with hostility and aggression learns to fight and bully. In contrast, a child brought up with approval learns to like himself or herself; a child frequently encouraged learns confidence; and a child who lives with acceptance can find love in the world.

RELATING TO OTHERS

Children learn how to relate to other people through the example of those around them. They learn from their parents or other carers how to care for children. Similarly they learn how to be a husband or wife, brother or sister, son or daughter, friend or neighbour. It is important not to believe that you can only succeed as a parent or partner if you are perfect, but to learn from your mistakes and from all your relationships, so that you constantly grow and mature. It is this openness and honesty that your children will benefit from most. A state of graceful imperfection, together with hopes and reasonable goals, is a much more human and encouraging act to follow than a constant striving for perfection. Children who can observe their parents engaged in the active and long-term process of learning to live together are likely to have a creative marriage or partnership later – far

more than children living with parents who refuse to allow themselves and each other permission to make mistakes and grow from them.

Communications skills are also picked up by example. Listening is an essential life skill. To be a good listener you have to want to hear what other people are saying. You have to believe that what they are saying and, more significantly, what they are feeling, are important, although you may not agree with the content of what they say. You also have to be able to put your own concerns and business temporarily to one side. Not only will your children learn about who they are and what makes them tick by being listened to attentively, but they will also learn how to listen. They will learn to pick up or resonate with the feelings behind the words, if that is what you have learned to do. They will also learn to let people know that they understand their feelings (as well as the verbal information imparted) by responding clearly and sensitively and naming the feelings they sense. Good listening is at the heart of most healthy relationships and can change lives. Encouragement and resolution of conflict come much more easily when you have learned listening skills as a child. Through being listened to, your children will learn to listen to themselves.

You need to make time to listen to your children. Other things can wait; listening cannot. Make time to focus on each child and make them feel special and important. Meal times can be good times for families to listen to each other. Shared meals are important because they can be islands in the day, when parents and children sit down together to listen and learn about each other. Some children like to talk as they play, while others like a chat at bathtime or at bedtime.

When you listen to your children, make sure you look at them. When someone listens to you without looking at you, it feels as though they are not listening properly or taking a genuine interest, and you are unlikely to feel understood if you are trying to communicate something that is important to you. Listen not just to the words but also to the body language, so you can sense the feelings behind the words. Try not to interrupt and always accept what the child says as being real for him or her at that time. Just as important as listening to your children is listening to yourself. Learn to listen to the emotional reality behind the buzz of thoughts and get to know yourself better.

Your compassion for people less well off than yourselves will come across to your children. Do they know that there are people starving? Do they realize the extent of suffering borne by people worldwide? Do you give time, money, old clothing or toys to those people, either via recognized charities or local distribution networks? The more you have, the more you can give. Your children could, perhaps, be encouraged to put some pocket money aside for others, or to accompany you if you help out locally. Learning a concern for other people may begin at home, but it does not have to end there.

MANAGING CHANGE & TIME

Parental example also shows children how to cope with change and the ups and downs that are a part of our lives. Any change implies both danger and opportunity. You can help your children by acknowledging your own feelings about change in your life, whether these emotions are positive or negative, obvious or underlying. If you can think of possible ways of coping and goals for the future, your children will learn to do the same rather than being unable to accept that life moves on. Your children will also learn how to apportion time through your example. The amount of time you give to each area of your life will influence your children's perception of what is important. It is essential to think carefully about how much time you give to key activities, such as work, recreation, relationships, helping others, laughter, creativity, relaxation and having a quiet time (perhaps through meditation, prayer or just being still). You demonstrate through your actions what is

valuable to you. If you are always busy, your children will believe that ceaseless activity is your priority in life. Some children go the opposite way to their parents as they grow up, but more often they follow in their parents' footsteps in one way or another.

Time is something that many of us squander. We fill it unproductively and unimaginatively, looking to the past or the future rather than living in the present. Time is an important natural resource and time management is therefore a green issue. Learning to make the most of each moment is the basis of intimacy. Children cannot learn to be emotionally intimate unless their willingness to share themselves as they are at one moment is fostered. If they are accepted as themelves, they will learn to communicate honestly and openly with others.

LEARNING BY DOING

Learning from first-hand experience is a potent way of learning and it tends to stick. Children learn by touching, manipulating, using materials creatively, watching and listening, meeting challenges and solving problems. Learning by experimenting, creativity and questioning has a life of its own and is a process which will continue throughout life. Helping children make the most of the instinctive drive to learn is an active, green process. Children enabled to learn in this way gain a self-confidence which is difficult to extinguish. Doing something unaided enables children to learn more quickly than any amount of demonstration and repeated explanation. By learning through doing, children become more and more able. As they grow in confidence, so their ability to take responsibility grows.

Inquisitiveness – a wish to find out or investigate – leads on to discovery and the urge to find out more. Any parent or child-carer knows, however, that a toddler who is 'into everything' can be a danger to him- or herself, and perhaps difficult to look after. There is a middle path between allowing no inquisitiveness and always being willing to encourage and to help children find out. Perhaps it lies in taking a real, genuine and focussed interest whenever you can, instead of giving half an ear or eye to all of your children's discoveries because you can never bring yourself to say that now is the wrong time for you. The more you give half your attention, the more difficult it may become to give it all.

On the other hand, young children can find it very difficult to understand the meaning of 'not now but later'. Perhaps, then, you need to give your full attention to the discoveries of a very young child more often than not. This implies that child care is a skilful and demanding process which takes time and effort to learn. It also poses a problem for some parents: unless you feel a real interest and delight in these discoveries, you are going to tire yourself out.

Perhaps you could let the child-like part of you experience the joy of discovering things with your children. Learning is, after all, a lifelong experience. If you cannot do this at least some of the time, it is worth assessing your needs. Ask yourself whether you are holding yourself back from having fun and playing and if so, whether life is becoming too serious. Ask if you are enjoying your job of child care. You may need more emotional space or more attention than you are getting. Perhaps being with a child so much is not right for you. Is it draining your resources instead of making the most of them? What steps can you take to ensure that your needs are met, both for your sake and so that you, or someone else, can be more fully with your child?

Many parents find that they are refreshed by having some time away from their children. Work can provide essential time out, but the stay-at-home parent needs time off too, although the amount varies from one person to another. Try to work out how your needs can be met while making sure your children are well cared for by another person: perhaps by your partner, a friend, a relative, a playgroup, a crèche, a nursery class, a teacher, a child-minder or a nanny.

Single parents are perhaps most in need of time to themselves, yet, according to a recent survey in the UK, they are the least likely to get it.

Television has become an alternative child-carer in many families and as such is a boon to busy parents. However, it effectively cuts children off from learning by doing. Watching other people doing something is never the same as doing it yourself. In the USA, by the age of 18 most children have spent more time watching television than they have at school. Some parents think their children do enough already and are happy for them to watch TV as a form of relaxation.

LEARNING BY IMAGINING

A child's imagination is a fantastic and powerful learning medium. Children's minds, hearts and souls weave vivid, colourful, magical and often strange pictures. Even a young child can get lost in a day-dream and explore all sorts of possible or impossible ideas. You can encourage your child's imagination through a variety of means. One is through making up stories of your own or reading other people's, or folk or fairy tales. Children can usually resonate emotionally with the symbolic characters – for instance, the good Little Red Riding Hood and the bad wolf – in books. This helps them learn that they are not alone in their experience of good and bad and of fear and trust.

Other ways of encouraging your children's imagination are through making up poems, rhymes or songs with them and for them, through teaching nursery rhymes and through singing songs. Yet another way is by taking an interest in their dreams and daydreams when they are old enough to tell them. Research by Dorothy Cohen, a child psychologist, found that extensive television-viewing prevented a child's imagination from growing. In the USA teachers have reported that children who watch television do not know how to play imaginative games – games of make-believe – possibly because they are so used to the pre-formed

Your children can learn about the cycles of nature by planting pips, seeds and indoor plants in pots and window boxes (*above*), then tending the plants as they grow and perhaps picking the flowers. They love to press flowers and to dry petals and mix them with sweet-smelling spices or oils to make a pot pourri. They enjoy harvesting mustard and cress, or herbs, and collecting fresh seeds.

television images that they have not developed the capacity to create their own ideas and images.

LEARNING THROUGH PLAYING

Children constantly use their imagination when they are playing: dolls become real people or a toy car a real car. Through play, children practise being adults. They also try to make sense of the world around them. Playing is, as it were, an introducion to the world. If you want to know what messages your children are receiving about life, their position in it and their value to it, listen to what they say as they play, and

play with them. Children grow visibly in confidence and understanding when adults play with them. Playing is, therefore, a rewarding way of making the most of their ability to learn and of making the most of your shared time.

Play is something children do spontaneously. They can make a toy or a game out of whatever is around and do not need the expensive custom-made variety. You cannot buy children's love through toys, but you can win it through a shared delight in play. You can provide playthings for your children from everyday household objects: a large cardboard box for a house, a pile of blankets to make a tent, or a comb covered with some tissue paper, which you blow through to improvise a mouth organ. You can help teach your children about the environment through play and through games that you make up together. With older children you can devise projects, word searches, treasure hunts, experiments and things to make and do. Your creativity will be soaked up by your children and will foster theirs.

Bear in mind that the preparation of a game or other pastime may be potentially much more interesting and valuable than the activity as a learning experience to your children. A child not allowed to take part in the preparation may easily see the result as fun for mummy or daddy only. The getting there may be greener than the goal.

Other childen are a valuable resource for your children and can provide hours of stimulation. Most young children are fascinated by other children. At first they just watch them, but as they get older they gradually play alongside each other and eventually together.

Some adults find it difficult, if not impossible, to be open and vulnerable enough to play. Their earnestness, seriousness, sadness, depression or anxiety get in their way. If no-one has ever played with you, you may have no play in you. Letting go of your burden may be the most difficult thing you have ever done, but it could also be one of the best. Many adults learn to play by following the example of their children. They can then allow themselves to play in adult life, for example, in their physical relationship with their partner and in activities such as sports or by playing with bubbles in a bubble bath, or with earth while potting up a plant.

LEARNING TO BE GREEN

Most religious and philosophical teachings are, at least in part, very green, stressing the importance of our relationship with the environment. Saint Francis of Assisi was a thirteenth-century Christian saint whose love for animals was renowned. Buddhists hold that all life is sacred and Hindus believe that every animal, however lowly, has a soul. Shintoism is a philosophy of life that stresses a one-ness or sense of identity with nature.

Bearing in mind that the way in which you teach your children about the environment is at least as important as what you teach, you can tune into the cycles of nature in small, practical ways: by eating seasonal, local foods; by choosing small household decorations in a colour and style to suit the season; and by matching the colour and shape of your dishes to the foods they contain. Your children's clothes (and your own) may reflect the changing seasons too. Flowers, leaves and fruits can bring a little of the outdoors into your home.

There are many things you and your children can do together to learn about the world around us. You can learn about the needs of plants by planting seeds in pots, preparing the soil with organic dressings; by watering; by keeping insects and other pests at bay with non-poisonous techniques (such as brushing greenfly off leaves with a paint brush or dousing them with soap solution, or putting out sticky yellow paper to catch whitefly).

If you have a garden you can enlarge the scope of your planting to include a wider variety of flowers, trees and vegetables, using many organic farming techniques, and establish a wildlife garden, perhaps with a pool. If you live in an area with few parks or gardens, but you know of some unkempt wasteground, find out from the owner if you could make a community garden out of it. Get together with other families to share out the work and maintenance. In the UK you may be eligible for funds (*see page 183–184* **Consumer Guide**).

In the UK several cities have established an urban farm where children can learn about agricultural life. This gives some town children more of a chance to learn about farm animals than some country children.

At home, you could help your children make a seed cake out of birdseed and melted-down solid fat and hang it out of the window. A nesting box fixed securely to a window ledge or a tree, or a feeding table for birds in a garden, will give a child hours of valuable instruction about the different species and their behaviour.

Children can learn a great deal from visiting wild, unspoilt places, such as moorland, hills, mountains, lakes, cliffs and beaches. But, before taking your children to a beach, try to choose a clean one. Look for obvious signs of pollution and find out from the local tourist board which beaches pass your national tests of water quality. Research in the USA indicates that it is possible to get gastro-enteritis and infections of the eyes, ears, nose and throat through swimming in polluted seas. EC requirements about the control of sewage pollution of bathing beaches mean that more and more are being cleaned up, but some countries, such as the UK and France, have a poor record and it is essential that the public continue to lobby for better conditions. In the UK seawater pollution is measured only in terms of the number of coliform bacteria (which come from human sewage) in each sample. The standards in the USA are ten times as rigorous and in Canada 20 times so.

Wise green parents do not use scare tactics when teaching their young children about the environment. Instead, they try to foster a delight in the world around; an awareness of the sensuality of nature; a sense of awe at the majesty and power of the ocean, the wind, the thunder and lightning; and a realization that each child can make a positive contribution to the environment.

LEARNING BY CELEBRATING

Family and community celebrations are essential parts of green learning. Through observing and joining in with the adults, children learn a great deal about the significance of important life events such as birth, coming of age, commitment to a partner and death. They also learn about the cycle of nature: the warming of the soil and the planting of the seed, the growing and harvesting of fruit and grain, and the excitement about the coming of a new season. They enter into life's essential rhythms and learn about the symbolic nature of many of our celebrations, both secular and religious, and how they bring to mind our own spiritual journey through life in an accessible way. Celebrating brings us into touch with our environment and the people in it. It focusses our attention on

turning points in our lives, so helping us to move on, at the same time as acknowledging what has gone before .

Your family can create its own special celebrations at any time. You can make the most of your shared time together by celebrating for the sake of it. You can celebrate at the beginning (or end) of each week with a special meal; you can celebrate the first tooth or the first leaves on the tree; you can make everyone's birthday, including your own, into a celebration; and you can have a celebration from time to time simply because you are all alive and well.

LEARNING FROM EXPERIENCE

As we have seen in this chapter, the green part of educating children lies as much in how you do it as in what you teach. Much of the joy in leading children the green way is in learning together. Something rediscovered is often surprisingly fresh and exciting, partly because you see it from a new viewpoint.

Each of us can learn from our own experiences as children and as parents. We can also learn from the lessons of history how to move forward without repeating mistakes or going up blind alleys already explored. To move forward instead of regressing we must look at history carefully and critically, try to spot the good and the bad in what happened before and work together to marry the best of the old and the new.

Take childbirth as an example. It would be misguided to do away with modern obstetric technology completely just because we are now recognizing the dangers of routine hospitalization, delivery by doctors and intervention in normal labour (*see pages 55-57*). What we need is the best of gentle and expert midwifery and the choice of delivering at home in familiar and relaxed surroundings, coupled with the reliable availability of superb modern obstetric opinion and intervention for the few who need it.

And it would be wrong to say that because young children benefit from committed one-to-one care, their mothers must stay at home full-time. In today's social climate, some mothers will not want – or be able – to do that. Yet it would be foolish to ape the experience of some countries, such as the USSR and Sweden, where day care provision for young children is well established, but many mothers find it impossible, for financial and/or social reasons, to stay at home. Large numbers end up neither enjoying their families nor their working lifestyles. They end up voting against the situation by not having any more children.

It is far better to provide a real choice for mothers and better conditions for children by ensuring that every mother is financially able to stay at home with her young children, full- or part-time, if she wishes; yet facilitating excellent alternative care for her child or children if she wants to work.

People who lobby for more State daycare or workplace nurseries perhaps do their children and themselves a disservice by setting their sights too low. They should be lobbying not just for nursery provision, if that is what they want, but for excellent conditions within the nursery. Women need to continue to press for far more sophisticated and sensitive arrangements for properly paid and protected part-time work (which many say they want); for career structures built around their potential child-bearing and child-rearing role; and for time off, or good child care provision, during school holidays. Women committed to the idea of returning to work after childbirth owe it to themselves to consider that staying at home for all or part of the time when their children are very young may bring benefits not only to their children but also to themselves.

The same principle of blending the best of the old with the best of the new holds for other green topics covered in this book, such as family planning, infertility, periconceptual care, family relationships, organic farming, food adulteration, housing, health care and education. We need to consider modern scientific findings and contemporary social needs in the light of lessons learned from our experience and from history, for everyone's benefit. This requires us to work with a mixture of honesty, humility and strength; to stop abusing positions of power; to offer and accept information and support; to walk with each other as we journey through life; to recognize and disentangle self-centred or profit-making motives from other-centred or altruistic ones and to realize that each of us is uniquely valuable.

AFTERWORD

Many people find that they struggle through life trying to make sense of it only to realize that the answer is very simple, and lay where they began. That may be why Christ taught that 'Unless you change and become like little children, you will never enter the kingdom of heaven'.

We are all connected with the environment, which makes us interdependent. Love, respect and reverence for each other, for nature, for our planet and for whatever is beyond is a part of worship and links spirituality with the green movement.

I believe that parenthood is a critical period for coming to know God, whether for the first time or in a deeper way; and that caring for our children offers us the chance to regain the simplicity, openness, trust and vulnerability we had as young children. Parenting challenges us to loosen our hold on the emotional defences we have built up over years. It challenges us – men and women – to release our locked-up 'feminine' qualities of caring, nurturing and reflecting; to experience our real feelings, and to play. Challenges can be frightening as well as exciting, but I believe we can find the courage to let go, to 'die to ourselves', in order to grow nearer to God by becoming more vulnerable and more truly ourselves. I believe that knowing God entails letting go; being passionate; trusting, hoping, loving and allowing ourselves to feel loved.

FURTHER READING

GREEN PREGNANCY & BIRTH BOOKS

Barnes, Belinda and Bradley, Suzanne Gail. *Planning for a Healthy Baby*, Ebury Press, 1990.

Flynn, Dr Anna and Brooks, Melissa. *A Manual of Natural Family Planning*, Unwin Publishing, 1985.

Gaskin, Ina May. *Spiritual Midwifery*, The Book Publishing Company, The Farm, Summertown, TN 38483, USA, 1977.

Leboyer, Frederick. *Birth Without Violence*, Fontana, 1975.

Odent, Michel. *Birth Reborn*, Souvenir Press, 1984.

Odent, Michel. *Entering the World*, Marion Boyars Inc., New York and Marion Boyars Ltd, London, 1984.

Palmer, Gabrielle. *The Politics of Breastfeeding*, Pandora, 1988.

Stanway, Dr Andrew. *Infertility*, Wellingborough, Thorsons, 1986.

Stanway, Drs Andrew and Penny. *Choices in Childbirth*, London and Sydney, Pan Books, 1984.

Tew, Marjorie. *Safer Childbirth*, Chapman and Hall, 1990.

Verny, Dr Thomas. *The Secret Life of the Unborn Child*, Sphere Books Limited, 1982.

GREEN BABY & CHILD CARE BOOKS

Berrien Berends, Polly. *Whole Child/Whole Parent*, Perennial Library, Harper & Row, 1983.

Campbell, Dr Ross. *How To Really Love Your Child*, Victor Books, 1980.

Jelliffe, Derrick B. and E.F. Patrice. *Human Milk in the Modern World*, Oxford, Oxford Medical Publications, 1978.

Kippley, Sheila. *Breastfeeding and Natural Child Spacing*, Penguin Books Inc, 1975.

Liedloff, Jean. *The Continuum Concept*, Futura Publications Limited, 1976.

London Food Commission. *Food Adulteration and how to beat it*, London, Unwin Hyman Limited, 1988.

Miller, Alice. *For Your Own Good – the roots of violence in child-rearing*, London, Virago Press Limited, 1983.

Miller, Alice. *Thou Shalt Not Be Aware*, London, Pluto Press, 1984.

Shaevitz, Marjorie. *The Superwoman Syndrome*, Fontana/Collins, 1984.

Stanway, Drs Penny and Andrew. *Breast is Best*, London and Sydney, Pan Books 1983.

Stanway, Drs Penny and Andrew. *The Baby and Child Book*, London and Sydney, Pan Books, 1983.

Thevenin, Tine. *The Family Bed*, P.O. Box 16004, Minneapolis, MN 55416, 1976.

Winnicott, D.W. *Home Is Where We Start From*, Penguin Books Ltd, 1986.

GREEN HEALTH BOOKS

Davies, Dr Stephen and Stewart, Dr Alan; Ed. Dr Andrew Stanway *Nutritional Medicine*, Pan Books, 1990.

Odent, Michel. *Primal Health*, Century Hutchinson Limited, 1986.

Stanway, Dr Andrew (ed.). *The Natural Family Doctor*, Century Hutchinson Ltd, 1987.

Stanway, Dr Penny. *Diet for Common Ailments*, London, Sidgwick & Jackson Limited, New York, Simon and Schuster, 1989.

Stanway, Dr Penny. *The Mothercare Guide to Child Health*, Conran Octopus, 1988.

GENERAL GREEN BOOKS

Albery, Nicholas and Kinzley, Mark (eds.). *How to Save the World*, Turnstone Press Limited, 1984.

Allaby, Michael. *Guide to Gaia*, Optima (Macdonald & Co. (Publishers) Ltd), 1989.

Button, John. *How To Be Green*, Century Hutchinson Ltd, 1989.

Levinson, Ralph. *Spring Clean Your Planet*, (Projects for young children), Beaver Books, (o.p.)

Porritt, Jonathon and Winner, David. *The Coming of the Greens*, Fontana/Collins. 1988.

Porrit, Jonathon (ed.). *Friends Of The Earth*, Macdonald & Co. (Publishers) Ltd, 1987.

Seymour, John and Giradet, Herbert. *Blueprint For A Green Planet*, London, Dorling Kindersley, 1987.

Shiva, Vandana. *Staying Alive: Women, Ecology and Development*, London and New Jersey, Zed Books Ltd, 1989.

Ward, Barbara. *Progress For A Small Planet*, London, Earthscan Publications Ltd, 1988.

DOMESTIC GREEN BOOKS

Christiansen, Karen. *Home Ecology*, London, Arlington Books, 1989.

Cuthbertson, Tom. *Enchanted Garden*, Rider & Company/Hutchinson and Co. (Publishers) Ltd, 1979.

Eklington, John and Hailes, Julia. *The Green Consumer Guide*, Victor Gollancz Ltd, 1989.

Eklington, John and Hailes, Julia. *The Green Consumer's Supermarket Shopping Guide*, Victor Gollancz Ltd, 1989.

Lobstein, Tim. *Children's Food*, Unwin Paperbacks, 1988.

Pearson, David. *The Natural House Book*, Conran Octopus, 1989.

Thorsons Organic Consumer Guide, Thorsons Publishers Ltd, 1990.

OTHER BOOKS

Davis, Bruce & Genny Wright. *The Magical Child Within You*, Celestial Arts, P.O. Box 7327, Berkeley, California, USA, 1985.

Fox, Matthew. *Original Blessing*, Bear & Company. Inc., 1983.

Huws, Ursula. *VDU Hazards Handbook*, London Hazards Centre, 3rd Floor, Headland House, 308 Grays Inn Road, London WC1X 8DS, 1987.

Jowell, Roger, Witherspoon, Sharon and Brook, Lindsay (eds.). *British Social Attitudes: Special International Report*, Gower Publishing Company Limited, 1989.

Osborne, Cecil G. *The Art of Learning to Love Yourself*, Zondervan Publishing House, Grand Rapids, Michigan, USA, 1976.

Randle, Damian. *Teaching Green*, Green Print (The Merlin Press Ltd), 1989.

Rubin, Theodore Isaac. *Compassion and Self-Hate*, New York, Ballantyne Books, 1975.

Ryman, Daniéle. *The Aromatherapy Handbook*, Century Publishing, 1984.

Scott Peck, M. *The Road Less Travelled*, Century Hutchinson Ltd, 1988.

Skinner, Robin and Cleese, John. *Families and how to survive them*, London, Mandarin Paperbacks, 1984.

Teyber, Edward. *Helping your children with divorce*, New York, Pocket Books, 1984.

Williams, H.A. *The True Wilderness*, Fount Paperbacks, 1979.

Woodman, Marion. *Addiction to Perfection*, Inner City Books, Box 1271, Station Q, Toronto, Canada M4T 2P4, 1982.

World Fertility Survey. Series and volumes published by Publications Office, International Statistical Institute, 428 Prinses Beatrixlaan, PO Box 950, 2270-AZ Voorburg, Netherlands.

CONSUMER GUIDE

CARPETS

The British Carpet Manufacturers Association, Royalty House, 72 Dean Street, London, W1, publishes a booklet of facts on carpet materials and stain removal.

DOMESTIC GREEN GOODS

The Whole Thing (catalogue for green household products), Millmead Business Centre, Millmead Road, Tottenham Hale, London N17 9QU.

ELECTRICAL GOODS

Full Spectrum Lighting Ltd., Unit 5, Wye Estate, London Road, High Wycombe, Buckinghamshire.

Thorn Lighting Limited, Elstree Way, Borehamwood, Hertfordshire WD6 1HZ will supply information on low-energy lighting.

FOOD

The Soil Association, 86 Colston Street, Bristol, BS1 5BB is producing five regional *Guides to Organic Produce* price £2 each. Available from bookshops, wholefood shops and directly from the Soil Association.

GENERAL GREEN PRODUCTS

Ventflex, Cover Plus, Hyde, Cheshire, supply covering for children's mattresses with Ventflex polyurethane coating to screen out dust mites.

NAPPIES (DIAPERS)

Biobottoms are available from: The Whole Thing (mail-order catalogue, *see above* for address); and Biobottoms, PO Box 6009, Petaluma, California 94953, USA.

Bumkins, 7720 E. Redfield Road, Suite 4, Scottsdale, AZ 85260, USA.

Eco-Matrix, 124 Harvard Street, Boston, MA 02146, and Tender Care, Rocky Mountain Medical Corporation, 5555 E. 71st Street, Suite 8300, Tulsa, OK 74136 distribute nappies manufactured with biodegradable plastic in the USA.

Fluffies (reusable nappy covers) are available from 'Fluffies' Knitwear Industries UK Ltd, PO Box 534, Seaford, East Sussex, BN25 1AQ.

Wunderpants, 28 Claremont Avenue, Bishopston, Bristol, BS7 8JE.

PAINTS

Auro Paints, 16 Church Street, Saffron Waldon, Essex CB10 14W, and Auro Pflanzenchemie GmbH, Postbox 1229, D-3300 Braunschweig, West Germany, supply non-toxic wood preservers.

Natural Paint Company, 101 Lansdowne Road, London N17.

PAPER

The National Association of Paper Merchants, Hamilton Court, Gogmore Lane, Chertsey, Surrey, KT16 9AP is currently standardizing the definition of recycled paper to help the consumer. The term will only be applicable to paper containing 75 per cent genuine recycled waste. The Association can supply further information on paper products.

Wiggins Teape Paperpoint, 130 Long Acre, London, WC2E 9AL sells good-quality speckletone recycled paper. A box of 500 sheets costs £32.59; a single sheet costs 14p.

TESTING

A *Cruelty-Free* product guide is available from BUAV (British Union for the Abolition of Vivisection), 16a Crane Grove, London, N7 8LB.

TOILETRIES

None of the companies listed below test their products on animals.

The Body Shop International PLC, Hawthorn Road, Wick, Littlehampton, West Sussex, BN17 7LR.

Cosmetics To Go (mail-order), 29 High Street, Poole, Dorset, BH15 1AB.

Creighton Products, Water Lane, Storrington, Pulborough, Sussex, RH20 3DP.

Elida Gibbs, Hesketh House, Portman Square, London W1A.

Marks & Spencer plc, Michael House, Baker Street, London W1A.

Weleda (UK) Ltd, Heanor Road, Ilkeston, Derbyshire, DE7 8DR.

WATER

Thames Water plc, Water Quality Centre, Room 90, 173 Rosebery Avenue, London, EC1R 4TP will analyze domestic water supplies from the mains in the London area. Charges vary from £30 to £100. Customers who think their water may be below standard will be given a free analysis. A free list of water constituents in London areas is also available.

Water Quality Analysis, Consumer Association of Canada, Box 9300, Ottawa ON, KIG 3TG.

USEFUL ADDRESSES

BMAC (Baby Milk Action), 6 Regent Terrace, Cambridge, CB2 1AA.

The British Retailers, Association, Commonwealth House, 1–19 New Oxford Street, London, WC1A 1PA, will supply information on consumer rights.

The Civic Trust, 17 Carlton House Terrace, London SW1Y 5AW. Apply to this organization for help with funding a community garden.

The Consumers' Association, 2 Marylebone Road, London NW1 4DX, supplies information on consumer rights and products currently available in the shops. They publish an action pack, Baby on the Way, containing information on baby products.

Friends of the Earth, 26–28 Underwood Street, London, N1 7JQ.

Greenpeace, 30–31 Islington Green, London, N1 0XE.

Environmental Investigations Limited, Netley House, Gomshall, Surrey GU5 9QA. (Specialists in diagnosis of building defects and the ecological control of timber decay).

Henry Doubleday Research Association, National Centre for Organic Gardening, Ryton-on-Dunsmore, Coventry CV8 3LG.

IBFAN (International Baby Food Action Network), PO Box 1045, 10830 Penang, Malaysia.

Institute for Complementary Medicine, 21 Portland Place, London W1.

National Children's Play and Recreation Unit, 359-361 Euston Road, London.

The National Radiological Protection Board, Chilton, Didcot, Oxfordshire OX11 0RQ, can arrange for a radon test to be carried out in your home and supply information. The test is free to people in areas with high levels of radon.

The Parent Network, 44-46 Caversham Road, London NW5 2DS.

GLOSSARY

Acid Rain causes the gradual corrosion of the environment by acid deposition via rainfall, snow, hail, fog, gas clouds and dry dust. This pollution (q.v.) was first discovered in the nineteen-fifties, yet acid deposition has now reached crisis proportions in many industrial countries. Rainfall is naturally acidic, but harmful acid rain is created by the absorption into the atmosphere of sulphur dioxide and oxides of nitrogen, gases emitted when coal and oil are burned for industrial purposes. When they combine with water vapour in the atmosphere, these gases make dilute sulphuric and nitric acids, which fall in rain, snow or sleet. The acidic solution may be carried by the wind for hundreds of miles before it falls. Trees under constant attack by acid rain eventually die when their natural defence systems are broken down. The acid rain also drains into the earth, where a chemical reaction releases poisonous metals, such as aluminium, cadmium and mercury, from their compounds in the soil. From the soil, the solution runs into streams and lakes, poisoning the plant and animal species dependent on them for survival. As well as 'wet deposition' via rainfall, more localized 'dry deposition' of sulphur oxides in city air eats away at buildings and poisons the soil. When sulphur oxides mix with fog and dust, corrosive, choking smogs form in inner city areas. These provoke respiratory illnesses and have been linked with SIDS (Sudden Infant Death Syndrome) in babies. The gradual poisoning of waterways by acid rain may eventually lead to the contamination of drinking water, as water pipes are eroded by acidic deposits.

Agrochemicals are insecticides, herbicides and other chemicals used in farming. Residues from pesticide-spraying can cling to food crops or remain in the soil and so enter the food chain. Nitrates used in chemical fertilizers leach from agricultural land into waterways (*see below* **Pollution**).

Amino acids: Proteins in food are made up of strings of molecules; the amino acids, of which there are 22. Eight are essential to our diet. Animal proteins contain all; vegetable proteins are 'incomplete', because they do not contain a full complement.

Biocides is the collective term for pesticides (insecticides and fungicides) and herbicides (weedkillers).

Bioflavonoids are crystalline substances, formerly known as vitamin P, found in certain vegetables and fruits, especially citrus fruits.

A **biohome** is house built using materials and techniques which prevent or combat the chemical pollution of indoor air.

Carbon dioxide (CO_2) is a colourless, odourless, non-combustible gas, the most prolific greenhouse gas. It is produced by biological processes on land; by changes in land use; and by human activities, including the combustion of fossil fuels (q.v.). Carbon dioxide is exchanged naturally between huge reservoirs in the atmosphere, the oceans and the living world. Human activities have upset the balance of this exchange: scientists estimate that the percentage of carbon dioxide in the atmosphere (about 0.03% by volume) has increased by one quarter since the industrial revolution. It is a major contributor to the greenhouse effect (q.v.), because it can trap the sun's heat and hold it in the air, stopping it from radiating away from the Earth. It is calculated that, unless drastic measures are taken to stop emissions, the amount of carbon dioxide in the air will double over the next three decades, causing the Earth to warm by 2° Centigrade, crating havoc with the climate, the seasons and the sea levels. Sources of carbon dioxide emissions vary from country to country. Currently about 45% of total emissions of human origin come equally from electricity generation and vehicle fumes. In France, power stations are fuelled mainly by nuclear energy, so carbon dioxide emissions are reduced.

CFCs (chloroflurocarbons) are compounds of fluorine, chlorine and carbon used in processes such as refrigeration, the manufacture of foam packaging and as propellants in aerosols. They are stable at high temperatures, non-flammable, relatively non-toxic and cheap, but ever time an aerosol is sprayed or a foam carton is crushed, long-lasting CFCs are released into the atmosphere, eventually reaching the

Earth's protective layer of ozone gas. The resulting chemical reaction causes chlorine oxide to form, thus breaking down the fragile layer of ozone and impairing its absoption of ultraviolet rays from the sun. These harmful rays cause sunburn and skin cancer in humans and other animals. CFCs are also greenhouse gases (q.v.). Manufacturers have been under pressure to stop using CFCs and in 1990 a world-wide agreement was reached to phase them out.

Deforestation is the cutting down of forest trees on a large scale. Between 50 and 60 million acres of tropical rainforest – notably in South America and South East Asia – are currently destroyed annually. Burning the felled trees contributes to the build-up in the atmosphere of carbon dioxide (q.v.). Trees absorb carbon dioxide from the air as they photosynthesize, so fewer trees means more carbon dioxide in the atmosphere.

Ecology is the study of the relationships between living organisms and their environment. The term stems from the Greek word *oikos*, meaning house.

Essential fatty acids are found in food fats of animal and vegetable origin. They are vital for health, but, unlike other fatty acids, cannot be synthesized by the body from other nutrients and have to be eaten in the daily diet. The 'omega-6' fatty acid, linoleic acid, is found in a wide range of foods, especially vegetables and grains; the 'omega-3' fatty acids, such as alpha-linolenic acid, are found in wheat, beans and spinach; and eicosapentanoic acid and docosahexanoic acid are found in seafoods. Essential fatty acid deficiency can cause dermatitis, slow the healing of wounds and cause reproductive failure and poor growth. A diet high in animal fat and processed foods may be low in essential fatty acids.

Fossil Fuels are energy sources such as coal, oil and natural gas, found in rock formations. They develop over millions of years, as the remains of vegetation and animal life are subjected to heat and pressure from the deposition of successive layers of rock and earth on top of them. Over the years fossil fuels have supplied a large proportion of the world's energy needs, but reserves are finite and alternative forms of energy are now being investigated.

The **greenhouse effect** may be causing the temperature of the atmosphere to rise, due to a build-up of greenhouse gases, created by intensive industrial and agricultural practices. These gases – carbon dioxide, CFCs, methane and nitrous oxides (q.v.) – trap heat in the air. The greenhouse effect is in fact essential to life: carbon dioxide and water vapour keep the Earth at a temperature that enables it to sustain life. However, when carbon dioxide, CFCs, methane and nitrous oxides are released into the air, they block the passage of heat back into space. Some scientists warn that unless steps are taken to reduce the emission of greenhouse gases, the greenhouse effect will worsen, possibly causing temperature rises of up to $4\frac{1}{2}°$ Centigrade, disrupting weather patterns, making violent storms more frequent and many countries hotter and wetter, thus playing havoc with crop yields. With climatic changes come changes in sea levels: widespread flooding is predicted by meteorologists. One third of the world's population lives within 40 miles of the coast. Some scientists believe that the dire prophesies about global warming are grossly exaggerated.

A **healthy diet** provides the proteins, carbohydrates, fats, vitamins and minerals essential to our bodies. Most wholefoods contain varying proportions of these nutrients; processing food usually reduces its nutrient content. Many people in industrialized countries eat too much refined and processed food, made of sugar, white flour and saturated fat; and too little wholefood, containing fibre, essential fatty acids, minerals and vitamins.

Methane (CH_4) is a colourless, odourless, flammable gas, the main constituent of natural gas and a dangerous greenhouse gas. It is produced by vegetable matter decaying in places where there is little oxygen; in swamps, for example, animals' guts and termite mounds. Intensive farming practices, particularly the cultivation of paddy fields (artificial swamps), are responsible for an increase of methane in the air. Breeding large cattle herds to feed the increasing world population contributes to the build-up, because cattle flatulence is a rich source of the gas. Methane, lingering in the air, traps and retains 27 times as much of the sun's energy as carbon dioxide, thus contributing to global warming on a similar scale to CFCs.

Nitrates are nitrogen compounds formed in the soil by the breakdown of animal manure and plant debris. In the nitrogen cycle, nitrates are taken up naturally as food by plants. The use of animal manure, sewage sludge and synthetic nitrogenous fertilizers to increase crop yields boosts nitrate levels in the soil. This distortion of the nitrogen cycle causes a build-up of nitrates, which leach through the soil into ground water (*see below* **Pollution**). Nitrates in water react with bacteria in the mouth and stomach to form poisonous nitrates. In babies nitrates are thought to combine with respiratory pigment in blood cells, reducing the supply of oxygen to the body and causing an illness called blue baby syndrome. They have been linked to stomach cancers in animals and humans.

Organic food is grown without the use of synthetic agrochemicals: fertilizers, pesticides (such as organochlorine and organophosphorous compounds), fungicides, soil fumigants and herbicides. The term 'organic' can be applied to meat, fish and poultry produced without the routine use of antibiotics, hormones and other drugs, and reared humanely.

Ozone is a pale blue, pungent gas that is poisonous to human and animal life at ground level. It is found in its greatest concentration as the ozone layer, a thin, fragile band about 25 miles (40 kilometres) above the Earth's surface. The ozone layer performs a vital protective role in the upper atmosphere, by absorbing ultraviolet radiation from the sun. Without such absorption, lethal levels of ultraviolet radiation would kill all life on Earth. Scientists have discovered holes in the ozone layer above the Arctic and Antarctic, which, they say, are directly attributable to constant emissions of CFCs (q.v.). The US Environmental Protection Agency has calculated that for every 1 per cent decrease in the concentration of ozone in the stratosphere there would be a 5 per cent increase in the number of skin cancers each year in the USA.

Pollution is the addition to the environment of substances that cannot be made safe by biological processes. Air pollution is caused by harmful gases, such as sulphur dioxide and nitrous oxides (produced by burning fossil fuels in power stations), and carbon monoxide and lead (from motor vehicles). Inhaled regularly, these pollutants can affect the brain and nervous system, particularly of children.

Water pollution is caused by acid rain (q.v.) contaminating rivers and lakes; by pouring barely treated sewage into rivers and seas, thus removing oxygen and effectively killing all life; by dumping poisonous waste from factories into waterways; and by intensive agriculture. Agrochemicals (q.v.) used to improve crop yields, seep through the soil into the ground water, and from there into rivers and streams. Fertilizers in a river accelerate the rate of grown of weeds and other vegetation, which eventually choke the river, destroying its ecosystem. Some harmful chemicals are absorbed by fish and small animals and enter the food chain when other animals, including humans, eat them.

Land pollution is the result of dumped waste, from poisonous chemicals and old cars to dropped packaging. Rubbish scars the environment, can injure humans and animals and can contaminate the soil.

Trans-cutaneous nerve stimulation is a method of relieving pain during labour based on the interruption of the nervous pathways of pain with electrical stimulation of the lower back and abdomen.

INDEX

ACKNOWLEDGEMENTS

I would like to thank my editor, Helen Varley, for her unfailing courtesy, warmth and skill, and for the laughs we have shared; her assistant Michele Doyle, for her enthusiasm, cheerfulness and attention to detail; Ronnie Haydon, for her careful comments on the manuscript; Nancy Anderson, for her striking artwork; David Williams, for his stylish design work; and Hayden Williams, for his helpful research.

Thank you also to my husband, Andrew, my children, Susie, Amy and Ben, and my mother-in-law, Diana, for their loving support and interest in this project.

EDDISON SADD

Editorial Manager	Helen Varley
Copy Editors	Michele Doyle and Ronnie Haydon
Researchers	Hayden Williams and Yvette Traxler
Art Editor	David Williams
Design Assistants	Karen Watts and Amanda Barlow
Production Controller	Claire Kane

Eddison Sadd Editions would also like to thank the following: the International Planned Parenthood Federation and MEAL for supplying helpful information. Yale University Press for the rights to reproduce *May Allah Give Me a True Friend*. Rena Cop Rain for *My Vision from this Pain is Born* on the inside front cover. Geoffrey Bownas and Anthony Thwaite for the Tanikawa Shuntaro quotation (p65). Angus & Robertson (Australia) for the extract from *Woman to Child* by Judith Wright (p27).

Dr Penny Stanway has spent time in general practice and was a senior medical officer to a large area health authority for several years. She sees the care of ourselves and each other, adults and children, as being at the heart of the green movement. She has written widely for magazines and journals, and is the author of several books, including the best-selling *Breast is Best*; *The Breast Book*; *The Pears Encyclopedia of Child Health*; *The Baby and Child Book*; *The Complete Book of Love and Sex* and *Choices in Childbirth* (with her husband, Dr Andrew Stanway); *The Mothercare Guide to Child Health* and *Diet for Common Ailments*. She is a member of the Professional Advisory Board of the La Leche League International and has worked closely with the National Childbirth Trust. Since having her three children, she has worked as a writer, lecturer and counsellor, setting up a women's discussion group and a mother and toddler group.